THE
BABYLON
FILE

VOLUME 2

Also available:

The Babylon File

THE
BABYLON
FILE

VOLUME 2

THE DEFINITIVE
UNAUTHORISED GUIDE TO
J. MICHAEL STRACZYNSKI'S TV
SERIES *BABYLON 5*

Andy Lane

First published in Great Britain in 1999 by
Virgin Publishing Ltd
Thames Wharf Studios
Rainville Road
London W6 9HT

The essay entitled 'Cast . . . in a Bad Light' is a revised version of an article originally published in *DreamWatch* magazine.

ISBN 0 7535 0233 X

Typeset by Galleon Typesetting, Ipswich
Printed and bound in Great Britain by
Mackays of Chatham PLC

DEDICATED TO . . .

Paul W Brown III and John Myler, for considering me enough of an expert to pay me money to write about what I love . . .

Andrew Dent, for being so appreciative when I lent him videos, and so restrained when he lent videos to me and I didn't give them back . . .

Terry Jones, for being keener than I was, and so keeping my interest in the subject going . . .

Rebecca Levene, for generally being a wonderful human being . . .

Paul Simpson, for letting me rehearse many of my arguments in the pages of *DreamWatch* (the best media magazine on the market), and supplying me with raw material . . .

Lee Whiteside, for sending me videos and cards regardless of the fact that I frequently didn't reply for weeks or even months on end . . .

and Kevin McCarron, for not being able to tell the difference between someone who is anti-intellectual and someone who is anti-pretension.

ACKNOWLEDGEMENTS

Thanks to the following people for being friendly and pointing out the stupid mistakes in Volume 1: Davida Gypsy Breier, Celeste Sullin Burris, Jarrod Buttery, Mark Chapman, Jeannette Crenshaw, Susan Defosset, Michael Gage, Philip Hallard, Beth Hopkin, Leigh Hunt, Derek Jeffrey, Morag Kerr, Dan Kimmel, Stephanie M Kwandr, Rob Langenderfer, Vesa Lehtinen, Charles Lurio, Katrina McDonnell, Joanne Moore, Dwayne H Olson, Ojala Pasi, Matthew Pinnock, Jerry Redondo, Katherine P Rhine, Jim Smith, Matt Snowden, Elizabeth Sweeny, Penny Turner and Christina Willrich.

CONTENTS

Foreword

by Jeffrey Willerth

A childhood friend, Doug Corring, grew up to be an Assistant Director. During one of our annual holiday phone calls he mentioned he started work on a new sci-fi series called *Babylon 5*, and asked if I would like to come be an alien for a day or two. Doug had worked on *Star Trek: The Next Generation* and *Star Trek: Deep Space 9*, so I trusted his judgement about alien work, and agreed to join him as soon as I finished the *Young Indiana Jones* photo-double job I was on. I still recall the disappointment I felt when I first saw the now infamous Sun Valley warehouse that housed the stages for *Babylon 5*. How could a TV show possibly be made in a small facility next to the freeway? Little did I know that once I stepped inside, it would take me five seasons, four cable films and two episodes of the spin-off series to get out!

The first season I spent as a background artist, the second and third as a stand-in, the fourth and fifth as Producer's Associate; oh yes, and most of that time I played the role of Ambassador Kosh. This employment history provided me a unique perspective on the inner workings of *Babylon 5*; a perspective I'm quite proud of and will make full use of in due course.

Upon arrival at *Babylon 5* I set out to acquaint myself with the crew, the on-set attitude and the story the episodes were telling. To my surprise, most of the crew I encountered seemed confident there was no way we'd get picked up for a second season. This made for a relaxed work environment.

In fact each and every season it was a common opinion among the cast and crew that *Babylon 5* would not get picked up again by Warner Brothers. All negotiation between WB and the series' producers was highly confidential and never leaked, and so rumours were always rife on set. The few comments that were made rarely turned out to be what really transpired, or so it seemed. As each season would end we would go into hiatus, not knowing if we had jobs at the end of the summer. The renewal notice would not be announced until very late in the year, which was hard on the crew. We all so wanted to keep our 'family' together, but at the same time had to be ready to accept any reasonable offer to take work when it became available. Despite the tardiness, there was relatively low turnover of crew in our five seasons. Many of those who did leave *Babylon 5* left when a job opportunity arose before notice of the pick-up.

I think that crew attitude, confidence in the future and a clearer understanding of the story arc began with the second season. The decision to bring Bruce Boxleitner on board gave the show a cowboy hero – someone we all could identify with. Now we had a 'good guy' and, despite the initial confusion of the whole Shadow/Vorlon arc, the presence of a hero meant that somebody would obviously turn out to be the 'bad guys'. Furthermore, Warner Brothers must have encouraged or assisted the producers to get some great guest actors on board. Attracting some recognised faces certainly helped the crew feel as if we were working on a real prime-time show with the possibility of a multiple season run.

Unfortunately, *B5* never received the level of publicity required for mass appeal. The major media outlets were given hardly any access to the *B5* stages. In contrast, WB's Marketing and Affiliate Relations Department was hugely supportive and made great efforts to promote the series. Fan appreciation for *Babylon 5* was conveyed to the individual, locally broadcast stations resulting in regional publicity that initiated a larger public awareness.

Despite the increasing visibility of the show, the crew were unhappy. From the very start of production only around 10% of all the talented people working on the show had union representation. To put this in context, nine out of ten crew members were entering into a third season of hard work without industry-standard benefits, health plans, or pension contributions. Further, the pay scale for most positions was way below the network show rates as a result of the tight budget governing the production. Perhaps the most momentous event that occurred behind the scenes was their decision early in season three to go on strike until union representation was allowed. Until then, only the directors, actors and writers (i.e. the people hired by the episode rather than by the season) were organised in their respective guilds.

The whole affair was over inside three days, and the producers wrangled a new agreement and contract out of the union. The new pay rates were still, as far as I know, below any other show of our kind being produced in Los Angeles. None of the crew received any substantial pay raise as a result, but at least they got benefits and the time put in was contributing toward their futures. Walking off the job for what the crew believed in was a tense, risky and unnerving undertaking. On his first day back to work after the strike, Peter 'Londo' Jurasik held up shooting for a moment to applaud the crew for, in his words, 'your efforts to improve yourselves. No one should ever fault you for that.'

Much of the information the crew received was either premature and never came to fruition, skewed from what was really going on, or offered up after the fact and usually discovered on the Internet or from sci-fi magazines. During the fourth and fifth seasons I supported Copeland, Straczynski and Netter as a Producer's Associate. Despite being closer to the sources, I found the information flow just as frustrating as when I was on set.

One by one and *en masse*, actors, too, would approach me for an insider tidbit that might put their minds at ease about their future employment. They assumed that because of my position I knew what the real deal was. Most times I did not. Often this put me in precarious and difficult situations. Once, I found an actor in Copeland's office searching an unreleased draft of a TNT TV movie script to see which characters were in it. Regrettably, as part of doing my job responsibly, I had to report the incident, which lowered my popularity rating among the cast. The point is, this actor was motivated by frustration. The actors had repeatedly, and justifiably, queried the Producers about their involvement in the *B5* episodes and movies and in the *Crusade* series. Granted, there is the painful negotiation process with agents before any acting job is a done deal, but a simple answer might have relieved many headaches.

Difficult as it was to get straight facts at work, things became more confusing as the Internet became popular. Information often appeared online ahead of the publicity machine or before it was common knowledge on set. This started to give credibility to the information that was circulating on the net and later matured into a rash of rumours, some of which could be said to have damaged reputations and stunted careers. At the same time, the Internet was a critical tool for the exposure of the show, its cast and crew. I know I spent many nights in various chat rooms trying to convince my cybermates that I really was the guy inside the encounter suit! As I didn't receive credit on the show for playing Kosh I used the net to my advantage to publicise my contribution to the show.

The Internet hosts a huge community of loyal *B5* fans which continues to grow today. I wonder how the show would have fared had the cyber-audience not been there? Would the show have been too heady for a mass audience if there had not been a cyber-forum to communicate understanding and interpretation of the story arc?

Would *B5* even have survived to season five?

Reflecting upon rereading the above, I must confess the truth about the bigger picture. *Babylon 5* was a wonderful, exciting and important chapter in my life. I've made friends there who will stand by me until my final days. I learned a tremendous amount from very talented people. I developed skills that I hone today. *B5* was a significant springboard for my career. I am proud to have been part of the process of making, arguably, one of the best shows on television. I am grateful for the opportunities the producers offered me and thankful I seized them. Most of all, *B5* led me to my soul-mate and partner for life, Patricia 'Lyta' Tallman. For this alone, the trip to the plywood space station was worth a journey of a thousand light-years. It would have been rewarding to leave Babylonian Productions under better circumstances, but as in all the great love stories, in the end I (the good guy) got the girl.

THE
BABYLON
FILE

VOLUME 2

Introduction

This book is the second and final volume in an unofficial, unlicensed analysis of the cult American TV series *Babylon 5*. Volume 1 covered the first 3 seasons and the first few episodes of season 4, as well as the ancillary material – such as comics and novels – which was available up to the time of printing. Volume 2 covers seasons 4 and 5, ditto the ancillary material. Astute readers will already have noticed that there is a slight overlap on the first few episodes of season 4. Rest assured: those entries have actually been updated for this volume.

Why unofficial and unlicensed? Well, it's as true of *Babylon 5* as of any other popular TV series or film that the material which has been licensed by its creator(s) is generally uncritical and superficial. This doesn't mean it's not good: there are a series of books about the making of *Babylon 5* that are well worth reading (and which are referenced in the bibliography at the end of this book), and Titan produce an official magazine that is chock-full of great photographs and informative interviews.

But . . .

But you could be forgiven, when reading any of that material, for thinking that episode 319 ('Grey 17 is Missing') was as good as episode 420 ('Endgame'). For thinking that the transfer from PTEN to TNT between seasons 4 and 5 caused no problems in the show's production. For thinking that writing sixty continuous episodes did not result in a discernible decay in the quality of J Michael Straczynski's writing. For thinking that the lack of a script editor from midway through season 2 onwards did not lead to passages of self-indulgent dialogue and muddled plotting that could easily have been spotted if anyone who knew anything about writing had dared to make a comment.

This book is the antidote.

As with Volume 1, it takes an honest, unflinching look at the series; praising it where it is good, condemning it where it is bad. Everything in here is my own opinion, and there are areas where you will undoubtedly disagree with me. That's fine: informed debate is a good thing, and if there is one thing I want this book to do it's to inform the debate.

Reading back through Volume 1 of *The Babylon File* now, I find that some of it is quite breathlessly adulatory about certain episodes. They deserve it: looking back, season 3 was probably the high spot of the show. This volume does not have the same engine pushing it on. Times have changed; the show has too.

In the summer of 1995, before I wrote Volume 1, I was operated on for a tumour of the pituitary gland. It was a serious operation and, as the time approached, I used to tell people, only half joking, that I couldn't die under the surgeon's knife because that way I'd never know what would happen in the final episode of *Babylon 5*. That's how important the series was to us then: some of the questions had been laid out for us, but none of the answers, and we needed to know. We needed that sense of resolution that comes at the end of a really great novel, and we trusted J Michael Straczynski not to let us down, to deliver what he had promised.

As I started to pull the disparate threads of this book together in October 1998, the final five episodes had not yet been transmitted. And yet, if I wanted, I could have gone downstairs, picked up a copy of Jane Killick's official *Babylon 5* book *The Wheel of Fire* and read exactly what happens in each of them, or just flicked through it and looked at the photograph giving away the last few moments of the final episode. The early publication of that book – a licensed, official product, endorsed by J Michael Straczynski – was a kick in the teeth for every single fan who has hung on for five years, waiting for that resolution. It's worse than someone telling you who the murderer is in *The Mousetrap* while you're queuing up for your tickets; it's almost as bad as James Cameron himself leaning over to you in the cinema while you're watching Leonardo di Caprio drawing Kate Winslett in *Titanic* and whispering: 'Of course, you know he drowns at the end?'

Apologies to anyone who hasn't seen *Titanic* by the way. But *The Mousetrap* is still safe.

Worse still, I found I actually didn't care very much, having come that far. After finishing Volume 1 I was desperate to know what happened in the remaining 37 episodes. By the time I had sat through the interminable first half of season 5, my enthusiasm had waned. For three weeks before its transmission I had a review copy of the last ever episode, 'Sleeping in Light', sitting by my video recorder, but I couldn't raise the enthusiasm to watch it. Not because I was over-familiar with the series; not because the waiting had caused my appreciation to burn out; not because questions are inherently more interesting than answers; but because *it's not the same series*. We've been let down with a final season that's weak, rushed, badly plotted and badly characterised. In his desperate quest to keep the series on the air, to make it to the end of that promised fifth season, J Michael Straczynski appears to have bargained the heart out of *Babylon 5*.

Writing Volume 2 I've been saddened to discover that there is less and less to say about the episodes. The literary, mythological and historical references have gradually vanished, reducing their resonances and the complexity. The small in-jokes are no more, giving us all less to look for. Those wonderful guest stars – Aubrey Morris, Roy Dotrice, Michael York – are but a memory, replaced with local Los Angeles 'talent' more familiar from TV soap opera than from the London stage. The richness and the diversity of the series has vanished, leaving a plot that has been emasculated by the loss of key cast members and the artificial compression of important elements of the plot and the expansion of the filler material.

There is nothing to replace *Babylon 5*. Some other series stand out from the usual TV pap – *Millennium* and *Brimstone* are the front runners – but there is nothing on the screen now that is so good I cannot wait for the next episode to be on. I wish I could pin my hopes on *Crusade*, but the stories that are beginning to emerge about its troubled production are not encouraging.

If *Babylon 5* was a television experiment, then it was an experiment that failed. It did not change TV production noticeably; it has left the face of science fiction unaltered; it may have transfigured the lives of some people for the better, but then there are people who claim to live their lives by the teachings of *Star Trek*. Its final moments have been dissipated rather than celebrated.

The book you are holding in your hands contains some 80,000 words. Volume 1 contained around 140,000 words. That difference can be ascribed directly to the reasons given above, but I prefer to think of the entire project as a 220,000 word critical dissection of a series that has had its ups and downs, but which has, at its best, exerted a fascination that few other series have managed.

I will always have a soft spot in my memory for *Babylon 5*, but I will remember it more for what it could have been than for what it was.

THE LISTS

Directors

Babylon 5 is a perfect example of *auteur* theory, given that its successes (and failures) are laid firmly at the door of one J Michael Straczynski. Fair enough, he *is* the creator and Executive Producer as well as being the most prolific writer on the show, but the individual episodes do showcase the talents of other individuals as well. The directors have almost as much influence on the 'look' of the episodes as Straczynski does, even allowing for the legendary detail of his scripts (which frequently describe everything down to the camera angles to be used). A John Flinn episode is different from a Jésus Treviño, for instance, and Mike Vejar brings different skills to bear from those of, say, Janet Greek.

A quick trawl through the list of directors who have worked on the show over the past five years throws up some interesting facts. There are eight who have directed only one episode – Lorraine Senna Ferrara, Kim Freidman, Goran Gajic, Doug Lefler, John McPherson, Stephen L Posey, J Michael Straczynski and Douglas Wise. Of these eight, Lefler, Gajic, Straczynski and Wise all directed their only episodes in the final season, and had little chance to do any more, but one has to wonder what Ferrara, Freidman and Posey did wrong. Their one-off episodes were shown in the first two seasons and, had Straczynski wanted them back, there was plenty of scope for their return. Perhaps they were too busy; perhaps they didn't enjoy working on the show; or perhaps their vision didn't fit alongside that of the Executive Producer. Alternatively, four directors obviously delivered the goods every time, given that they have all directed more than ten episodes. David Eagle clocks in with thirteen; Janet Greek has twelve plus two TV movies; Jim Johnston gets eleven; but Mike Vejar is the overall winner with fourteen episodes to his credit plus two TV movies. Oddly, only one director has actually worked on all five seasons of the show: the series' own cinematographer, John C Flinn III.

So, for those of you who want to delve among the data and

come up with your own conclusions, here is the list of all the directors who have worked on *Babylon 5*:

Menachem Binetski
- 213 – 'Hunter, Prey'
- 305 – 'Voices of Authority'

Richard Compton
- TVM – *The Gathering*
- 101 – 'Midnight on the Firing Line'
- 104 – 'Infection'
- 107 – 'The War Prayer'
- 110 – 'Believers'
- 115 – 'Grail'

John Copeland
- 420 – 'Endgame'
- 512 – 'The Ragged Edge'
- 521 – 'Objects at Rest'

Kevin G Cremin
- 206 – 'Spider in the Web'
- 218 – 'Confessions and Lamentations'
- 301 – 'Matters of Honor'
- 307 – 'Exogenesis'
- 318 – 'Walkabout'

Mario DiLeo
- 205 – 'The Long Dark'
- 211 – 'All Alone in the Night'
- 215 – 'And Now For a Word'

Kevin James Dobson
- 402 – 'Whatever Happened to Mr Garibaldi?'
- 406 – 'Into the Fire'

Tony Dow
- 409 – 'Atonement'
- 414 – 'Moments of Transition'
- 421 – 'Rising Star'
- 507 – 'Secrets of the Soul'
- 510 – 'A Tragedy of Telepaths'

David Eagle

Lorraine Senna Ferrara

John C Flinn III

Kim Freidman

Stephen Furst

Goran Gajic

Janet Greek

108 – 'And the Sky Full of Stars'
113 – 'Signs and Portents'
118 – 'A Voice in the Wilderness' Part One
119 – 'A Voice in the Wilderness' Part Two
122 – 'Chrysalis'
201 – 'Points of Departure'
209 – 'The Coming of Shadows'
222 – 'The Fall of Night'
501 – 'No Compromises'
504 – 'The View From the Gallery'
515 – 'Darkness Ascending'
519 – 'Wheel of Fire'
TVM – *The River of Souls*

Bruce Seth Green

103 – 'Born to the Purple'
106 – 'Mind War'
109 – 'Deathwalker'
117 – 'Legacies'
120 – 'Babylon Squared'

Jim Johnston

102 – 'Soul Hunter'
105 – 'The Parliament of Dreams'
111 – 'Survivors'
112 – 'By Any Means Necessary'
116 – 'Eyes'
202 – 'Revelations'
204 – 'A Distant Star'
208 – 'A Race Through Dark Places'
210 – 'GROPOS'
212 – 'Acts of Sacrifice'
309 – 'Point of No Return'

John Lafia

405 – 'The Long Night'
416 – 'Exercise of Vital Powers'
418 – 'Intersections in Real Time'

Doug Lefler

508 – 'Day of the Dead'

John McPherson
403 – 'The Summoning'

Adam Nimoy
304 – 'Passing Through Gethsemane'
322 – 'Z'ha'dum'

Stephen L Posey
216 – 'Knives'

J Michael Straczynski
522 – 'Sleeping in Light'

Jésus Treviño
219 – 'Divided Loyalties'
312 – 'Sic Transit Vir'
315 – 'Interludes and Examinations'
410 – 'Racing Mars'
TVM – *Thirdspace*
520 – 'Objects in Motion'

Michael Laurence Vejar
203 – 'The Geometry of Shadows'
214 – 'There All the Honor Lies'
221 – 'Comes the Inquisitor'
302 – 'Convictions'
308 – 'Messages From Earth'
313 – 'A Late Delivery From Avalon'
314 – 'Ship of Tears'
316 – 'War Without End' Part One
317 – 'War Without End' Part Two
413 – 'Rumors, Bargains and Lies'
415 – 'No Surrender, No Retreat'
417 – 'The Face of the Enemy'
TVM – *In the Beginning*
503 – 'The Paragon of Animals'
514 – 'Meditations on the Abyss'
TVM – *A Call to Arms*

Douglas Wise
518 – 'The Fall of Centauri Prime'

Thematic Episodes

Your partner has gone away for the weekend, all your friends are at weddings or funerals and there's nothing on TV apart from athletics and Open University documentaries. Now's the perfect chance to rewatch some of those *Babylon 5* tapes you bought (or recorded off the Sci-Fi Channel). But there are so many episodes to choose from, and the last thing you want to do is start halfway through a plot. Here's an idea: why not follow one particular plot strand from beginning to end, ignoring the side issues? To be used in conjunction with the list in Volume One of *The Babylon File*, here's a rundown of which episodes from the last two seasons contribute in a major way to the five major plot strands in the series.

Telepathy and Psi Corps
402	'Whatever Happened to Mr Garibaldi?'
403	'The Summoning'
407	'Epiphanies'
410	'Racing Mars'
412	'Conflicts of Interest'
414	'Moments of Transition'
416	'Exercise of Vital Powers'
417	'The Face of the Enemy'
501	'No Compromises'
503	'The Paragon of Animals'
506	'Strange Relations'
507	'Secrets of the Soul'
509	'In the Kingdom of the Blind'
510	'A Tragedy of Telepaths'
511	'Phoenix Rising'
513	'The Corps is Mother, the Corps is Father'
519	'The Wheel of Fire'
520	'Objects in Motion'

President Clark and the War to Retake Earth

The Narn/Centauri War

The Shadow War and its Legacy

Recurring Characters

More than in most shows, the complexity of *Babylon 5*'s plot structure has meant that many characters – some major, some minor – have recurred over the years. This is a list of the ones that get credits on screen during seasons 4 and 5. They may have been credited in various ways – the Centauri Official became the Centauri Minister and then the Centauri Regent, for instance – but I've tried to list them under their most commonly recognised title.

Note that I've left out some of the more uncertain characters. Kim Strauss, for instance, has appeared as a Drazi on numerous occasions, but it's difficult to tell whether it's meant to be the same Drazi every time. Others, such as a couple of Byron's telepaths, turn up once or twice but never get an on-screen credit.

Character	Actor	Episodes
Alexander, Lyta	Patricia Tallman	401, 403, 404, 406, 407, 416, 417, 420, 503, 506, 507, 508, 509, 510, 515, 517–20
Allen, Zack	Jeff Conaway	401, 403, 404, 407, 412–14, 416, 501, 502, 504, 505, 506, 507, 508, 509, 510, 513, 514, 520–2 *Thirdspace, The River of Souls, A Call to Arms*
Bester, Alfred	Walter Koenig	407, 414, 417, 421, 506, 509, 510, 513
Byron	Robin Atkin Downes	501, 503, 504, 506, 507, 508, 509, 510
Centauri Emperor	Wortham Krimmer	401–5
Centauri Regent	Damien London	401–3, 406, 407, 509, 518, 519
Clark, Morgan	Gary McGurk	420
Cole, Marcus	Jason Carter	406, 409–11, 415, 417, 419, 420
Corwin, David	Joshua Cox	415, 501, 504, 506, 517, *Thirdspace, The River of Souls*
Cotto, Vir	Stephen Furst	401, 403, 405, 406, 415, 502, 514, 517, 518, 520–2, *Thirdspace*

Character	Actor	Episodes
Delenn	Mira Furlan	401–4, 406–11, 413, 414, 417, 420–506, 508, 514–18, 520–2, *In the Beginning*
Edgars, William	Efrem Zimbalist Jnr	412, 414, 416, 417
Franklin, Dr Stephen	Richard Biggs	402–4, 408–13, 415–17, 420–507, 510, 513, 515–22, *In the Beginning*, *Thirdspace*, *The River of Souls* (but it's not him)
G'Kar	Andreas Katsulas	401–5, 408, 412, 415, 421–504, 506, 508, 509, 514–18, 520, 521, *In the Beginning*
Garibaldi, Michael	Jerry Doyle	402–4, 407, 408, 410, 412, 414–17, 419–501, 503–6, 508–10, 514–22, *The River of Souls*, *A Call to Arms*
Hampton, Lise	Denise Gentile	412, 416, 417, 421, 513, 515, 520, 521
Ivanova, Susan	Claudia Christian	401, 403, 404, 405–8, 411–16, 419, 420 (unconscious), 421, 522, *In the Beginning*, *Thirdspace*
Kosh	Ardwright Chamberlain	401–4
Lennier	Bill Mumy	401–3, 408–11, 413, 414, 417, 419, 420–21, 502, 514–22
Lochley, Elizabeth	Tracy Scoggins	501, 503, 504, 505, 506, 507, 509, 510, 517, 519–21, *The River of Souls*, *A Call to Arms*
Lorien	Wayne Alexander	401–6, 522
Mollari, Londo	Peter Jurasik	401–8, 412, 413, 415, 421–504, 506, 508, 509, 514–21, *In the Beginning*
Morden	Ed Wasser	401, 404, 406, 511
Number One	Marjorie Monaghan	410, 411, 417, 419, 420, 520, 521
Na'Toth	Julie Caitlin Brown	510
Neroon	John Vickery	413, 414
Sheridan, John	Bruce Boxleitner	401–506, 508–22, *A Call to Arms*
Wade	Mark Schneider	410, 412, 416, 417
Zathras	Tim Choate	412

Culture Shock

We've been introduced to a plethora of alien races in *Babylon 5*, each with their own distinctive physiognomy and their own distinct customs and ways of doing business. Some of these races are so similar to humanity that we could almost be genetic cousins (the Centauri, for instance) while others are significantly different (the Pak'ma'ra, or the Trackallans). Most, however, have two arms, two legs and eyes at the right height to gaze into a human's – evidence either of an amazing degree of evolutionary convergence on worlds across the galaxy (aided perhaps by the Vorlons) or of a desire to reduce costs by using real actors as opposed to animatronics or computer-generated characters.

Just for the hell of it, here's a list of all the races that have appeared or been mentioned over the years, both in the TV series itself and also in the various spin-off items:

The Abbai originated on the planet Ssumssha (also known as Abba IV – not to be confused with the fourth album released by the Scandinavian pop group Abba, of course). They are, or are descended from, what appears to be an amphibious race: their skin is slightly scaled and they have a rill or crest, like that of certain newts, running down the centre of their bald heads. The Abbai are ruled by a matriarchy whose authority passes down from mother to daughter in the ruling family. Their society is peaceful and, in technological terms, is several hundred years ahead of that of Earth. Their primary appearances have been in episodes 107 ('The War Prayer') and 109 ('Deathwalker').

The Anfran come from the planet Anfras. Little more has been revealed about them so far (novels only).

Antareans exist in the *Babylon 5* universe, although we don't know what they look like. They do cook flarn, however.

The Balosians send the odd spacecraft to Babylon 5, but are never seen.

The Baltans have been mentioned but not described (novels only).

The Brakiri hail from either the planet Brakos (according to one source) or Brakir (according to another). They are very humanoid in appearance, with prominent bony ridges around their eyes. Most of the Brakiri we have seen have been the proud possessors of long, black hair, although one bald Brakiri often turns up at League meetings. They can be regarded primarily as a planet of businessmen and corporate interests whose rulers are those who make the most money for the planetary economy. They tend to be in many of the episodes from about season 3 onwards, but their moment of glory comes in episode 508 ('Day of the Dead').

All we know about **the Bremmaer** is that they are furry (novels only).

The Cauralline are reptiles with six eyes (novels only).

The Centauri homeworld is Centauri Prime. The Centauri are superficially a humanoid race, but they have two hearts and six sets of sexual organs (the males having six tentacular 'appendages' emerging from their backs which are capable of independent movement, the females having six openings in their backs). Although claiming to be a Republic, the Centauri are in fact ruled by an Emperor whose power is conferred onward through his family. Beneath the Emperor, the power resides in certain families whose fortunes fluctuate depending on how close the members of the family are to the Emperor and to the ruling body – the Centarum. Alliances are forged between these families, and are sealed by intermarriage. The Centauri were once considered an aggressive race who conquered and subjugated planet after planet, but now the Centauri Republic is sliding into depravity and dissolution (they used to own most of the sector of space in which Babylon 5 is located, but now they have control of only twelve worlds). Despite their practical natures, there is a spiritual side to the Centauri – certain of their women can foretell the future, and all Centauri know how, and sometimes when, they are going to die (the knowledge comes to them in a dream). The Centauri have a number of household gods, much like the lares and penates of the ancient Romans. They also have massive feasts which alternate bingeing and purging – also much like the Romans.

A race known as **the Ch'lonas** attacked the Earth colony at Ross 128 IV in 2170. We do not know what they look like or, indeed, why they attacked (role-playing game only).

The Cthulhin have been mentioned as having a presence on Babylon 5, but no more details have emerged about them as yet (novels only).

The inhabitants of the planet **Cotswold** are amphibians (novels only).

The Deneth have been referred to, but not in any detail (novels only).

The Dilgar used to be the scourge of many of the races listed here. A highly intelligent but amoral and militaristic people, they were wiped out by an alliance of the very races they had oppressed (see episode 109 – ' Deathwalker' – for a sight of the last of the Dilgar).

The Drazi are a green-skinned race who are descended from nocturnal ancestors on the planet Zhabar. There appear to be two types of Drazi – one whose heads are covered with small scales and one whose heads are smooth and hard. The Drazi used to be an outdoor race who came indoors only for sleeping. Aggressive, warlike, argumentative and unpleasant – that just about sums up the Drazi. They have a number of colonies and research establishments scattered about the local area, and their region of space is generally known as the Drazi Freehold. Episodes with more Drazi in than usual include 203 ('The Geometry of Shadows') and 512 ('The Ragged Edge').

The Enphili are a peaceful race who have yet to achieve space flight and who have been treated almost as a slave race by the Drazi for some time.

The First Ones are a disparate collection of those races who evolved first in the galaxy. Apart from the Vorlons and the

19

Shadows, the only First One we have ever seen (as far as we know) has appeared in two different forms – that of a tall, distinguished humanoid with gold eyes and long, thin fingers (perhaps its original form) and also that of a glowing ball of energy (probably what it evolved into, over the years). Many of the First Ones have vanished from the galaxy; others hang around in vastly powerful spacegoing habitats, whiling away the long years.

The Froon visit Babylon 5 from time to time (novels only).

The Gaim are an insectoid race from the planet N'chak'fah, whose atmosphere is hostile to most other races. The few Gaim we see in *Babylon 5* wear all-enclosing metallic suits within which they can breathe their own atmosphere. The Gaim are ruled by a number of Queens and are expert genetic engineers (whose knowledge is largely instinctive rather than taught). The ambassadors they send to other worlds are specially bred to be bipedal. True Gaim do not look very much like the ones we've seen in the programme. We get to see what a Gaim ambassador (but not a true Gaim) looks like in episode 501 ('No Compromises').

Gigmosian ceremonies are mentioned in passing, but who holds them and what they are for is anyone's guess (novels only).

Golians have rough, greyish skin and long hair, and are otherwise human in form. We saw one named Trakis in episode 103 ('Born to the Purple'). The Golians were once Centauri slaves (throw a stone in the *Babylon 5* universe and you're likely to hit someone who was a Centauri slave).

The Grome are bald bipedals with a roughened pink skin and a ridge running down the centre of their skulls (one of them harangues Garibaldi and Walker Smith in episode 114 – 'TKO'). Their homeworld is Gromahk, and they are one of the least powerful races to have achieved space flight.

The Hurr are from the planet Androma, and tend to stay there, given their low technological level. They are very human in appearance, except for their rather squashed, piglike snouts. One of them can be seen in episode 121 ('The Quality of Mercy') gambling with Londo and Lennier.

The Hyach are an old, peaceable organisation whose home planet is Shri-shraba. They wear long robes and have pink skin and bald heads, and their skulls appear to have two distinct lobes (covering, it is rumoured, two distinct brains). They are a gerontocracy, ruled by the eldest of their kind, and get on better with the Drazi than with any other race. The Hyach have been civilised for some seven thousand years – that's a good few thousand longer than humanity. In a similar manner to *Homo sapiens* and *Homo neanderthalis*, the Hyach evolved alongside a more primitive race known as the Hyach-do. The two races were close enough genetically for interbreeding to take place – in fact, it was the genetic input from the Hyach-do that kept the Hyach race fertile. The Hyach-do were discriminated against by the Hyach and, several hundred years ago, the Hyach had the Hyach-do completely wiped out. This, alas, has rendered the Hyach increasingly infertile and, unless something is done, the entire race will die off within a few generations. Members of the Hyach race appear in many episodes, but their high point is undoubtedly 506 ('Strange Relations').

The Ikaarans are a humanoid race who are extinct now, but they called the planet Ikaara home. A recording of one of them can be seen in episode 104 ('Infection').

The Ipsha haven't been seen yet, but we know they were one of the races oppressed by the Dilgar.

An extinct alien race known as **the J/Lai** were an offshoot of the Brakiri (novels only).

The Kandarians get a name check, but little else as yet (novels only).

A race known as **the Koulani** attacked the Earth colony at 61 Cygnus A II in 2169 but, as with the Ch'lonas, we don't know why, nor what they look like (role-playing game only).

Little is known about an extinct alien race known as **the Krich** (novels only).

The Llort come from the planet Vartas. They are subterranean and look vaguely reptilian, with small mouths, eyes spaced further apart than a human's and tortoiseshell patterns on their wide foreheads. They frequently appear at meetings of the League of Non-Aligned Worlds and later the Interstellar Alliance, but they never say anything and rarely seem to take part in any military action. They are known as collectors of souvenirs and trinkets (many of which don't actually belong to them).

The Lumati are humanoid, differing physically from humanity in their large foreheads and interesting noses. They are superior, if not downright snobby, and refuse to deal with any race they consider to be their inferior. They oppress their underclass – the poor, the dispossessed – with ruthless efficiency. Their one appearance so far has been in episode 212 ('Acts of Sacrifice').

The Markab are now more or less extinct (although one or two might still be around, having avoided the plague that devastated their homeworld and their colonies). Humanoid and bald, with skulls patterned like broken eggshells, they appear to have been a deeply spiritual race with strongly held moral beliefs. The events that lead up to the sudden and tragic extinction of the Markab can be seen in episode 218 ('Confessions and Lamentations').

The Minbari originate on the planet Minbar, although the Minbari Federation covers twenty worlds in eighteen systems. They are physically very similar to humanity, to the point where members of each race can be transformed into members of the other using sufficiently advanced technology (but, then, sufficiently advanced technology could probably transform a human into a Trackallan, and wouldn't *that* have come as a shock to Jeffrey Sinclair?). Minbari have almost translucent red blood, and they can lose an awful lot of it without dying (although in some later stories their blood is as dark as that of humans). They are ruled by a mysterious Grey Council, whose leader never leaves the Council chamber (which is on a War Cruiser kept distant from Minbar). Beneath the Grey Council is a caste system into which Minbari are born – the castes being

Religious, Warrior and Worker. That said, the Minbari caste structure cuts across a number of clans, the most important being the Wind Swords (generally militant), the Star Riders (who usually become starship personnel), the Night Walkers (who act as the custodians of the Minbari homeworld), the Fire Wings (generally explorers and inventors) and the Moon Shields (the guardians and healers). Minbari do not react well to alcohol – they become subject to psychotic impulses and homicidal rages – and neither do they sweat, but instead secrete a fluid while they are asleep that serves a similar purpose. Minbari can fast for up to fourteen days without too much physical harm, and can enter trancelike states to conserve energy. The Minbari race have three languages – one for each caste. On Minbar, the Minbari are told what they need to know and no more. Undue curiosity is frowned upon. Minbari sleep at an angle, because they believe sleeping horizontally to be tempting death.

The Morellians pop up on the station from time to time (novels only).

The Narn (whose homeworld is known only as the Narn Homeworld) may look like reptiles, but in fact they give birth to live young and look after them in pouches, much like kangaroos. Originally a peaceful species of farmers and herdsmen, the Narn transformed themselves into a race of warriors following the (first) invasion of their homeworld by the Centauri. Following their successful fight to throw off the yoke of Centauri slavery, they started to buy and sell weapons and do everything they could to build up the strength of their armed forces. Following the *second* Centauri invasion of their homeworld, and the abrupt withdrawal of Centauri forces following the 'death' of the Centauri Emperor, there are signs that the Narn are becoming more spiritual and less warlike (they have several different religions). It is a Narn tradition that, for the first ten years of their lives, they have temporary names. After they are ten, they can choose the faith they wish to follow and the name they wish to use. Narn can hibernate for six days at a time.

The Norsaii are a peaceful, agrarian race.

The Pakkel are mentioned briefly but never seen (comics only).

The Pak'ma'ra home planet is Melat according to one source but Pak'ma according to another. They're grey-skinned and bulky, and the lower halves of their faces are covered in tentacles. They are essentially a race who enjoy the process of thought and the sharing of ideas. Their eyes can see further into the ultraviolet than humans and they have at least three lungs and two pulmonary systems. The Pak'ma'ra would appear to be a religious race who believe themselves to be the chosen of God. They can digest almost anything apart from fish, but prefer rotting carcasses. All Pak'ma'ra that we have seen in *Babylon 5* are male: the humps on their backs are rumoured to be the females of the species, who are symbiotically attached to their mates.

The Piridians are briefly mentioned, but not described (novels only).

The Raugans were just about to evolve into a life form with no need of physical form when the Shag'Toth (the Soul Hunters) came along and imprisoned all of them within one of their Soul Spheres.

The Shag'Toth are bald humanoids with deep-set eyes and strange gemlike objects embedded in their foreheads. They are better known as 'Soul Hunters', and they live for many thousands of years. Little is known about them, save that the ones seen out at large in the universe are solitary creatures who seek out successful, powerful members of alien races at the moment of their death and capture the essence of their life force – their 'soul' – for adding to their collections (kept in large buildings known as Whisper Galleries). Only three times in their entire history have the Soul Hunters 'collected' an entire species. The Shag'Toth regard this as an altruistic act, saving these beings from death, but the rest of the universe think of them as scavengers and fight them off whenever possible. The Shag'Toth have made two main appearances in *Babylon 5* – one in episode 102 ('Soul Hunter') and again in the third TV movie (*The River of Souls*).

The real name of **the Shadows** is a thousand characters long and unpronounceable by humans. Originating from the planet Z'ha'dum, they were among the first races to evolve in this galaxy (see **First Ones**). Hard-skinned, six-legged and spiky, they resemble nothing so much as giant, black praying mantises – or at least they would if they weren't able to shield themselves at will from observation, phasing themselves somehow from out of the visual spectrum and into the ultraviolet. The Shadows believe passionately that the 'lesser' races should be allowed to (or indeed actively encouraged to) fight among themselves so that the weak perish and the strong survive to evolve. The Shadows have, as far as we know, all vanished from our universe now, having travelled 'beyond the rim' with the rest of the First Ones.

The Sh'lassa are mentioned once or twice, and receive military aid from Earth during season 2, but so far we have not seen them (as far as we know).

The Streibs are distantly related to the Vree, and are similarly small and bald, with large eyes (red and slitted, in the case of the Streibs). Their primary purpose in life seems to be to travel around abducting specimens of alien races and examining them for weaknesses – in their resistance to torture, stamina and so on – as a preparatory measure for invasion. The Minbari appear to know more about them than anyone else, having been on the receiving end of their attentions and having subsequently taught them a lesson.

The Tak'cha are a spindly, gnarled race who were associated with the Minbari and Valen during the last War Against the Shadows but were thrown out of the alliance because of their rather aggressive interpretation of Valen's teachings. They are still around (comics only).

The Thalatine are highly humanoid in form, but oviparous (i.e. they lay eggs rather than hatch their young live). They are a deeply spiritual people who believe that any break in the skin will allow their souls to escape and thus render them animals rather than rational beings. Their moment of glory in the programme was in episode 110 ('Believers').

The Thrantallil breathe liquid metal hydrogen (novels only), which would make serving them in the Fresh Air restaurant a trifle tricky.

The Throxtil are big aliens with five legs and five arms (novels only).

The Tikar have spacecraft that look like great glowing green clouds. Captain Sheridan initiated contact with them and found the experience quite memorable.

The T'llin are a humanoid race from the planet T'll with sharp features, nictitating membranes on their eyes and a blue, scaled skin. They are well adapted to life on a desert world, and are able to voluntarily enter a state of hibernation in which their vital signs slow down so much they appear to be dead. They were once a slave race of the Narn, in that short period between the liberation of Narn and its subjugation again (novels only).

The Tokadi are represented on Babylon 5, although we never get to see them.

The Trackallans are bipedal insects that stand about as tall as a human but probably have a greater body mass.

Trivorians have three eyes, and their tears are corrosive (novels only).

The Tuchanq are a humanoid race with sensory organs shaped like a mane of spines instead of eyes. Sometimes they are biped, sometimes quadruped, and they never sleep (novels only). They were once a slave race of the Narn, in that short period between the liberation of Narn and its subjugation again (novels only).

The Vendrizi are an ancient form of life who were artificially created by an unnamed race on an unnamed planet half a million years ago. They consist completely of genetically neutral material (looking rather like a large earwig), and are able to infiltrate a host creature and join with its neural system, effectively forming a joint creature with the memories of both its components. The Vendrizi appear to have a collective mind, with everything known by one of them being accessible to all of them. Once a Vendrizi is removed from its host organism, the host cannot accept another Vendrizi without causing severe damage to its neural system. They are very sensitive to 'impurities' such as drugs in the host's blood. The 'purpose' of the Vendrizi is to travel through the galaxy memorising everything they see and hear. They are a mobile repository of knowledge, and, when darkness falls across the galaxy and everything that was known is lost, they will keep the memories alive. They refer to themselves as 'keepers of the past, the present and the future'.

Before their sudden disappearance from our universe, **the Vorlons** had been one of the earliest races to have evolved. Once humanoid, they had evolved to the point where their bodies were semicrystalline energy forms (although they still breathed an atmosphere composed of methane, carbon dioxide and sulphur) and they had the power to make other races see them as they wished. Mysterious, secretive and private, the Vorlons kept their own borders inviolate while 'guiding' the development of the lesser races: interfering in their genetic make-up to produce telepaths and ensuring that they were conditioned to follow orders from 'higher beings'. The Vorlons are dedicated to the principles of order and stability: they would far rather issue edicts on what other races can and can't do than allow them to make their own mistakes. The Vorlons have a fondness for semiorganic technology: their spaceships appear to be living beings in their own right. The body that rules the Vorlon Empire is referred to as the Vorlon High Command. Up to the pilot episode ('The Gathering') it was alleged that no human had ever seen a Vorlon, although there are legends of one who had and was turned to stone. In fact, we now know that several humans had been abducted by the Vorlons and used as their agents throughout history.

The Vree call the planet Vreetan home. They are small and pale, with large skulls and large, black eyes, and are genetic cousins of the Streib. Their ships resemble flying saucers, and pack some terrific fire power. Although they never turn up to meetings of the League of Non-Aligned Worlds or the Interstellar Alliance, their ships are always at the forefront of any military action.

Little has yet been revealed in *Babylon 5* about **the Xoth** (novels only).

All we know about **the Ylinn** is that they are reptilian and squat (novels only).

The Ynaborian Sinining remains something of a mystery in the series (novels only).

The Yolu originated on the planet Pa'ra. They are an ancient race who have possessed space flight for some 3,000 human years. The only one we have seen is bald and lined (it's in charge of the fight in episode 114 – 'TKO'), but who knows if they all look like that? In fact, the Yolu that appears in the comic strip *In Valen's Name* looks nothing like it, having orange skin, a big, toothy mouth and red eyes. The Yolu refused to take part in the War Against the Shadows a thousand years ago, and there is no evidence that they took part in this one either.

Other races have appeared in passing, but no names have yet been assigned to them. The pilot episode ('The Gathering') is chock-full of aliens who have never subsequently reappeared, while in season 1 N'Grath's bodyguards (big, burly, bald creatures) were rather impressive. Zathras's race have never been given a name, and neither have the race who built the Great Machine on Epsilon 3 (assuming Varn was one of them) or the ones who claimed it as theirs in episode 118 ('A Voice in the Wilderness' Part One). The invaders who test the station's defences in episode 504 ('The View From the Gallery') don't get named either. In later episodes, 'The Ragged Edge' has a humanoid alien with a series of what appear to be gills where the mouth and nose are on a human, while in

Thirdspace a red-skinned, bald-headed being whose eyes appear to be on stalks projecting from its cheeks is wandering around the station. And, to finish, perhaps the most alien of them all, the creatures who live in thirdspace are bigger than humans, and can survive in a vacuum. They look rather like house mites with six legs and tentacles, and are older even than the Vorlons.

Other Worlds

During five seasons of *Babylon 5*, as well as ten books, various comics and a couple of role-playing games, we've had a wealth of planets and colonies thrown at us. These names have, in the main, been slipped past us in ones or twos – a colony here, a homeworld there – and so here, for the first time anywhere, is a comprehensive list of the worlds we know exist in the *Babylon 5* universe:

Abba IV (otherwise known as Ssumssha), Akdor, Alzeral (a Vree colony), Anara VII (books only), Andat, Androma, Anfras (books only), Antares, Antareus (books only), Ares Colony, Arisia III, Arkada VII (destroyed by the Vorlons)

Balos, Batain VI (RPG only), Beata (a Centauri colony, RPG only), Berlin II (an Earth colony, RPG only), Beta Durani, Beta System (including Beta XII and Beta IX: all Centauri possessions), Betelgeuse IV (books only), Betelgeuse VI (books only), Brakos

Canton I and Canton III (Earth colonies, RPG only), Centauri Prime, Cestus, Ceti II (RPG only), Comac IV, Cooke I and Cooke III (Earth colonies, RPG only), Corianus VI, Cotswold (books only), Contor II (RPG only), Cyrus III

Dakota I and Dakota II (Earth colonies, RPG only), Daltron 7, Davo, Delphi IV (Earth colony, RPG only), Deneb IV, Deruzala (a Vree colony), D'Grn IV, Disneyplanet, Dorac VII, Dras (a Narn world), Drathun II (a Drazi colony), Draxis colony, Dura 7

Earth, Eridani III (an Earth colony, RPG only)

Fendamir Research Colony (a Drazi possession), Fensalir (books only), Frallis XII

G'Halmaza (a Centauri colony, RPG only), Glasir (books only), Gorash 7 (a Centauri world), Greater Krindar, Gromahk

Halax, Handhi III (an Earth colony, RPG only), Harat (a Narn colony, RPG only), Heptharg III (a Drazi colony), Hutchinson Colony, Hyach VII (a Narn colony)

Ikarra III, Immolan V (a Centauri colony), Iridan Colony

Janos VII

Kara (a Brakiri colony), Kazomi VII, Khefti, Kitab III (a Yolu colony)

Latec IV, Leonis V and VII (Earth colonies, RPG only), Lesser Krindar, L'Gn'Daort, Lorra Outpost (RPG only)

MacArthur Mid-Range Colony, the Markab Homeworld, Melat, Mentab II (RPG only), Minbar, Mjollnir (books only), Myoto VI (an Earth colony, RPG only)

Nacambad Colony, Narn Homeworld, N'chak'fah, Nemus (a Yolu colony), New Jerusalem, Nippon (a human colony)

Omelos, Oqmrritkz, Orion IV, Orion VII (an Earth colony, RPG only)

Pak'ma, Pa'ra, Photikar (a Vree colony), Proxima III

Ragesh III, Ragesh IX, Rauga, Ross 128 IV (an Earth colony, RPG only)

7 Lukantha, Shambah (a Drazi colony), Shi (a Narn world), Sh'lek'k'tha (a Minbari colony, RPG only), Shri-shraba, Sigma 957, 61 Cygnus A II (otherwise known as the Signet outpost, an Earth colony, RPG only), Skirnir (books only), Ssumssha (also known as Abba IV)

Tau Ceti IV (an Earth colony, RPG only), Tavita (Abba III, a colony of the Abbai), Thalatine, Theta Omega 2 (books only), Tirolus, Tizino Prime, T'Lad'Tha II (RPG only), T'll (a Narn colony, books only), Tolonius VII (a Centauri colony), Trepani VII, Tr'es's'na (a Minbari colony, RPG only), Trivorian (books only), Tuchanq (a former Narn colony, books only), Tulok I (RPG only), Turan I (RPG only)

Vartas, Vega Outpost, Vega VII, Velatastat, Ventari 3, the Vorlon Homeworld, Vreetan

Wolf V (RPG only)

Ymir (books only)

Zagros VII (a Drazi world), Zander Prime, Zathran VII, Zhabar, Z'ha'dum, Zok (a Narn world)

Key to Episode Guide Entries

The episode entries which constitute the majority of this book follow the same form as for Volume 1. For those of you who missed Volume 1, or whose grylor ate their copy, here's what the various entries mean:

Transmission Number: This is the standard notation that tells you which season and where in the season the episode was transmitted. For instance, 411 is the eleventh episode of the fourth season, and 102 is the second episode of the first season. Although some of the episodes were swapped shortly before transmission for various reasons, this is the order in which, for continuity purposes, we assume that the events happened. Any mentions of episode numbers in this book refer to the transmission number.

Production Number: This operates in the same way as the transmission number, but tells you in what order the episodes were made, rather than transmitted (with the exception of 523 which, bizarrely, was made at the end of season 4). Most of the time this constitutes redundant information, but sometimes it can help clarify problems in continuity. Episode 507 ('Secrets of the Soul') for instance, is followed in transmission order by episodes 508 ('Day of the Dead') and 509 ('In the Kingdom of the Blind'). Internal evidence, however, indicates that 'In the Kingdom of the Blind' follows directly on from 'Secrets of the Soul' with scant space for another story. Looking at the production numbers makes it clearer: 'Secrets of the Soul' is 507, 'Day of the Dead' is 511 and 'In the Kingdom of the Blind' is 509. The episodes were swapped around (for reasons which will be made clearer later in the book).

Story by: This entry is a new one, given that on two episodes in seasons 4 and 5, J Michael Straczynski collaborated with Harlan Ellison over the story.

Written by: Well, this was reasonably important in seasons 1 and 2, but it's almost completely redundant for seasons 4 and 5. Of the twenty-two episodes and four TV movies listed herein, only one has anything apart from 'J Michael Straczynski' under this item.

Directed by: As with Volume 1, there has been some attempt here to ensure at least a modicum of consistency between entries. Jésus Treviño, for instance, decided at some stage to have himself listed as Jésus Salvador Treviño (although I sincerely doubt there was a Jésus Treviño already listed as a Directors' Guild member), and both John Flinn and David Eagle have been listed in different ways.

Cast: As before, I haven't bothered listing every bit part actor who walked past in the background, only the characters who have had some major impact on the story or otherwise made themselves memorable. One of these was, of course, Peter Brown, who was listed as 'Minister' in episode 418 ('Intersections in Real Time') but who made himself instantly memorable by not actually being in the episode.

Date: There's been much less of an attempt in seasons 4 and 5 to tie the events down to specific dates, but where that's occurred, or where it can be inferred, I've mentioned it.

Plot: As before, a brief overall review of the story will be followed by a breakdown into three sections: the 'A' plot, the 'B' plot and the 'C' plot. It's a semi-standard template for action/adventure series like *Babylon 5* to have three plots working together. Cutting between them stops the viewer from getting bored and provides a richer, multi-layered texture to the proceedings. That's the theory, anyway.

The 'A' Plot: this is the action/adventure plot, where things explode and there's lots of jaw-clenching and dramatic one-liners.

The 'B' Plot: this is usually more reflective, and is more about emotions than explosions. Internal conflict rather than external conflict, if you will. In the hands of a good writer, the events of the 'B' plot will parallel the 'A' plot; in the hands of a bad writer they will be about completely different things.

The 'C' Plot: this is usually the comic relief.

The Arc: This section attempts to draw your attention to the material in each episode which is part of J Michael Straczynski's five-year story arc. During season 4 this primarily concerns the Shadow War and the War to Retake Earth. Uncertainties over the commissioning of season 5 meant that most of Straczynski's arc was used up in season 4, and so there is a certain perception that season 5 was made up on the spur of the moment. Nevertheless, certain issues such as the tragic events to befall Londo Mollari were set up back in season 1 and are worth mentioning.

Observations: Odd things such as alternative castings, clips reused from other episodes, scenes moved wholesale from one episode to another, anything that adds to the viewing enjoyment and which couldn't be squeezed in anywhere else in the entries.

Koshisms: Well, by the time season 4 started Kosh was dead, but he still managed to get a line or two anyway.

Ivanova's Life Lessons: For as long as she was around.

Dialogue to Rewind For: Those lines that sparkled like gems and deserve to be remembered.

Dialogue to Fast-Forward Past: Those lines that drew attention to themselves by being completely out of kilter with the rest of the dialogue; usually when J Michael Straczynski was letting a character talk like him rather than like themselves.

Ships That Pass in the Night: Not as many as in seasons 1 to 3, but some spaceships do still arrive at the station.

Other Worlds: Planets that get a name-check in the *Babylon 5* universe.

Culture Shock: By this stage we've discovered most of what we need to know about the main races, but there are still some interesting little facts to unearth.

Station Keeping: Not much call for this during seasons 4 and 5, given that it's the section where I list things we discover about Babylon 5 itself. Still, estimating what colour Babylons

2 and 3 had to be based on the colours of 1, 4 and 5 is interesting, in a train-spotter kind of way . . .

Literary, Mythological and Historical References: Seasons 1 to 3 were a cornucopia of references to other writers. Seasons 4 and 5 have been less of a treasure trove, but there are still some odd references here and there worth mentioning.

I've Seen That Face Before: Actors who have been in the series before, or who are recognisable from other things.

Accidents Will Happen: It's impossible to avoid them, and I think it's symbolic of something or other that the very last episode of *Babylon 5* contains one of the oldest and most common accidents in the book.

Questions Raised: One would have hoped that all the questions would have been answered by the end of the series, but there are still some left hanging.

THE TV EPISODES

Seasons 1 to 3:
Addenda and Corrigenda

It's always the way: you spend months of your life writing a book about a TV series and then, just after it's published, you find a whole bag of facts that you really wish you'd incorporated. So, until that happy day when Volumes 1 and 2 of *The Babylon File* are published in a single, massive, completely revised version, below is a list of the things I've discovered about seasons 1 to 3 since the last book.

Observations: During auditions for the pilot TV movie, 'The Gathering', Andreas Katsulas and W Morgan Sheppard were neck and neck for the part of G'Kar. Sheppard returned to play the first Soul Hunter in episode 102 ('Soul Hunter') and G'Kar's uncle in episode 220 ('The Long, Twilight Struggle'). It would have been a completely different series, wouldn't it?

And, continuing on the theme of odd casting, Julie Caitlin Brown auditioned for the roles of Delenn and Ivanova before getting the part of Na'Toth.

Curtis Laseter (construction coordinator on the series) played the casino barman in episode 116 ('Eyes').

Stephen Posey (director of episode 216 – 'Knives') is married to the show's 2nd Assistant Director, Pam Eilerson.

The UK video release of 'Divided Loyalties' (episode 219) and 'The Long, Twilight Struggle' (episode 220) had the episodes the wrong way round, resulting in Delenn referring to a conversation she had with Sheridan (the 'abso-fraggin'-lutely' one) before she has even had it.

One of the Narn in episode 221 ('Comes the Inquisitor') is played by a CNN entertainment reporter named Dennis Michael.

Episode 310 ('Severed Dreams') won the 1997 Hugo Award for Best Dramatic Presentation.

Literary, Mythological and Historical References: The

title of 'There All the Honor Lies' (episode 214) comes from Alexander Pope's *An Essay on Man* (1733):

> Honour and shame from no condition arise;
> Act well on your part: there all the honour lies.

The title of 'The Long, Twilight Struggle' (episode 220) might derive from President John F Kennedy's inaugural address, in which he issued a call to arms (now there's a phrase) in 'a long, twilight struggle . . . against the common enemies of man: tyranny, poverty, disease and war itself'.

I've Seen That Face Before: Beth Toussaint, who played Anna Sheridan in episode 202 ('Revelations'), also appeared as Tasha Yar's sister Ishara in the *Star Trek: The Next Generation* episode 'Legacy'.

Mark Rolston, who played Karl Mueller in episode 121 ('The Quality of Mercy'), was Private Drake in James Cameron's film *Aliens*.

Carel Struycken, who played the alien trader in episode 207 ('Soul Mates'), appeared many times in *Star Trek: The Next Generation* as Mr Hom.

Accidents Will Happen: There's a running discrepancy over how old Susan Ivanova was when her mother committed suicide. In 'The Long Night' (episode 405) Ivanova tells Sheridan that she was ten years old when her mother committed suicide. In episode 114 ('TKO') it emerges in conversation that Ivanova's brother, Ganya Ivanov, was killed in the Earth–Minbari War one year after their mother committed suicide. This would make Susan Ivanova eleven years old when her brother dies, which she patently is not in the TV movie *In the Beginning*. Similarly, in 'Midnight on the Firing Line' (episode 101) Ivanova says that her mother committed suicide ten years after she started taking the sleepers to suppress her telepathic abilities, but in 'Eyes' (episode 116) Harriman Grey says to Ivanova, 'She must have been in your mind numerous times before she was given the sleepers, your mother.' Not likely if Ivanova was only one year old.

In episode 120 ('Babylon Squared') we're told that the

Leader of the Grey Council never leaves the Council Chamber, but Dukhat was all over the ship in episode 409 ('Atonement') and the TV movie *In the Beginning*. Perhaps they changed the rules after Dukhat's death.

Apparently (and I can't be arsed to check), although Ivanova is lighting Hannukah candles in episode 222 ('The Fall of Night'), Hannukah will fall earlier than the date of this episode in the year 2259.

In 'Messages From Earth' (episode 308) Lennier says two scientifically meaningless things in as many minutes. First he claims that the atmospheric pressure is approaching two standard gravities, but 'gravity' is a unit of field strength rather than a unit of force (I'm a physicist, I knew that). He also talks about the ship's energy blast igniting the hydrogen in Jupiter's atmosphere, but hydrogen will ignite only in the presence of free oxygen, and there's precious little of this in Jupiter's atmosphere.

In 'War Without End' Part Two (episode 317) the beam that falls on Zathras is rectangular as it falls but cylindrical by the time it hits the ground.

In episode 322 ('Z'ha'dum') Sheridan reminds Delenn that 'You and Kosh came to my quarters. You showed me images from Z'ha'dum . . .' Er, no . . . they were in Delenn's quarters.

At the bottom of page 252 of Lois Tilton's *Babylon 5* novel *Accusations*, Sheridan briefly turns into Sinclair.

Now, having made the amendments, I turn my attention rather shamefacedly to the corrections. The British Newspaper the *Guardian* has a policy of apologising for, and correcting, every single mistake in every issue. Provoked by their example, I hereby present a list of every error that has been discovered in Volume 1 of this mammoth work. Get your pencils ready:

Page 56   There's no episode listing for Marcus Cole.

Page 57   I missed out Garibaldi's appearance in episode 318 ('Walkabout').

Page 68	All that effort to get the US military ranks correct, and I make a mistake. In the US Army, the lower enlisted structure goes from E1 at the bottom up to E9. It runs as follows: Private (E1) (a basic recruit); Private (E2); Private First Class (E3); Specialist (E4) (which is the same pay grade as a Corporal, but is not a leadership position, and is the only grade that can be used as either an NCO or lower enlisted rank); then up through E4 (Corporal); E5 (Sergeant); E6 (Staff Sergeant); E7 (Sergeant First Class); E8 (where a soldier can be either a Master Sergeant (MSG) or a First Sergeant (1SG)) and E9 (where a soldier can be either a Sergeant Major (SGM) or a Command Sergeant Major (CSM)). The highest Warrant Officer rank is currently Master Warrant (MW5). In descending order come the Chief Warrant Officer Four (CW4), Chief Warrant Officer Three (CW3), Chief Warrant Officer Two (CW2), and Warrant Officer One (WO1). You'll be tested on this later.
Page 86	In **The Arc** for episode 101 ('Midnight on the Firing Line') I claim that it contains scenes of Delenn working on her transformation device. It doesn't.
Page 101	In **The Arc** for episode 105 ('The Parliament of Dreams') I say that Delenn is 'the One that is to come'. Arrant rubbish: Delenn is 'the One who is'; Sheridan is 'the One who will be'.
Page 116	In the **Observations** on episode 108 ('And the Sky Full of Stars') I stated that, as there were nine members of the Grey Council shown, they must have replaced the dead Dukhat. What I had failed to appreciate, of course, is that the Grey Council has nine members *plus* the Leader of the Council.
Page 120	In the **Observations** section for episode 109 ('Deathwalker'), I'm informed that Gilbert

Gottfried was never a host of *Saturday Night Live*, merely a temporary member of the resident comedy troupe during the show's sixth season.

Page 133   In **The Arc** section for episode 113 ('Signs and Portents') I suggest (wrongly) that episode 217 is 'The Shadow of Z'ha'dum' rather than '*In* The Shadow of Z'ha'dum'.

Page 134   As page 133.

Page 144   In the **Plot** for episode 116 ('Eyes') I claim that Harriman Grey is a Psi Cop. He's not, he works for the military. As a P10, he couldn't be a Psi Cop if he tried.

Page 148   In the **Plot** for 117 ('Legacies') I state that Neroon's rank is Shai Alyt: it isn't, it's just Alyt.

Page 169   In **The Arc** section for episode 122 ('Chrysalis') I say that the Shadows hold their forelimbs like a preying mantis. I actually meant a pr*a*ying mantis (I actually knew that, but it took a vet to remind me).

Page 170   In the **Questions Raised** section for episode 122 ('Chrysalis') I wondered what the jammers in Deveraux's crates were for, given that communications from Earthforce 1 were being jammed pretty effectively without them. The answer, of course, is that one of the ships carrying the jammers had engine trouble, and never left Babylon 5. The rest did, and carried out the job just fine.

Page 176   Under **Ivanova's Life Lessons** in episode 201 ('Points of Departure') I quote Sheridan as saying one of Ivanova's lines. Look, I was tired. I missed it, my readers missed it, the editor missed it, the proofreader missed it . . . We were *all* tired.

Page 177   In the **I've Seen That Face Before** section for episode 201 ('Points of Departure'), Robert

	Foxworth should have appeared in the *Outer Limits* episode 'Trial By Fire', not 'Worlds Apart'.
Page 181	In the **Dialogue to Fast-Forward Past** in episode 202 ('Revelations') it's Elizabeth Sheridan who tells John Sheridan that his wife died 'on a deep-space exploration vessel that exploded', not the other way around. Whichever way round it goes, it's still a clumsy, exposition-heavy piece of dialogue.
Page 186	In **Dialogue to Rewind For** in 'The Geometry of Shadows' (episode 203) it is the green Drazi leader who explains why Ivanova's trick worked and not the purple one.
Page 191	The single most pointed-out error in the book: in the **Plot** of 'The Long Dark' (episode 205) Amos actually survives the encounter with the 'Dark Soldier' and does not, as I said, die.
Page 222	In the **Plot** for episode 214 ('There All the Honor Lies') Lennier's clan is the Third *Fane* of Chudomo, not the vaguely Shakespearian Third *Thane* of *Chodomo*.
Page 223	In the **Observations** section of episode 214 ('There All the Honor Lies') I refer to the baseball scene between Garibaldi and Sheridan. That's not in this episode, it's actually in episode 216 ('Knives'). In the same section I describe the 'priceless moment' when a Markab takes off a human mask and a human takes off a Drazi mask in the new Babylon 5 emporium. Actually, it's a human wearing a Markab mask and a Drazi wearing a human mask. Easy mistake to make . . .
Page 228	In the **Accidents Will Happen** entry for episode 215 ('And Now For a Word') I stated that Sheridan's middle name is known to be David even though his initial is here given as 'J'. This

is, of course, nonsense. His middle name has *never* been said to be David.

Page 248   In the **Literary, Mythological and Historical References** for episode 221 ('Comes the Inquisitor') I foolishly stated that it was Faustus who said 'Why, this is Hell, now am I out of it,' in Marlowe's *Doctor Faustus*. It isn't: it's Mephistopheles.

Page 252   In **I've Seen That Face Before** for episode 222 ('The Fall of Night') I make that Alyt/Shai Alyt mistake again for Neroon.

Page 263   In the **Dialogue to Rewind For** in episode 302 ('Convictions') the Centauri joke that culminates in the punch line 'hundreds of servants would screw in a thousand light bulbs at our slightest command!' should be 'hundreds of servants would *change* a thousand light bulbs at our slightest *whim*!'

Page 266   In the **Observations** for episode 303 ('A Day in the Strife') I say that this was the first episode in which Corwin was given a name. Incorrect: he was named in episode 215 ('And Now For a Word'). In the same section, 'A Voice in the Wilderness' Part Two should be episode 119, not 319.

Page 267   In **Ivanova's Life Lessons** for episode 303 ('A Day in the Strife') the quote, 'I don't want to get killed because of a typo – that would be stupid', contains a typo. How stupid. It should read, 'I don't want to get killed because of a typo – it would be embarrassing'.

Page 273   In the cast list for episode 305 ('Voices of Authority'), it should be Julie Musante rather than Julie Masante.

Page 276	In the **Observations** on episode 305 ('Voices of Authority'), it should *still* be Julie Musante rather than Julie Masante.
Pages 286–7	In **I've Seen That Face Before** for episode 307 ('Exogenesis'), how could I mention Aubrey Morris without listing his best-known role as Mr Deltoid in Stanley Kubrick's 1971 film of Anthony Burgess's *A Clockwork Orange*? How? Because Stanley Kubrick won't let the film be shown in the UK any more, that's how.
Page 289	In **The Arc** for episode 308 ('Messages From Earth'), episode 201 isn't 'Chrysalis', it's 'Points of Departure'.
Page 296	In **The Arc** for episode 310 ('Severed Dreams'), episode 201 should be 'Points of Departure', not 'Matters of Honor'.
Page 308	In **The Arc** for episode 313 ('A Late Delivery from Avalon'), Marcus compares himself to Galahad, not Lancelot.
Page 327	In the **Observations** on episode 317 ('War Without End' Part Two), 'A Voice in the Wilderness' Parts One and Two are episodes 118 and 119, not 318 and 319.
Page 336	In the **I've Seen That Face Before** section of 319 ('Grey 17 Is Missing') Neroon is maintaining his unwarranted promotion to Shai Alyt.
Page 350	The overall title for season 4 is 'No Surrender, No Retreat', not 'No Retreat, No Surrender'. There's a rather embarrassing story attached to that mistake which I won't go into now . . .
Page 358	In the **Observations** on episode 402 ('Whatever Happened to Mr Garibaldi?') I should have stated that it also contained flashbacks to episode 308 ('Messages From Earth').

Page 364	In the **Plot** for episode 404 ('Falling Toward Apotheosis') the Vorlens are obviously an off-shoot of the Vorlons.
Page 380	In the **Date** for John Vornholt's *Babylon 5* book *Voices* I refer to episode 203 as 'A Day in the Strife' as opposed to 'The Geometry of Shadows'.
Page 387	In the **Date** for John Vornholt's *Babylon 5* book *Blood Oath* I rather foolishly again refer to episode 203 as 'A Day in the Strife' as opposed to 'The Geometry of Shadows'.
Page 392	In the **Ships That Pass in the Night** section for Jim Mortimore's *Babylon 5* book *Clark's Law*, I erroneously list episode 305 as being 'Voices From Earth' when everyone knows it's 'Voices of Authority'.
Page 403	In the **Observations** on the comic strip 'In Darkness Find Me', I said that it contained a two-page article on customs in the series, written by *Babylon 5*'s Costume Designer. I actually meant 'costumes', not 'customs'. Of course.
Page 409	In the **Observations** on the comic strip 'Shadows, Past and Present' I state that episode 122 is 'Signs and Portents'. It's not: episode 113 is 'Signs and Portents'. I actually meant 122 ('Chrysalis').
Page 410	In the **Date** section of the entry on the comic strip 'Laser – Mirror – Starweb' I claim that episode 204 is 'Distant Star' whereas, in fact, it's 'A Distant Star'.

Season 4:
'No Surrender, No Retreat'

'It was the year of fire; the year of destruction; the year we took back what was ours.

'It was the year of rebirth; the year of great sadness; the year of pain and a year of joy.

'It was a new age; it was the end of history; it was the year everything changed.

'The year is 2261; the place – Babylon 5.'

– Lennier, Zack Allen, G'Kar, Lyta Alexander, Vir Cotto, Marcus Cole, Ambassador Delenn, Londo Mollari, Dr Stephen Franklin, Commander Susan Ivanova, Security Chief Michael Garibaldi, Captain John Sheridan.

Regular and Semi-Regular Cast:

Captain John Sheridan: Bruce Boxleitner
Commander Susan Ivanova: Claudia Christian
Security Chief Michael Garibaldi: Jerry Doyle
Ambassador Delenn: Mira Furlan
Londo Mollari: Peter Jurasik   **G'Kar:** Andreas Katsulas
Dr Stephen Franklin: Richard Biggs
Vir Cotto: Stephen Furst   **Lennier:** Bill Mumy
Marcus Cole: Jason Carter   **Zack Allen:** Jeff Conaway
Lyta Alexander: Patricia Tallman

Observations: In order to avoid the problem of having to choose a particular character to read the opening narration – and thus admit by default that they survive long enough to have some kind of historical perspective on events – J Michael Straczynski had originally toyed with the idea of changing the narrator every few episodes. In the end, he chose to have everyone narrate a part of a line, thus having what must be the first opening of a TV series to be narrated by twelve separate actors.

The title sequence and title music were changed again for season 4, reflecting a more upbeat, triumphant feel for the series.

Cast changes were fairly restrained this time around. As was expected, Andrea Thompson did not return as the telepath Talia Winters. In her place, Patricia Tallman returns as Lyta Alexander, and gets promoted into the title sequence.

In an unexpected turn of events, Foundation Imaging lost the contract to provide computer-generated special effects for the series. Rumours abound as to why that happened (neither party is allowed to discuss publicly the terms of the settlement between Babylonian and Foundation, or the circumstances surrounding it, which at least indicates that there was a legal problem) and the true story is unlikely ever to be made public, but the replacement effects provided by Netter Digital Imaging are indistinguishable in terms of quality from their predecessors'. Foundation went on to provide effects for *Star Trek: Voyager*: a contract that was awarded *after* they were replaced on *Babylon 5* by NDI.

J Michael Straczynski's original intention was for Bruce Boxleitner not to be in the first few episodes of season 4, but sensibly he changed his mind and introduced the scenes between Sheridan and Lorien.

The umbrella title for season 4 was not released until Straczynski started work on the last six episodes of the season, because it wasn't until then that he knew whether the arc would have to be compressed into four seasons or whether Warner Brothers would allow it to extend to its full length of five seasons. That decision would influence which of two titles was given to the season.

The biggest problem facing Straczynski during the making of season 4 was, of course, the uncertainty over whether Warner Brothers were going to commission a fifth season, or whether he was going to have to wrap up the story in four seasons despite all his promises to the fans and the public at large. The pressure was intense, and Straczynski's solution was, characteristically, the one that would be hardest for him to pull off but would make him look like a magician if he could. In essence what he did was to structure the rest of the story so that he could transmit the final episode at the end of either season 4 or season 5. This meant, of course, that the story would divert from the one he had planned out so many years ago.

The biggest factor affecting the shape of the fourth season was, of course, the uncertainty as the season approached its end on whether Warners Brothers would commission a fifth and final year. Toward the end of the filming of season 4, J Michael Straczynski claimed that he was writing alternative scenes or alternative scene endings into the last six or so episodes, and that he would not know until those episodes were actually filmed which versions he was going to use.

Had he been told early enough that season 5 had been commissioned, Straczynski has confirmed that season 4 would have ended on episode 418 ('Intersections in Real Time'), i.e. after the War to Retake Earth had begun, but before it concluded. This indicates that, despite intense fan speculation at the time, the Shadow War was always scheduled to conclude in season 4, although in the 'original' mix of season 4 (i.e. before the compression of the plot), there would have been one or two episodes leading up to the climactic events of episode 406 ('Into the Fire'). Straczynski has said, however, that all the events in that episode – the confrontation between the Shadows and the Vorlons, the support of the First Ones and the vanishing of all of them beyond the Rim – were meant to be contained entirely in that episode.

'The Hour of the Wolf'

Transmission Number: 401
Production Number: 401

Written by: J Michael Straczynski
Directed by: David J Eagle

Morden: Ed Wasser
Emperor Cartagia: Wortham Krimmer

Centauri Minister: Damien London
Lorien: Wayne Alexander
Drazi Ambassador: Mark Hendrickson
Brakiri Ambassador: Rick Ryan

Plot: Intense isn't a strong enough word. Nothing actually happens in this episode, but it's still immensely watchable. And by this time we would all sit entranced while Andreas Katsulas read out the Los Angeles telephone directory.

The 'A' Plot: It's seven days since Sheridan's disappearance, and the League of Non-Aligned Worlds are pulling back the majority of their ships from Babylon 5, either because they think the war is over or because they want to protect their homeworlds. Ivanova is walking around in a daze, unable to sleep. Delenn demands that Ambassador Kosh help them look for evidence of what happened to Captain Sheridan, but Kosh refuses. Lyta Alexander, discomfited by Kosh's refusal, offers her own help. If the White Star can take her to Z'ha'dum, she might be able to detect whether or not Sheridan is alive.

A trip is quickly arranged, and the White Star drops out of hyperspace near Z'ha'dum. While Lennier sends messages on all frequencies calling for Sheridan to respond, Lyta Alexander attempts to shield them from the Shadows while simultaneously attempting to 'feel' Sheridan's presence. Both attempts fail and the Shadows detect their presence. Their minds are affected by the Shadows' powers, but Lennier has programmed the White Star's computer to return them to hyperspace if he appears to be affected by anything, and when it does so the spell is broken.

Back on Babylon 5, Ivanova accepts that Sheridan is dead, and starts planning to continue where he left off.

The 'B' Plot: Londo returns to Centauri Prime to take up his post as Adviser on Planetary Security. He discovers pretty quickly that the Emperor is barking mad, and has allowed the Shadows to use a small island on Centauri Prime as a base of operations. As a badly radiation-scarred Morden tells him, 'The incident at Z'ha'dum has forced us to look for outside support sooner than we had intended.' Londo confides his worries to a Centauri Minister, but the Minister warns him to keep quiet about the Emperor's mental state. It is rumoured that Cartagia has secretly beheaded those people who have criticised his actions, and talks to their heads. Londo calls Vir on Babylon 5 and tells him to return to Centauri Prime as soon as possible, where they will conspire against the Emperor together.

The 'C' Plot: (a) G'Kar decides to go in search of the vanished Mr Garibaldi. (b) On Z'ha'dum, Sheridan is eking out an existence when he meets a mysterious alien named Lorien.

The Arc: The Great War has paused for a while. The Shadows are regrouping and reconsidering their tactics after what is effectively their capital city has been destroyed by Captain Sheridan and two large atomic bombs (not to mention a medium-sized spacecraft).

Londo's dream of multiple Shadow ships crossing the sky of Centauri Prime comes appallingly true in this episode. He first had the dream in episode 209 ('The Coming of Shadows') and remembered it again in episode 301 ('Matters of Honor'). A similar vision later recurs in episodes 516 ('And All My Dreams, Torn Asunder') and 517 ('Movements of Fire and Shadow'). It had been speculated earlier by some fans that the Shadows invaded Centauri Prime at some stage in the future. Not many people had expected them to have appeared by invitation.

We learn in this episode that the Shadows wish to set up a base on Centauri Prime, on the small island of Celene. It was back in episode 301 ('Matters of Honor') that G'Kar said, 'They came to our world over a thousand of your years ago – long before we went to the stars ourselves. They set up a base on one of our southern continents. They took little interest in us. G'Quan believed they were engaged in a war far outside our own world.' History repeats itself – Emperor Cartagia is well aware that the Shadows spread their ships around 'like seeds' a thousand years before.

It becomes clear in this episode that Lyta Alexander is able to carry Vorlons around inside her mind, allowing them to reach places and observe things without themselves being observed. We first suspected this in episode 304 ('Passing

Through Gethsemane'). The experience is more draining and more painful with the new Kosh, to the point where she asks him whether everything is OK. His answer – 'Yes' – could be construed as being said in a tone of voice indicating that he has a much darker motivation than the original Kosh.

When the occupants of the White Star are broadcasting to Sheridan on Z'ha'dum, they are spotted by the Shadows. An image of a Shadow head with glowing eyes forms against the star field – as it does in episode 305 ('Voices of Authority'). The Shadows appear to be able to influence human minds, as their minions do in issues 5 to 8 of the *Babylon 5* comic (the four-part comic series 'Shadows Past and Present'). The Shadows also talk to Ivanova and Delenn in the voices of their fathers, a trick Kosh uses on G'Kar in episode 306 ('Dust to Dust') and on Sheridan in episode 315 ('Interludes and Examinations'). This symbolism – speaking with the voice of a progenitor – implies that the Shadows and the Vorlons are both, in some sense, forerunners or ancestors of the various races currently at large in the galaxy.

At the end of the episode, Ivanova says she will need help to continue with Sheridan's work, and says she knows where to go to get it. She's referring either to Draal on Epsilon 3 or to the First Ones near Sigma 359. Or both.

Observations: It's supposed to be seven days since Sheridan vanished off to Z'ha'dum, which would make it 27 December 2260, but the opening narration tells us that the year is 2261.

The Hour of the Wolf is, allegedly, the hour between three and four in the morning where all worries are magnified and 'all you can hear is the sound of your own heart'.

Lorien is not named during the episode, but his name appears in the credits.

Koshisms: On Sheridan: 'He has opened an unexpected door. We do now what must be done now. His purpose has been fulfilled.'

'No one returns from Z'ha'dum' (but he's lying, and Delenn knows he is).

'Respect is irrelevant.'

Dialogue to Rewind For: Lennier: 'Initiating "getting the hell out of here" manoeuvre.'

Londo to Vir: 'I need a friend, Vir, and I need a patriot, and you are both.'

Ships That Pass in the Night: The White Star again, despite its having been destroyed in episode 322 ('Z'ha'dum'). We'll be charitable, and assume they just renamed one of the fleet they built.

Literary, Mythological and Historical References: There is a distinct parallel with Robert Graves's books *I, Claudius* and *Claudius the God* (or with Graves's historical source – the Roman historian Suetonius) in *Babylon 5*. Claudius was a tongue-tied youth whom everyone looked down on but who was destined to become Emperor of Rome, while Vir is a tongue-tied youth whom everyone looked down on but who is destined to become Emperor of the Centauri Republic. Caligula was a lunatic youth who became Emperor before Claudius and whose behaviour became so increasingly insane that he had to be assassinated, whereas Cartagia is a lunatic youth who has become Emperor before Vir, and whose behaviour is becoming so increasingly insane that he will have to be assassinated. And that leaves the obvious question – what role is Londo fulfilling? Later events indicate that perhaps he might be Nero, fiddling while Centauri Prime burns.

I've Seen That Face Before: Wayne Alexander, the actor playing the stately Lorien, previously appeared as Sebastian in episode 221 ('Comes the Inquisitor') and as the Narn G'Dan in episode 320 ('And the Rock Cried Out, No Hiding Place').

Damien London turns in another performance of barely suppressed hysteria as the Centauri Minister. He previously appeared in episodes 121 ('The Quality of Mercy') and 312 ('Sic Transit Vir').

Accidents Will Happen: During the 'Previously, on *Babylon 5* . . .' section before the episode opens, we see again the shot of Sheridan throwing himself into the abyss from episode 322

('Z'ha'dum'). It appears he says 'Goodbye' as he jumps, whereas in episode 322 he doesn't. What has happened is that the audio track from an earlier shot, of Sheridan's farewell message to Delenn, has been allowed to run on over his jumping. Clumsy, but understandable.

Questions Raised: Why do the Shadows sometimes choose inhabited planets and sometimes uninhabited planets upon which to base their ships? Sometimes the planets are uninhabited (Mars and the Jupiter moon Io are examples) but sometimes there is an indigenous race (as in the case of the Narn Homeworld and Centauri Prime). Do they sometimes need new recruits for their ships? It's unlikely to be anything to do with using living beings as shields against attack, otherwise they would do it all the time.

'Whatever Happened to Mr Garibaldi?'

Transmission Number: 402
Production Number: 402

Written by: J Michael Straczynski
Directed by: Kevin James Dobson

Lorien: Wayne Alexander   **Isaac:** Lenny Citrano
Harry: Anthony DeLongis
Emperor Cartagia: Wortham Krimmer
Centauri Minister: Damien London
Centauri: Rick Scarry

Date: The episode starts on 3 January 2261.

Plot: This episode moves slowly but unstoppably, like an avalanche. Quite breathtaking.
The 'A' Plot: G'Kar is following the trail of Mr Garibaldi, and has discovered that what appears to be a fragment of his Starfury has been sold by a scrap dealer on a storm-racked planet. He questions the dealer in a seedy bar to discover how he came by the fragment, but provokes a fight instead. He is rescued by Marcus Cole, who has followed him to the planet. They leave the bar in a hurry, but the owner reports G'Kar's

presence to a Centauri friend of his. Marcus forces the scrap dealer to admit that he was told about the derelict Starfury by a contact in Interplanetary Expeditions named Montaigne.

While Marcus returns to Babylon 5 to trace Montaigne, G'Kar prepares to leave for the area of space in which the Starfury was found drifting. He is kidnapped by the Centauri instead and shipped as a captive to Centauri Prime, where the Emperor gives him to Londo Mollari as a gift. Londo offers G'Kar a deal: he will save him from death – if not actually from torture – if G'Kar will help him kill the Emperor. G'Kar agrees, on one condition – that Londo arrange for Centauri forces to be withdrawn from the Narn Homeworld.

The 'B' Plot: Captain Sheridan is still on Z'ha'dum with the enigmatic Lorien, but is beginning to realise that something is wrong. He hasn't eaten for nine days but he isn't hungry; he's been walking in a straight line but he's ended up back where he started; and, most puzzling of all, he doesn't appear to have a pulse. Lorien tells Sheridan that he is trapped between life and death, and needs to let go of life if he is to escape. If he has something to live for, he will survive. Lorien also admits that he is, effectively, the first of the First Ones – the oldest being in the entire galaxy. Sheridan, trusting him, relinquishes his grip on life and relives his fall into the chasm . . .

The 'C' Plot: (a) Delenn has not eaten anything since Sheridan disappeared, but Franklin persuades her to set aside her grief by showing her an extract from Sheridan's diary in which he admits how much he loves her. Revitalised, Delenn calls the Rangers together and tells them that they are to mount a last-ditch attack on Z'ha'dum.

(b) Mr Garibaldi is being held in a cell by unknown captors. They keep asking him what he remembers about the ship that captured him, and he keeps replying that he doesn't remember. He starts smashing the cell up, and they tranquillise him. A man in an opaque face mask and wearing a Psi Corp badge enters the cell and stares down at Mr Garibaldi's body.

The Arc: Sheridan dreams of being held in the grip of a glowing, hazy creature of light, who asks him, 'Who are you?

What do you want?' The creature, he later discovers, is a representation of Lorien – the first of the First Ones. It's interesting to note that 'Who are you?' is the question Sebastian was so set on having answered in episode 221 ('Comes the Inquisitor') while 'What do you want?' is the question Morden was asking in episode 113 ('Signs and Portents').

Lorien disapproves of the conflict going on in the galaxy at large – 'It is a terrible thing when your children fight,' he says.

'I must watch,' Londo says to G'Kar, 'and you must endure, until the time is right.' It's that phrase again – 'when the time is right'.

Observations: Delenn tells Franklin that she once said to Sheridan she would see him again, 'where no shadows fall'. She did this in episode 218 ('Confessions and Lamentations').

This is the first episode of *Babylon 5* (except for the pilot episode) in which Ivanova does not appear. A scene filmed for this episode with her asking Delenn if she can borrow a White Star ship was moved to the next episode.

Interplanetary Expeditions have been mentioned before, in episodes 104 ('Infection'), 215 ('And Now For a Word') and 322 ('Z'ha'dum').

Sheridan's log entry is dated 14 May 2260. This would put it somewhere between episode 311 ('Ceremonies of Light and Dark') and 312 ('Sic Transit Vir').

The scene with Delenn reaching out to touch the screen with Sheridan's image on it is a parallel with the scene in episode 202 ('Revelations'), in which Sheridan reaches out to touch a screen with Anna's image on it.

There are flashbacks in this episode to episodes 308 ('Messages from Earth'), 321 ('Shadow Dancing') and 322 ('Z'ha'dum').

Look for the really clumsy cut just as Marcus leaves the hovel where G'Kar is hiding: the camera pulls back, as if to reveal someone emerging from hiding, but then the scene cuts away to something else. It looks as if a few seconds have been removed here.

Dialogue to Rewind For: Lorien to Sheridan: 'You are quite, quite dead.'

G'Kar to Marcus: 'I've never had a friend before who wasn't a Narn.' Marcus to G'Kar: 'I've never had a friend before who *was* a Narn.'

Sheridan to Lorien: 'You're one of the First Ones!' Lorien to Sheridan: 'No, not *one* of the First Ones . . . I *am* the First One.'

Lorien to Sheridan: 'Do you know you have a Vorlon inside you?'

Other Worlds: Zathran VII.

Culture Shock: Minbari can fast for up to fourteen days, and do so as part of their grieving ritual.

I've Seen That Face Before: Wayne Alexander returns as Lorien, and Damien London returns as the wonderful Minister.

Accidents Will Happen: At the beginning of the episode, Stephen Franklin says that it's been fourteen days since Captain Sheridan was presumed killed at Z'ha'dum and nine days since Mr Garibaldi disappeared while on patrol. This is a script mistake: Garibaldi disappeared on the same day Sheridan is supposed to have died. The script should have said it has been fourteen days since Captain Sheridan left for Z'ha'dum. J Michael Straczynski has explained that the problem arose during the editing of script drafts and remained uncorrected by accident.

I may be seeing things, but there is a long shot of a ship entering the Babylon 5 docking bay in which the ship appears to vanish before it gets in.

Questions Raised: Whatever happened to Mr Garibaldi?

'The Summoning'

Transmission Number: 403
Production Number: 403

Written by: J Michael Straczynski
Directed by: John McPherson

Emperor Cartagia: Wortham Krimmer
Lorien: Wayne Alexander
Ambassador Lethke: Jonathan Chapman
Verano: Eric Zivot

Date: 17 January 2261.

Plot: A great deal happens in this episode – to the point where there are three 'B' plots and nothing as trivial as a 'C' plot – and it's all deeply affecting. This season just keeps hitting you in the gut.

The 'A' Plot: It is Delenn's intention to amass a fleet to attack Z'ha'dum, but the Vorlons refuse to help her. When Lyta Alexander tries to find out their plans, the new Kosh lets her have access to his mind, and the sheer shock renders her powerless. Many of the League of Non-Aligned Worlds aren't happy about Delenn's plans, and they hold an open rally to protest against her actions. The rally looks set to degenerate into a brawl when Captain Sheridan appears, having returned to Babylon 5 on board a mysterious spacecraft with Lorien. His presence galvanises the crowd, and he manages to swing them behind Delenn's plan.

The 'B' Plot: (a) Ivanova and Marcus set out in one of the White Star ships to search for the First Ones. The intention is to find some more First Ones, apart from those at Sigma 957. What they find instead is a Vorlon fleet hidden in hyperspace – thousands of ships, including some three or four miles across. The fleet is attacking Shadow bases, eliminating entire planets that have any contact with the Shadows, irrespective of how many innocent inhabitants might also be on them.

(b) Zack Allen has got a lead on the whereabouts of Mr Garibaldi: the man who salvaged Garibaldi's Starfury has filed a flight plan for his freighter, and Zack intends going after him and questioning him. He leads a mixed fleet of shuttles and Starfuries to intercept the freighter, but, when they suggest it prepare for boarding, it ejects a lifepod and blows itself up. The lifepod contains Mr Garibaldi, but there are indications (unnoticed by his rescuers) that he may be under some form of control. He is taken back to Babylon 5, where he claims not to remember what happened to him. It seems clear that he is lying.

(c) Emperor Cartagia is torturing G'Kar, but is annoyed at the fact that G'Kar will not cry out. No pain that he or his 'pain technicians' can inflict will make G'Kar scream, but he keeps on trying and promises Londo he will either get his scream or G'Kar will die. When Londo pleads with G'Kar to scream, otherwise he will be killed and Londo's plan to assassinate the Emperor will founder, G'Kar resists. To scream, he points out, would be to submit to a conqueror, and he would not be a Narn if he did that. Finally, less than a second before Cartagia would kill him, he screams – not to save his life but to save his race.

The Arc: 'We must play along,' Londo tells Vir, 'until the time is right.' It's that line again.

So – the Vorlons reveal their true colours. During the first half of season 1 they were presented as very powerful and domineering; it was only during seasons 2 and 3 that Kosh lightened up and we were encouraged to think of them as, in some sense, angelic. Now the wheel has come full circle, and we see again the same Vorlons that were prepared to destroy Babylon 5 to prevent anyone finding out what one of them looked like. They're on the warpath, encouraged by the sudden catastrophe to befall the Shadows to launch a strike against all their bases. And the other races in the galaxy are caught in the middle – anyone who has ever sheltered or aided the Shadows, including Earth and Centauri Prime, is on their list.

The episode makes the strong point that the original Kosh was not a typical Vorlon – he had come to have feelings for the lesser races around him. The distinction between Kosh as we knew him and the new Ambassador ('We are all Kosh') is still not completely clear. Are they all the same Kosh? And what about the original Kosh's second name – Naranek? How does that fit into the equation?

We discover in episode 417 ('The Face of the Enemy') that the Babylon 5 personnel were intended to rescue Mr Garibaldi all along: that was part of the plan.

Observations: Ivanova says that the last time she looked up and saw sky was six years ago. That immediately invalidates the third *Babylon 5* book (*Blood Oath*) in which she spends some time on the Narn Homeworld.

There are brief flashbacks in this episode to episodes 322 ('Z'ha'dum') and 402 ('Whatever Happened to Mr Garibaldi?').

The scene early on with Ivanova asking Delenn if she can borrow a White Star ship was actually filmed for episode 402 ('Whatever Happened to Mr Garibaldi?') but was shifted to this episode for time reasons during the editing of episode 402.

Koshisms: To Lyta Alexander when she asks for a little respect to be shown her: 'Respect? From whom?'

To Lyta Alexander when she tries to scan him: 'Would you know my thoughts? Would you?'

Ivanova's Life Lessons: Her attempt at speaking Minbari – 'Engines at full . . . high power, hatrack ratcatcher, to port weapons . . . brickbat lingerie.'

Dialogue to Rewind For: Marcus, on board the White Star, telling Ivanova where they are headed next – 'Sector 87 by 20 by 42. At least a dozen ships have reported seeing something rather godlike in the area, and since neither you nor I were there it must be one of the First Ones.'

Lyta Alexander, on the Vorlons: 'I don't think they care about what happens to us any more.'

Drazi, to Sheridan: 'I'm sorry, we thought you were dead.' Sheridan: 'I was – I'm better now.'

Ships That Pass in the Night: Lorien's beautiful ship, which seems to have some echo in the sculpture of Thailand.

Other Worlds: The planet Arkada VII is destroyed by the Vorlon fleet. It had over 4 million inhabitants.

Culture Shock: When the open rally against Delenn is going on, there are two aliens on the platform, making speeches to the crowd. One of them is a Drazi, the other a Hyach. The Hyach have been around for some time in *Babylon 5*, but this is the first time I've been able to indicate one unambiguously and say, 'There, that's a Hyach.'

Literary, Mythological and Historical References: At the beginning of the episodes, G'Kar is wearing a crown of thorns. Although a fairly common punishment, it may be a reflection of the biblical tradition that Jesus also wore a crown of thorns when he was being martyred. The biblical parallels don't end there – G'Kar is to be whipped forty times, probably a nod towards Deuteronomy 25:1–3, which states: 'When men have a dispute, they are to take it to court and the judges will decide the case, acquitting the innocent and condemning the guilty. If the guilty man deserves to be beaten, the judge shall make him lie down and have him flogged in his presence with the number of lashes his crime deserves, but he must not give him more than forty lashes. If he is flogged more than that, your brother will be degraded in your eyes.'

Just after Marcus tells Ivanova he's a virgin, he says he's picking something up on the ship's scanners. 'A unicorn?' Ivanova quips. This refers to the mythological basis of unicorns, which suggests they are attracted to virgins.

I've Seen That Face Before: Wayne Alexander and Wortham Krimmer, of course. Eric Zivot, who plays Verano, previously played Spragg – a member of Zathras's race – in episode 316 ('War Without End' Part One).

Questions Raised: How did Sheridan and Lorien leave Z'ha'dum without the Shadows realising? Why did they leave? Does that ship belong to Lorien? And, most importantly, how did that tall, thin ship get through the short, wide docking-bay entrance of Babylon 5 without turning sideways?

'Falling Toward Apotheosis'

Transmission Number: 404
Production Number: 404

Written by: J Michael Straczynski
Directed by: David J Eagle

Emperor Cartagia: Wortham Krimmer
Lorien: Wayne Alexander   **Morden:** Ed Wasser

Plot: Given that we have come to know and love all of these characters (with the possible exception of Emperor Cartagia, and I'm even developing an odd fondness for him), it's gut-wrenching to see what happens to them in this season. The final shot of this episode is probably the single most disturbing moment in this entire series, and all we see is a door closing. Gulp.

The 'A' Plot: Given what is happening with the Vorlon fleet, Captain Sheridan wants to get rid of the new Vorlon Ambassador. He orders Garibaldi and some of his security guards to try to force the Ambassador to leave, knowing that they will fail and thus lull the Ambassador into a false sense of security. They do indeed fail – the Ambassador is far too powerful and protected to be bothered by their PPG fire. Lyta Alexander tells the Ambassador that there is a part of Kosh inside one of the people on the station, and that she will lead the Ambassador to him so that Kosh can be retrieved. The Ambassador, as expected, finds this 'intolerable', and is lured into a trap – at Sheridan's request Lyta has brought the Ambassador to a position in a cargo bay where massive electrical charges can be passed through him. What with the electrical discharges and the PPG fire from Garibaldi's guards, his encounter suit cracks to reveal the true Vorlon form – a creature like a jellyfish made of light.

At the same time as the Ambassador is attacked, the Vorlon ship in Bay 13 begins to break free, and Ivanova clears it to leave before it rips the station apart.

The part of Kosh that was within Sheridan leaves him, along with some of Sheridan's life force and some of Lorien as well, and confronts the Ambassador. Intertwined and fighting, they pass through the hull of the station and explode along with the departing ship. Sheridan has been injured in the struggle, and Lorien replenishes his life force. Sheridan has to admit to Delenn that being recalled from death on Z'ha'dum has its price – he will live for only another twenty

63

years. In a moment of tenderness and honesty between them, Sheridan proposes to Delenn.

The 'B' Plot: With the Vorlons using immense planet-killer craft to attack any colonies and planets who have had contact, however unwitting, with the Shadows, Londo is worried that Centauri Prime is in the firing line. After all, there are over 100 Shadow ships based there. Neither the Emperor nor Morden is worried, however: Morden doesn't believe the Vorlons will dare attack Centauri Prime, while the Emperor is convinced they will but sees it a pyre to celebrate his imminent apotheosis. Londo suggests that the Emperor travel to the Narn Homeworld to put G'Kar on trial in order to ensure that the Emperor will be remembered by someone after the Centauri have all been immolated. The Emperor agrees.

The 'C' Plot: Garibaldi is worried about Lorien – he doesn't know who he is, what he wants or why he is following Sheridan around. He's also getting worried that Sheridan is keeping things from him. As if that weren't enough, Garibaldi is *also* getting worried that people keep asking what happened to him when he was lost during the Shadow attack.

The Arc: A pretty stationary story in arc terms, but there are some features of interest. The Vorlon Ambassador dies in a fight with the remains of Kosh, of course. Also, Emperor Cartagia makes passing reference to Centauri Prime ending 'in fire' ('Let it all burn, Mollari. Let it all end in fire'), which is exactly what Kosh told Emperor Turhan would happen in episode 209 ('The Coming of Shadows'). And, of course, we have G'Kar's blinding by Emperor Cartagia – a moment prefigured in episodes 209 ('The Coming of Shadows') and 317 ('War Without End' Part Two) when we see G'Kar seventeen years in the future, minus an eye.

Observations: It's a three-day trip from Centauri Prime to the Narn Homeworld.

Doctor Franklin suggests using the nearby planet Epsilon 3 as a refugee camp for those people fleeing the depredations of the Vorlons. Let's hope he has a lot of face masks – it has a poisonous atmosphere for oxygen breathers.

Franklin tests Garibaldi for Shadow implants in the back of his neck (as seen in episodes 314 ('Ship of Tears') and 322 ('Z'ha'dum')). There aren't any – which doesn't mean he's not under *someone*'s influence, of course.

This isn't the same Garibaldi who went away. In episode 318 ('Walkabout') he gets really irritated with G'Kar over the apparent reluctance of the Narn captain Na'Kal to risk his life when ordered to. He even has a little speech about how sometimes you have to trust your leader when he orders you into an apparently hopeless situation – you have to trust that he knows best. Well, Garibaldi ain't trusting his boss in this episode – he is very reluctant to go into the Vorlon Ambassador's quarters to confront him.

Koshisms: 'A human imprisons one of us? Intolerable.'

Other Worlds: We're positively inundated with planets in this episode, many of them being names you couldn't possibly pronounce but which more or less work when they are shown on screen. Dura 7, Tizino Prime and Ventari 3 are believed to have fallen to the Vorlons, while 7 Lukantha, D'Grn IV, the Drazi Fendamir Research Colony, Kazomi VII, Lesser Krindar and Greater Krindar, L'Gn'Daort, Mokafa Station, Nacambad Colony, Oqmrritkz and Velatastat are at risk.

Literary, Mythological and Historical References: 'Right now, our greatest enemy is fear,' Ivanova says. This echoes several past writers and speakers, including the American president Theodore Roosevelt ('Let me assert my firm belief that the only thing we have to fear is fear itself') and the writer Henry David Thoreau ('Nothing is so much to be feared as fear').

Emperor Cartagia has had the head of Minister Dugari removed because said Minister was always coughing. The Roman Emperor Caligula did a similar thing to Tiberius Gemellus, as reported in Robert Graves's novel *I Claudius*. The Roman historian Suetonius reported, however, that Caligula had Gemellus killed because his breath smelt of an antidote to poison and this was an insult to Caligula's hospitality, although

Suetonius claims that Gemellus's breath actually smelt of medicine taken for a persistent cough. The parallels between Cartagia and Caligula also point up the fact that Vir's career is paralleling that of the stuttering Claudius – the unlikeliest Emperor of them all.

I've Seen That Face Before: Wortham Krimmer (as the Emperor Cartagia) and Wayne Alexander (as Lorien) and a remarkably short appearance by Ed Wasser as Morden.

Questions Raised: 'The Vorlons have gone mad,' says Morden. By 'gone mad' he means they are attacking people with disproportionate force for an aim far above the comprehension of most species. So what does that make the Shadows?

'The Long Night'

Transmission Number: 405
Production Number: 405

Written by: J Michael Straczynski
Directed by: John Lafia

Ericsson: Brian Cranston
Emperor Cartagia: Wortham Krimmer
Centauri No. 1: Carl Reggiardo
Centauri No. 2: Mark Bramhall
Drazi Ambassador: Ron Campbell   **G'Lorn:** Kim Strauss

Plot: It's compulsive viewing: an episode that ranges effortlessly between long, deeply touching personal conversations concerning guilt and big strategy sessions concerning the fate of the galaxy.

The 'A' Plot: Cartagia has gone to the Narn Homeworld, accompanied by Londo. There he intends putting G'Kar through a show trial and then executing him.

Londo's conspiracy to kill Cartagia has widened to include other Centauri officials, and the signal for the attempt to begin is when G'Kar distracts Cartagia's personal guard by snapping his (preweakened) chains and runs amok. Londo will then take the Emperor aside and stab him between his hearts with a syringe containing an undetectable neurotoxin.

The plan starts to go wrong when Cartagia has G'Kar's chains replaced, thinking they look weak, but G'Kar's righteous anger gives him the strength to snap them anyway. Cartagia manages to unwittingly knock the syringe from Londo's hand, but Vir picks it up and stabs Cartagia, killing him. Londo is named Prime Minister, and recommends that the Centauri leave the Narn well alone from now on. They leave for Centauri Prime, with three days left to get rid of the Shadows.

The 'B' Plot: Sheridan is almost ready to strike against the Vorlons, but a report from a ship passing through Sector 900 – on the edge of Vorlon space – indicates that the Shadows are using a new weapon, something equivalent to the Vorlon planet-killer. White Star 14, which is in the area, reports back that the weapon fires millions of missiles into a planetary crust. When the missiles detonate, they split the crust open and turn the planet inside out. Sheridan orders Ericsson, the captain of White Star 14, to sacrifice himself and his ship in order to get false information to the Shadows, luring them to Corianus 6 – the next planet on the Vorlons' list. Sheridan knows that the Shadows and the Vorlons are dancing around each other, avoiding direct confrontation, and he intends putting them face to face.

The 'C' Plot: Following the Centauri withdrawal, G'Kar realises that his people wish to take their revenge, and start the entire cycle over again.

The Arc: Emperor Cartagia finally gets his comeuppance in this episode, but any man who dresses like a Morris dancer deserves everything that happens to him. Unexpectedly, it is Vir who kills him, rather than Londo.

Observations: There is a reference to Lord Refa having Prime Minister Malachi killed (an event shown in episode 209 – 'The Coming of Shadows'). There is also a reference to Londo having Lord Refa killed (as shown in episode 320 – 'And the Rock Cried Out, No Hiding Place').

Corillium is a very hard metal.

The original intention, up until the episode was being written, was for Londo to have killed the Emperor, but J Michael Straczynski changed things at the last moment when he realised Vir would be the perfect, and the most unexpected, assassin.

A scene filmed for this episode involving Ivanova and Lorien talking was moved to the following episode (406 – 'Into the Fire') instead.

Dialogue to Rewind For: G'Kar: 'I did not fight to remove one dictator just to become another myself!'

Dialogue to Fast-Forward Past: Captain 'Call Me Subtle' Sheridan's way of telling Ericsson that he won't be coming back: 'You're not a married man, are you Ericsson?' So – what would have happened if Ericsson had said yes?

Ships That Pass in the Night: White Star 14.

Other Worlds: Coriana VI (in sector 70 by 12 by 5) has over 6 billion inhabitants.

Dorac VII has a small Shadow base on it.

Culture Shock: Centauri have at least two hearts.

Literary, Mythological and Historical References: 'My eye offended him,' G'Kar says, explaining why Cartagia had his eye plucked out. This is a reference to the Bible, Matthew 18:9: 'If thine eye offend thee, pluck it out, and cast it from thee: it is better for thee to enter into heaven with one eye, rather than having two eyes to be cast into hell fire.'

Sheridan reveals that, when he took command of Babylon 5, he found a poem left on his desk. The poem is Tennyson's 'Ulysses', indicating that the person who left it was Ambassador Sinclair (see the pilot episode, 'The Gathering').

'Into the Fire'

Transmission Number: 406
Production Number: 406

Written by: J Michael Straczynski
Directed by: Kevin James Dobson

Lorien: Wayne Alexander   **Durano:** Julian Barnes
Centauri Minister: Damien London   **Morden:** Ed Wasser

Plot: And so it ends. The war is over; the Vorlons, the Shadows, the rest of the First Ones and Lorien himself have all left. We're on our own now. And what an exit they get!

The 'A' Plot: Sheridan draws the line at Corianus VI – placing his ships in the way of the Vorlon fleet and attracting the Shadow fleet to the same point. He calls in reinforcements from the First Ones to hold the two fleets at bay and attempts to communicate with both sides. It works: the Vorlons take Sheridan's mind elsewhere to reason with him, and the Shadows do the same with Delenn. Lorien, unbeknown to both the Vorlons and the Shadows, transmits images of the negotiations to everyone else in the fleet. Sheridan and Delenn are offered the chance to choose between the Vorlons and the Shadows, but they both refuse to make that choice. Both of them point out that there is a third option – not to join in the game that the two sides are playing. Sheridan asks both sides to leave the younger races in peace, pointing out that neither side knows who they are or what they want any more. Lorien throws his weight behind Sheridan and, after some discussion, both the Shadows and the Vorlons agree to leave the galaxy, passing beyond the Rim to whatever lies beyond. Lorien and the rest of the First Ones agree to go with them. The war is over, and the younger races are on their own . . .

The 'B' Plot: Londo and Vir have 24 hours to get rid of every trace of Shadow influence on Centauri Prime before the Vorlon fleet arrives. Londo offers Morden the chance to withdraw the Shadow ships from the island of Selene, and when Morden refuses Londo has Morden's 'associates' killed and blows up the island. He then kills Morden in order to eradicate what he thinks of as the last remaining Shadow influence on the planet, but he has forgotten one last source of contamination. He, too, has been touched by Shadows. The

Vorlons arrive, and Londo orders Vir to kill him. The Vorlons are about to fire when they are recalled to provide reinforcements at Corianus VI. Centauri Prime is safe – for the moment.

The 'C' Plot: Ivanova and Lorien contact the six remaining First Ones and persuade them to join with them against the Vorlons and the Shadows.

The Arc: After Londo has Morden killed, he places Morden's head on a pike in the garden and tells Vir to go outside. Vir gazes up into Morden's dead eyes and remembers the conversation he had with Morden in episode 217 ('In the Shadow of Z'ha'dum'): 'I'd like to live long enough to be there when they cut off your head and stick it on a pike as a warning to the next ten generations that some favours come with too high a price. I want to look up into your lifeless eyes and wave – like this.' We even get a flashback to that very speech.

In episode 309 ('Point of No Return') Lady Morella prophesies that Londo has three chances to avoid the fire that lies before him. One of them is, 'And, at the last, you must surrender yourself to your greatest fear, knowing that it will kill you.' In this episode, Londo begs Vir to kill him, rather than let the Vorlons destroy his world. Is this what Lady Morella was referring to?

Captain Sheridan turns upon the Shadows and the Vorlons the two questions they have been asking all along: 'Who are you?' and 'What do you want?' Unsurprisingly, neither race can answer the question.

To cap the episode, Captain Sheridan defines the three ages of mankind (as set up in the opening narration for the pilot episode – 'The Gathering' – and the first season). The First Age is when the races of the galaxy are too primitive to make decisions about their own fate; the Second Age is when they are manipulated from outside by more powerful forces; the Third Age is when they are able to stand on their own and make decisions about their own fate.

Observations: There is a discussion of Adira, the dancer Londo fell in love with in episode 103 ('Born to the Purple'), and who was killed by Morden's associates in episode 315

('Interludes and Examinations'). We still don't know how Morden's agents got on to the Centauri liner to poison her.

Sheridan's ploy with the mined asteroids is very similar to the stunt he pulled in order to destroy the *Black Star* during the Earth–Minbari war.

The Vorlon saying 'Understanding is a three-edged sword' gets another airing in this episode. It was previously said in episode 109 ('Deathwalker').

The voice of the Shadow spokesman is provided by Ed Wasser (Morden).

A scene filmed for the previous episode (405 – 'The Long Night') involving Ivanova and Lorien talking was moved to this episode instead.

In the 'original' mix of season 4, when season 5 was planned but before J Michael Straczynski pulled events from season 5 into season 4 in case the series was not renewed, there would have been one or two episodes leading up to the events of 'Into the Fire'. Straczynski has stated, however, that all the events occurring in the episode as it was finally transmitted were meant to be in that episode – they were never meant to take place over a longer period (say, a two-part story).

Straczynski and the director Kevin Dobson clashed over Dobson's interpretation of 'Into the Fire'. Tellingly, perhaps, Dobson has directed no more episodes of the series.

Koshisms: To Sheridan: 'You thought we could not touch you. You were wrong.'

'You do *not* understand.'

Dialogue to Rewind For: Londo, on the damage after Morden's associates have been killed: 'I will have to have that painted over, I suppose.'

Sheridan, blowing up some nuclear mines to get the attention of the Vorlon and Shadow fleets: 'Good morning, gentlemen – this is your wake-up call.'

Lyta Alexander, when the Vorlon and Shadow fleets turn and head toward Sheridan's ragtag fleet: 'Captain – they're pissed.'

Sheridan to the Vorlons and the Shadows: 'Who are *you*? What do *you* want?'

Marcus: 'Did we just win?' Ivanova: 'Don't jinx it.'

Sheridan: 'It's a new age, Delenn – a Third Age. We began in chaos, too primitive to make our own decisions. Then we were manipulated from outside by forces who thought they knew what was best for us. And now – now we're finally standing on our own.'

Dialogue to Fast-Forward Past: Londo talking about Morden having poisoned Adira: 'He played me – he played me like a puppet!' (You play violins, but you don't play puppets – you manipulate them.)

Ships That Pass in the Night: White Star 9. The *Stra'kath* – a Drazi warship.

Culture Shock: There are over two dozen races taking part in Sheridan's crusade (how many can *you* name?).

Lorien and his race were born immortal. Lorien believes that subsequent races were given life spans because the sentient universe realised that, for there to be change and growth, lives had to be limited.

Questions Raised: Where do we go from here?
What happened to Lorien's ship? Is it still on Babylon 5?

'Epiphanies'

Transmission Number: 407
Production Number: 407

Written by: J Michael Straczynski
Directed by: John C Flinn III

Bester: Walter Koenig
Centauri Minister: Damien London
Psi Corps Official: Victor Iunidin
Earth Alliance Pilot: Robert Patteri
News Anchor: Lauren Sanchez

Plot: A new start; a new direction.
The 'A' Plot: President Clark, worried at the sudden loss of

his Shadow allies, is becoming increasingly concerned over the threat posed to him by Babylon 5. He sets in motion a four-pronged attack, with Psi Corps, Earthforce, Nightwatch and the Ministry of Peace each advancing a piece of the plan, but none of them knowing what the others are doing. Following an ISN announcement that Babylon 5 is now off limits to all humans following reports of possible terrorist activity emanating from it, Psi Cop Bester is ordered to attack a squadron of Earthforce Starfuries with his own Black Omega Starfuries and then leave evidence making it look as if Babylon 5 was responsible. Bester has his own plans, however, and travels to Babylon 5, where he offers to help Sheridan fight Clark's plans if Sheridan will take him to Z'ha'dum. Ivanova travels to the jumpgate in Sector 49 with Alpha Squadron, where they help the Earthforce Starfuries there to destroy the attacking Black Omega forces. President Clark is wrong-footed, but Bester is not completely 'onside', and may have been involved in sending a coded message to Garibaldi which has caused him to resign as Head of Babylon 5 Security.

The 'B' Plot: Bester wants to ransack Z'ha'dum in an attempt to discover whether the Shadows left behind any technology that could be used to remove the organic components from his lover, Carolyn – held in cryogenic suspension on Babylon 5. Sheridan, Delenn and Lyta Alexander accompany him there, and find a fleet of the Shadows' Dark Servants leaving, having (probably) stripped the planet. Sheridan suspects a trap, and turns tail. Moments later, the planet explodes. They return to Babylon 5, where Sheridan accuses Lyta of having deliberately triggered the explosion telepathically. She admits it, giving as her possible reasons (a) the fact that she might be still operating under unconscious Vorlon instructions, (b) that she doesn't think Shadow technology should fall into anyone else's hands, or (c) that she hates Bester and will thwart whatever he wants to do.

The 'C' Plot: The Centarum vote to delay deciding upon a new Emperor. In the interim, they elect the ubiquitous Minister as Regent, and Londo returns to Babylon 5. The Regent wakes up during the night and discovers that an alien parasite has been attached to his neck by Dark Servants of the now departed Shadows.

The Arc: The Shadows are gone, but their Dark Servants remain. They are undoubtedly the beings responsible for placing an organic 'controller' on the new Centauri Regent's neck. We saw that Londo had one of these in his future in episode 317 ('War Without End' Part Two), and we see the preparations being made for his fitting in episode 517 ('Movements of Fire and Shadow'), as the Regent draws to the end of his unhappy life.

After some twenty episodes in which Earth had remained quiet, President Clark makes his long-awaited next move against Babylon 5. He's using Bester, among others, not realising that Bester had come to an arrangement with Sheridan in episode 314 ('Ship of Tears') – the episode in which we found out about his lover, Carolyn, and what the Shadows had done to her.

Lyta Alexander has come out of her time with the Vorlons with some hidden extras. As well as the methane gills we saw in episode 304 ('Passing Through Gethsemane') she also appears to have enhanced telepathic abilities – she can block Bester's telepathy and can send messages over many light years. What else did they do to her? Events in season 5 indicate that she herself does not know, while the second *Babylon 5* TV movie (*Thirdspace*) shows us that remnants of the Vorlons remain in her subconscious mind.

Bester knows something about Lyta's past: something she doesn't want anyone else to know about.

Observations: We get a flashback to Mr Garibaldi's experiences in episode 402 ('Whatever Happened to Mr Garibaldi?').

Zack Allen has a problematic past, and Garibaldi was the only person who would hire him. Further reference to this is made in season 5.

Some material was obviously snipped out during Delenn and Sheridan's conversation aboard the White Star: after Delenn says, '. . . the picture always ends with your head imploding!', their postures and relative positions suddenly change.

A group of Elvis impersonators arrives on the station in this episode. The lead Elvis is actually Mark Walters, who, at various times in the series, has been a prop maker, the Assistant Art Director, the Prop Master and the Art Director.

Dialogue to Rewind For: The new Regent, admiring the curtains in the Throne Room: 'I'm thinking . . . pastels.'

Other Worlds: Disneyplanet (but does it have twin moons that rise above its horizon like huge ears?).

Station Keeping: The jumpgate in Sector 49 is the last stopover point for vessels heading from Earth to Babylon 5.

Literary, Mythological and Historical References: Ivanova's quip about 'Reports of our disloyalty have been greatly exaggerated' refers to Mark Twain's famous put-down, 'The report of my death was an exaggeration.'

I've Seen That Face Before: Walter Koenig returns as Bester.

Questions Raised: What did the Vorlons do to Lyta's telepathic abilities?

What does Bester know about Lyta's past?

What is Bester's 'ace in the hole', and does it have anything to do with the coded message received by Mr Garibaldi?

What are the separate plots launched by Earthforce and the Ministry of Peace against Babylon 5 (the ISN plot in episode 408 – 'The Illusion of Truth' – is presumably the Nightwatch one)?

'The Illusion of Truth'

Transmission Number: 408
Production Number: 408

Written by: J Michael Straczynski
Directed by: Stephen Furst

Dan Randall: Jeff Griggs
Dr William Indiri: Henry Darrow
Alison Higgins: Diana Morgan   **Ramirez:** Albert Garcia

Date: The ISN broadcast takes place on 12 April 2261, and the ISN team arrive on Babylon 5 about two weeks beforehand. It's been 259 days since Mars was taken by President Clark.

Plot: This episode doesn't play as well in England as in America – we're already too used to programmes telling us how the media twist the truth. The episode's message is old news, and, apart from the message, what else does it have? It has other problems as well – in order to ensure that the dialogue during the interview sections can be quoted out of context, J Michael Straczynski has had to write it in such a way that nobody would really say it. The whole episode is staged.

The 'A' Plot: ISN reporters turn up on the station, claiming to want to tell something of the truth about what is going on, although they admit that ISN is deep in the pocket of President Clark. With the agreement of Sheridan they conduct interviews with all the major players on the station, but, when the ISN special is finally transmitted, the interviews have been re-edited into a terrifying accusation that Sheridan and Delenn are genetically re-engineering humans from Downbelow into a half-human, half-alien army, with the White Star fleet being readied for an invasion of Earth.

The 'B' Plot: Doctor Franklin wants to move the comatose, Shadow-enhanced telepaths into storage. ISN reporters discover what is going on, and twist the truth to suit their own ends – claiming that the medical staff on Babylon 5 are carrying out genetic experiments on the lurkers in Downbelow.

The 'C' Plot: Mr Garibaldi is carving out a living as a recovery agent for lost articles and people. Approached by ISN and asked about Captain Sheridan, he manages to say exactly the wrong thing.

The Arc: We discovered in episode 407 ('Epiphanies') that President Clark had set in train a four-pronged plot against Babylon 5, involving Psi Corps, EarthForce, Nightwatch and the Ministry of Peace. None of them know the plots the others are hatching. In that episode, Psi Corps had their go at the station. In this episode, it's probably Nightwatch who have a crack, on the assumption that they are the ones who used the twisted-logic arguments in season 3.

Observations: There's a lovely scene where Lennier is bothered by a floating camera, and 'nuts' it when nobody is looking.

The Foundation for Luna Colony was laid on 12 April 2018. Psi Corps was founded on 12 April 2061.

We get another flashback to Mr Garibaldi's experiences in episode 402 ('Whatever Happened to Mr Garibaldi?').

In the opening scenes, Sheridan is playing with a model of a Starfury. Allegedly, it was an unauthorised model confiscated by J Michael Straczynski at a convention.

Alas, we lose a joke in England that was included in the USA transmission. When Sheridan, Ivanova and Delenn sit down to watch the ISN broadcast, Sheridan switches on the screen, saying, 'Let's see what's on – with our luck, it'll probably be a commercial.' In the US transmission the episode then went straight to a real set of commercials, but in the UK transmission the episode went straight to the ISN broadcast.

When Dan Randall is sneaking in to see the cryo-units in medlab, we can see the names Carolyn Sanderson and John Flynn on two of the units. Carolyn Sanderson is the character we saw in episode 314 ('Ship of Tears') – Bester's lover. John C Flinn III is the show's Director of Photography and occasional episode director.

Stephen Furst – the actor who plays Vir – directed the episode. He's the first (and, by episode 522, last) actor in the series to have done so.

Dialogue to Rewind For: Londo: 'When I said my quarters were cold, I did not mean, "Oh, I think it's a little chilly in here, I think I'll put a blanket on the bed." No, I said it was cold, as in, "Oh look, my left arm has snapped off like an icicle and shattered on the floor!"'

Dialogue to Fast-Forward Past: Randall: 'Can I sit?' Garibaldi: 'That's between you and your chiropractor – I don't get involved.'

Other Worlds: The Iridan Colony.

Culture Shock: Shokola is a minor Drazi deity – patron god of pilots.

Literary, Mythological and Historical References: The Tri-vid producer, Lee Parkes, names those people who helped him in his supposed acts against President Clark. They include Carleton Jarrico, Beth Trumbo and Adrian Mostel. These are actually combinations of names of some of the people who faced the House Commission on Un-American Affairs in the 1950s (the centre of the McCarthy witch-hunts against communist sympathisers in Hollywood), including the actor Zero Mostel and the writers Dalton Trumbo and Paul Jarrico.

I've Seen That Face Before: Henry Darrow came to fame back in the era of black-and-white television in *The High Chaparral*. Since then he has appeared in many American TV series, although his most recent genre appearance has been as Chakotay's father in the *Star Trek: Voyager* episode 'Tattoo'.

Accidents Will Happen: 'This place has been declared dead more times than Lazarus,' says Sheridan. Well, Lazarus was declared dead only once, according to the Bible, so it's not much of a distinction.

The well-known phenomenon of hostages sympathising with their captors is referred to in this episode as the 'Helsinki Syndrome'. It's actually called the 'Stockholm syndrome'.

Yuri Gagarin's name is misspelt by ISN as 'Gargarin'.

The ISN report takes a humorous argument between Sheridan and Londo and twists it to make it look as if Londo is giving Sheridan orders. They do this by playing the confrontation without sound for most of its length, except that anyone who can lip-read can tell that Londo is not saying what ISN claim he is.

Dan Randall claims during the ISN broadcast that Earth taxpayers are funding repairs to the White Star fleet. He then goes on to say that Babylon 5 broke away from Earth some time ago. How does he expect his viewers to accept both of these contradictory statements?

'Atonement'

Transmission Number: 409
Production Number: 409

Written by: J Michael Straczynski
Directed by: Tony Dow

Dukhat: Reiner Schöne **Callenn:** Brian Carpenter
Morann: Robin Atkin Downes

Plot: Up there with the best of episodes, 'Atonement' gives us a new perspective on what we thought we already knew.

The 'A' Plot: A Minbari cruiser arrives at Babylon 5 in order to take Delenn back to Minbar. She is told that she must go through a ceremony known as 'the Dreaming'. No Minbari has ever polluted the purity of the Minbari race by taking an off-worlder for a mate before, and Delenn's caste must determine her reasons for doing so – is she following the calling of her heart, or does she have another reason? The Dreaming – a type of guided hallucination – will help them discover, by exposing Delenn's inner reasons to her conscious mind.

Back on Minbar, Delenn enters the Dreaming with Lennier as her protector and guide (she previously fulfilled the same function for Dukhat). In the Dreaming she discovers, from things she subconsciously knew but never consciously realised, that, when the human Jeffrey Sinclair became the Minbari Valen a thousand years ago, human DNA became mixed with Minbari DNA. Many Minbari now are the descendants of Valen, and have remnants of this human DNA. Delenn's argument is that she cannot be diluting the purity of the Minbari race by marrying Sheridan as she herself carries human DNA, and is therefore not herself pure. Callenn, it appears, already knew about the DNA and does not want it revealed to the populace. He and Delenn come to an arrangement – it used to be an old tradition during Minbari battles that the winning side would donate a female to the losing side to enable them to renew their forces. Callenn suggests that the tradition be revived, and that Delenn be handed to the humans (or, more precisely, to Sheridan) as a symbol of life.

The 'B' Plot: During the Dreaming, Delenn relives the first meeting of humans and Minbari, and the tragic mistake that led to war. The Minbari ships approached the human ships with their gunports open as a mark of respect, but this was misinterpreted as a hostile action by the humans, who fired back. Dukhat was killed, along with many Minbari, and it was Delenn who gave the order for retribution while overcome with emotion at the death of Dukhat. In effect, Delenn gave the order for the war to start.

The 'C' Plot: Marcus and Franklin are sent to Mars to coordinate resistance against President Clark.

The Arc: The triluminary glows when Delenn is introduced to the Grey Council. We discover in this episode that it glows when exposed to Valen's DNA (which is why it glows when placed next to Sinclair in 'And the Sky Full of Stars' – episode 108). The triluminaries were, or so legend has it, a gift from Valen, although it is said that they originally came from the future. We see the story behind this legend in episodes 316 and 317 ('War Without End' Parts One and Two).

After Sinclair had become Valen and travelled back one thousand years to lead the Minbari against the Shadows, he married and had children. He left Minbar and his body was never found. His children returned to Minbar to settle down. Background hints in the eighth *Babylon 5* novel (*To Dream in the City of Sorrows*) and in the comic miniseries *In Valen's Name* indicate that his wife was actually Catherine Sakai (having gone through the chrysalis process herself, one assumes).

Observations: Zack Allen has taken Garibaldi's place as Head of B5 Security.

G'Kar has been fitted with a prosthetic eye that can still transmit images to his brain when removed from its socket. I would have laid good money on that eye coming in useful later in the series, but I would have been wrong.

Delenn is of the family of Myr. She was chosen to be

Dukhat's aide by Dukhat as an apology for placing her into a position where she embarrassed the Grey Council.

Soul Hunters arrive just before the shooting starts between the humans and the Minbari. We were told that this happened as far back as the first season (episode 102 – 'Soul Hunter').

The character of Morann is not named until the TV Movie *In the Beginning*. In this episode he is credited only as 'Grey Council No. 1'.

It will take Marcus and Franklin between two and two and a half weeks to get from Babylon 5 to Earth, but they are taking the long route.

The end credits of the episode discard the usual theme music, and instead have Jason Carter singing Gilbert and Sullivan's 'I Am the Very Model of a Modern Major-General', ending with an aural out-take.

The TV movie *In the Beginning* covers much the same set of events as the 'B' plot of this episode.

Dialogue to Rewind For: Dukhat to Delenn: 'I cannot have an aide who will not look up – you will be forever walking into things.' This mirrors an early line from her to Lennier in episode 105 ('The Parliament of Dreams').

Delenn's words of war: 'Strike them down! No mercy! No mercy!'

Morann's bitter words: 'We are a world gone mad.'

Lennier's explanation of how he obtained Valen's scrolls from their archives: 'The guards resisted at first . . . I managed to explain matters to them. They will recover – in time.'

Franklin: 'Marcus, this is the kind of conversation that can only end in a gunshot.'

Culture Shock: It used to be an old tradition during Minbari battles that the winning side would donate a female to the losing side to enable them to renew their forces.

I've Seen That Face Before: Reiner Schöne played a character called Esoqq in the *Star Trek: The Next Generation* episode 'Allegiance' – a member of a race known as the Chalnoth.

'Racing Mars'

Transmission Number: 410
Production Number: 410

Written by: J Michael Straczynski
Directed by: Jésus Treviño

Captain Jack: Donovan Scott
Number One: Marjorie Monaghan
Number Two: Clayton Landrey
Dan Randall: Jeff Griggs **Wade:** Mark Schneider
Brakiri Woman: Carrie Dobro

Plot: Length, breadth and depth: everything that *Babylon 5* should be. This episode will probably never be viewed as one of the classic ones – it's too transitional for that – but it's damn near perfect as it stands.

The 'A' Plot: Franklin and Marcus are approaching Mars and are ready to make contact with the Resistance. A rather bizarre travelling companion who calls himself Captain Jack turns out to be their contact, and he leads them to the underground tunnels where the Resistance are based.

Captain Jack seems strangely eager for them to be taken straight to Number One, but the Resistance Number Two wants to check their identifications first. The identifications don't check out, and Number Two is on the verge of killing them when Number One appears. She wants to see their faces before they are killed. Captain Jack pulls a gun and tries to kill Number One, but Franklin manages to save her life. Marcus grabs a gun and fires at Captain Jack, missing him but hitting an invisible alien on his shoulder. It dies and Jack runs off.

Jack communicates with them via radio, and tells them that the alien was controlling his actions and wanted Number One killed. He cannot return, as the alien controller is growing back, so he blows himself up.

The 'B' Plot: Sheridan wants to find out why Garibaldi was so negative when talking to ISN. There appears to be some small chance of a reconciliation, but it's blown when an alien woman treats Sheridan like a demigod and Garibaldi reacts badly. Sheridan reads the riot act to him, telling him that one small infringement of the rules means he will be thrown off the station. Garibaldi is approached by a man named Wade, who recruits him into a mysterious organisation who believe that Sheridan has to be stopped for his own good.

The 'C' Plot: Having spent their three nights together, as decreed by Minbari tradition, Delenn and Sheridan must now discover each other's 'centres of pleasure'. This is done, much to Sheridan's discomfort, with a contingent of Minbari outside the bedroom to ensure that the ceremony is properly followed.

The 'D' Plot: The blockade by Earthforce of Babylon 5's supplies is biting home, and Ivanova determines to do something about it. Contacting all the smugglers operating through the station, she offers them a deal: if they will smuggle food, medicines and technical supplies, she will provide their ships with escorts, maintenance and support. They accept.

The Arc: The alien parasite on Captain Jack is obviously the same sort of creature we saw on the future version of Londo in episode 317 ('War Without End' Part Two) and on the Centauri Regent in episode 407 ('Epiphanies'). It shows that the Shadows' Dark Servants are active in the universe, and in this instance probably working for President Clark.

Observations: There's a lovely tracking shot from space right into a porthole through which Marcus is staring, then in through the porthole and into the cargo bay in which Marcus is standing, all in one seamless shot.

Captain Jack's real name is John Demeter.

Franklin and Marcus are masquerading on Mars as a married couple, indicating that same-sex marriages are perfectly acceptable in the future (and quite right too). We also discover from throwaway dialogue that the Pope is female.

Mr Garibaldi's hair fell out thanks to the contents of a black-market bottle not being as advertised.

We discover in season 5 that Number One's real name is Theresa Halloran.

Dialogue to Rewind For: Captain Jack: 'The thing of it is . . . the damn thing of it is . . . they grow back. They always grow back.'

Lennier to Sheridan after the ceremony: ' "Whoo-hoo?" '

Dialogue to Fast-Forward Past: Captain Jack talking about his daughter: 'She's the alpha and omega of my soul.'

Other Worlds: Deneb IV has the biggest market in the area near Earth.

Culture Shock: The controlling alien creature on Captain Jack is covered with microfibres which are built like synaptic relays. They cut into the neural pathways and override them.

I've Seen That Face Before: Marjorie Monaghan (Number One) played a recurring role on the juvenile SF TV series *Space Rangers* (alongside Cary-Hiroyuki Tagawa, who appeared as Morishi in episode 302 – 'Convictions').

Jeff Griggs is credited as reprising his role as Dan Randall, the ISN reporter from episode 408 ('The Illusion of Truth'), but the character appears only in clips from that episode.

Questions Raised: Marcus has his arms around Captain Jack's shoulder at one point. Can he not feel the controlling alien creature, or is it insubstantial as well as invisible? The Shadows were actually insubstantial, given that two of them accompanied Morden everywhere, even in narrow corridors, without anyone bumping into them.

'Lines of Communication'

Transmission Number: 411
Production Number: 411

Written by: J Michael Straczynski
Directed by: John C Flinn III

Number One: Marjorie Monaghan **Phillipe:** Paulo Seganti
Forell: GW Stevens (sometimes known as G Wesley Stevens)
Drakh Emissary: Jean-Luc Martin
ISN Reporter: Carolyn Barkin

Plot: Although there had previously been hints that the lesser races who had worked for the Shadows were still around, this episode brings them out of the . . . ahem, shadows and gives them form. In passing, it also takes the first steps along the path that leads to *Crusade*. A good, tense, intriguing episode.

The 'A' Plot: Delenn becomes aware that there have been attacks on races along the edge of Minbari space. The Norsaii – a peaceful, agrarian race, have suffered, as have the Pak'ma'ra. Delenn takes a fleet of White Star ships to patrol near the location of the attacks, accompanied by Lennier and Forell – the Minbari who first drew the problem to her attention.

When they arrive, Forell pulls a gun and forces Delenn to take the White Star fleet to a particular location in space, where they are met by a huge mothership accompanied by a number of fighters. The ships belong to the Drakh, the race who have been making the attacks. Forell tells Delenn that the Drakh are a powerful race who are looking for allies. There is trouble on Minbar, with the Warrior caste taking arms against the Religious caste, and Forell recommends allying the Religious caste with the Drakh.

A Drakh emissary comes aboard Delenn's ship and offers a deal, but Delenn realises from things that are said that the Drakh were allied to the Shadows. The Drakh emissary suddenly realises who Delenn is, and what she has done, and Delenn knows that the White Star fleet will be wiped out when the emissary returns to its ship. The fleet makes off rapidly, using the mothership for cover, but when they are in hyperspace Delenn gives them the order to return and destroy the Drakh, who must not be allowed to survive.

The 'B' Plot: Franklin and Marcus have arranged a meeting with the local resistance leaders on Mars, but a bomb placed by the resistance in a Martian hotel without Number One's knowledge kills a number of innocent civilians and jeopardises the Resistance's aims. Franklin gives a speech to the Resistance leaders, offering the help of Babylon 5 but stressing that acts of random violence are counterproductive.

The 'C' Plot: Sheridan has been watching the incessant outpouring of propaganda and lies about Babylon 5 on ISN, and comes up with a plan. During the Shadow War, they were providing information on safe havens and dangerous sectors from the station, broadcast around the galaxy, around the clock. Why not do the same now, and call it the Voice of the Resistance? He tells Ivanova that she will be fronting it, and he converts the former War Room into the studio for the broadcasts.

The Arc: The long-awaited appearance of the Shadows' servants is interesting. The Shadows could render themselves visible or invisible at will. The Drakh Speakers are halfway along that path, given that their appearance is blurred as if they were caught halfway between one state of being and another.

Delenn becomes aware that things are not as they should be on Minbar.

Observations: One of the Minbari on Delenn's ship is played by a CNN entertainment reporter named Dennis Michael. He was also a Narn in episode 221 ('Comes the Inquisitor').

The Speaker for the Drakh is a fascinating creature. Photographs show an amazingly effective face that resembles a huge snake skull with red eyes set into the bony sockets. The creature would (as far as I can tell) have been amazingly effective and spooky – especially if kept to the shadows (as opposed to the Shadows) but someone has made the unfortunate decision to have it walk in a kind of very slow breakdance. Perhaps the idea was to make it look as if it is jointed in a different way from most other races, but the final result was so unintentionally humorous that J Michael Straczynski immediately imposed a special effect on top of the creature, blurring it so that it looks half real, half mirage. It almost manages to cover over the broken-legged walk of the thing, but I can't help feeling that the original creature, gliding around mysteriously, would have been better.

Dialogue to Rewind For: Delenn: 'John it pleases me that you care for what I have become, but never forget who I was, what I am and what I can do.'

Sheridan: 'You have a face people trust.' Ivanova: 'I'd rather have a face people fear.'

Delenn: 'End this.'

Dialogue to Fast-Forward Past: Phillipe (one of the Mars Resistance) to Number One, making his pitch for best 'as you already know' line this season: 'Tell me, is this how you treat all your former lovers?'

Ships That Pass in the Night: The *Juno*, an Earthforce ship.

Other Worlds: Marcus was raised on Arisia Colony (see **Literary, Mythological and Historical References** below).

Alien Races: The Drakh, or the Speaker for the Drakh (see **Questions Raised**, below) – one of the races that served the Shadows. The Norsaii are also mentioned, but not seen.

Literary, Mythological and Historical References: The Arisia Colony may well be a reference to the planet Arisia from EE 'Doc' Smith's epic *Lensman* SF series. The *Lensman* series has some marked similarities to *Babylon 5*, what with its hierarchy of good and evil races (led by the Arisians and the Eddorans at the top) fighting it out across the galaxy, using the younger races as their pawns.

Accidents Will Happen: Sheridan claims that during World War Two the French Resistance made radio broadcasts telling the French what was really happening. This is an overly romanticised view on either Straczynski's or Sheridan's part – the French Resistance were peddling as much propaganda as the Germans were, just in a different direction.

Questions Raised: Is the Drakh emissary actually a Drakh, or a member of another race who is being used as an emissary? The script is very careful never to refer to it as a Drakh itself, and the Drakh as seen in episode 517 ('Movements of Fire and Shadow') are quite different.

'Conflicts of Interest'

Transmission Number: 412
Production Number: 412

Written by: J Michael Straczynski
Directed by: David J Eagle

Zathras: Tim Choate   **Lise Hampton:** Denise Gentile
Wade: Mark Schneider   **Ben:** Charles Walker
William Edgars: Efrem Zimbalist Jnr (uncredited)

Plot: Very much a transitional episode, with a handful of plots being given a boost, but good to watch, nonetheless.

The 'A' Plot: Garibaldi is making a go of his independent locator service – so much so that he can afford to reduce his rates for deserving cases. Just when things are going so well, Sheridan sends Zack Allen to confiscate Garibaldi's link, identicard and weapons. This, to what in Garibaldi's eyes is unwarranted interference in his affairs, provokes him into accepting a job from the mysterious Wade. The job will be to act as expediter and bodyguard to the wife of Wade's boss. She will be coming through the station in the near future, and she has to be protected.

When Wade's boss's wife arrives, she turns out to be Garibaldi's old girlfriend Lise Hampton – now Lise Hampton-Edgars. Her husband – and, by extension, Wade's boss – is William Edgars, a millionaire industrialist who 'owns half of Marsdome'. Lise tells Garibaldi that Edgars has identified a genetic weakness in telepaths that might turn into a debilitating or deadly virus, and that he is working on a cure. Other forces are trying to stop him, however, because they want all telepaths to die. Lise is on the station to pick up the results of experiments into this genetic weakness – carried out by alien scientists. As she does so, they are attacked.

Garibaldi gets Lise and Wade out of danger, and alerts Zack Allen to the location of their attackers (one of whom is a telepath). Garibaldi gets Lise and Wade safely off the station, complete with their package of genetic material, and when

Zack tries to arrest the attackers they kill themselves rather than be taken.

The 'B' Plot: Ivanova travels to Epsilon 3 to ask Draal if she can use the vast energy resources of the Great Machine to help broadcast the messages from the Voice of the Resistance. Draal is busy, but Ivanova meets another of what turn out to be ten Zathras brothers. He agrees to help provide the power they require.

The 'C' Plot: Sheridan calls G'Kar and Londo to a meeting. Worried about the increase in attacks on alien borders, caused primarily by Raiders, the servants of the Shadows such as the Drakh and other opportunistic aliens, he wishes to deploy the Rangers along the borders between the various alien sectors. Aware that this might seem provocative to the League of Non-Aligned Worlds, he asks the Narn and the Centauri to set a good example by agreeing. After some discussion, they do.

The Arc: This episode gives a healthy kick of life to the Garibaldi storyline, which has been relatively dormant for some time. We know from episodes 402 ('Whatever Happened to Mr Garibaldi?') and 403 ('The Summoning') that Garibaldi has had some contact with Psi Corps and may have had a secondary personality implanted: in this episode he is manoeuvred on to the path that Psi Corps want him to travel. The scene where the telepathic killer fails to shoot Garibaldi is a hint that Psi Corps are using him as their agent – a hint that will be put into context in episode 417 ('The Face of the Enemy').

Observations: Garibaldi is watching old (Warner Brothers) Loony Tunes cartoons again. Interestingly, in the cartoon he is watching, Daffy Duck realises he is being controlled by an outside influence – the cartoonist – who turns out to be Bugs Bunny. This foreshadows later revelations about Garibaldi's life, as shown in episode 417 ('The Face of the Enemy').

Although Efrem Zimbalist Jnr provides the voice of William Edgars, albeit uncredited, he will not appear in person for another two episodes.

We get flashbacks in this episode to episodes 120 ('Babylon Squared') and 119 ('A Voice in the Wilderness' Part Two).

Dialogue to Rewind For: Zathras, explaining to a confused Ivanova who he is: 'You work up there; Zathras work down here. You dress like that; Zathras dress like this.' Ivanova: 'That's not –' Zathras: 'Just covering all possibilities. Zathras does not want you being confused.'

Zathras again – 'There are ten of us, all of family Zathras. Each one named Zathras. Slight differences in how you pronounce "Zathras".'

And more from Zathras, concerning his time-travelling sibling: 'Zathras was quiet one in family.'

More from Zathras (and why not?): 'Zathras trained in crisis management!'

Ships That Pass in the Night: The ship that Lise Hampton arrives on sounds like the *Mo'fak'cha*.

Other Worlds: Ares Colony gets a mention.

'Rumors, Bargains and Lies'

Transmission Number: 413
Production Number: 413

Written by: J Michael Straczynski
Directed by: Mike Vejar

Alyt Neroon: John Vickery
Religious Minbari No. 1: Guy Siner
Religious Minbari No. 2: Chard Heywood
Alien Ambassador: Ron Campbell
Brakiri Ambassador: Jonathan Chapman

Plot: Lashings of irony and a nice, light-hearted plot on Sheridan's part – the calm between storms. A shame, however, that the default phrase for an invisibility device has to be 'a cloaking device'. *Star Trek* has, alas, become a part of the language.

The 'A' Plot: Returning to Minbar, where civil war has

broken out, Delenn arranges to meet her old adversary in the Warrior caste, Neroon. She tells Neroon that neither the Warrior nor the Religious caste can be allowed to win the civil war. He agrees, but feels it is too late to stop the fighting, and says that it must burn itself out.

A passing member of the Religious caste mishears what is being said, and assumes that Delenn is offering to surrender to the Warrior caste. In order to prevent this, the senior members of the Religious caste on board the ship plot to poison its occupants by releasing a gas into the air recycling system. The lifeless ship will then drift onward in hyperspace and will never be found. Lennier discovers their plan and disconnects the gas from the air supply, suffering injuries in the process. He then covers up the involvement of the Religious caste, having first ensured that they realise they were in error.

The 'B' Plot: Sheridan is concerned that it will take some time to get the League of Non-Aligned Worlds to agree that the White Star fleet can patrol their borders and act against Raiders and Drakh, and so he comes up with a plan. By setting up a series of deceptions – White Star ships attacking asteroids, Londo Mollari denying that the White Star ships are patrolling Centauri borders, Ivanova announcing as the Voice of the Resistance that nothing happened in the sector of space where the asteroids were attacked – he fosters a paranoid attitude among the members of the League. Believing that invisible enemies are encroaching on their borders, they demand that the White Star fleet patrol their borders as well.

The 'C' Plot: Delenn and Neroon agree to work together to stop the civil war, but Neroon appears to have a secondary agenda. He leaves the ship and goes on ahead to meet the Warrior caste, transmitting a message to them indicating that he is double-crossing Delenn.

The Arc: The episode acts as a bridge between the temporarily suspended Shadow ally arc from the previous episode and the Minbari civil war arc that will occupy the next episode.

Observations: Lennier has part of his lung removed as a result of breathing in the poison gas.

Delenn points out to Lennier that this is the second time

she has seen him injured. The first time was, of course, during episode 302 ('Convictions').

The less said about the so-called comedy team of Rebo and Zootie, the better. They appear, of course, in episode 508 ('Day of the Dead').

Dialogue to Rewind For: Sheridan: 'I'm tired of doing things the hard way.'

Dialogue to Fast-Forward Past: Sheridan to Marcus: 'You have your orders. I have neither the desire nor the inclination to explain them to you.' Isn't desire the same as inclination?

Ships That Pass in the Night: The Minbari ship sounds like the *Tikari*.

I've Seen That Face Before: Guy Siner will be a familiar face to British viewers, having played Lieutenant Gruber in the long-running comedy series *'Allo, 'Allo*. He also played General Ravon in the *Doctor Who* story 'Genesis of the Daleks'.

John Vickery returns as Neroon. His last appearance was in episode 319 ('Grey 17 is Missing').

Accidents Will Happen: Sheridan tells Marcus to take the White Star fleet to Sector 87 and attack some asteroids. Later, the attack appears to have occurred in Sector 83.

'Moments of Transition'

Transmission Number: 414
Production Number: 414

Written by: J Michael Straczynski
Directed by: Tony Dow

William Edgars: Efrem Zimbalist Jnr (uncredited)
Shakiri: Bart McCarthy   **Neroon:** John Vickery
Bester: Walter Koenig   **Mr Adams:** Scott Adams

Plot: Superb stuff: politics and drama playing out hand in hand. It's a shame to lose Neroon – a character who has been around since season 1 – but he dies in style.

The 'A' Plot: Delenn has arrived on Minbar and is trying to stop the fighting between the Religious and Warrior castes. The Warrior caste have surrounded the capital city and are demanding the surrender of the Religious caste, otherwise they will destroy it. With no options left to explore, Delenn tells Lennier that the Religious caste are prepared to surrender.

Neroon meets with Shakiri, the leader of the Warrior caste, and makes it clear that, although the Religious caste believe he is working with them, he is actually still loyal to the Warrior caste. Neroon suggests to Shakiri that the surrender take place in an ancient Minbari temple as a symbolic act, and Shakiri agrees.

During the ceremony, Delenn invokes an ancient rite in which the leaders of the castes come together in a trial of strength. Under the gaze of the entire Minbari race she calls down the starfire wheel – a column of intense white light – and invites Shakiri to step inside with her. Goaded by Delenn and by Neroon, Shakiri steps inside the circle, but he cannot endure the pain and leaps out, his body smouldering. Delenn remains inside, martyring herself, and so Neroon follows her in, removes her, and remains inside himself. He dies in Delenn's place, making a death-bed conversion from Warrior caste to Religious caste. Delenn re-forms the Grey Council, ensuring that the Worker caste have a controlling interest.

The 'B' Plot: Lyta Alexander is trying to get a job, but nobody will take her on as she does not have a Psi Corps licence. Bester arrives on Babylon 5 and offers to take her back into Psi Corps, taking her off the rogue list and putting her on a list of deep-cover agents. All he wants is her body, after she has died, for research purposes. She refuses, but soon afterwards Zack Allen tells her that she has to move to smaller quarters. She persuades Garibaldi to offer her a job, but he has to fire her after his boss, William Edgars, tells him to. Reluctantly, Lyta takes up Bester's offer.

The 'C' Plot: Garibaldi receives transmission from William Edgars. A package will be arriving on Babylon 5, Edgars tells him, and Garibaldi is to shepherd that package on its way to Io. Edgars claims that the package contains pharmaceutical supplies for the research arm of his company, supplies that he does not want getting into the hands of his competitors. Zack Allen spots the package being passed to Garibaldi in the customs hall but cannot get Garibaldi to admit that anything is going on.

The 'D' Plot: Sheridan is provoked into fighting back against President Clark by an attack made by one of Clark's ships on an unprotected refugee convoy.

The Arc: William Edgars displays his almost paranoid distrust of telepaths in this episode. His paranoia will be explained further in episode 417 ('The Face of the Enemy').

Bester indicates here for the first time that he has plans for Mr Garibaldi. As with William Edgars, his plans will reach their fruition in episode 417 ('The Face of the Enemy').

Delenn tells the Grey Council, 'And this place is reserved in memory of Neroon, until the day it is taken by the One that is to come.' The One that is to come is established as being John Sheridan in episode 317 ('War Without End' Part Two).

Observations: There's a seven-hour time difference between Babylon 5 and Mars.

From 2247 to 2257, Lyta Alexander worked for Xenocorp.

Lyta Alexander refers in passing back to her first arrival in 'The Gathering'.

This episode has an appearance by Scott Adams, creator of the cult cartoon character Dilbert. Adams is a great fan of the programme, and has referred to it a couple of times in his *Dilbert* strip. In a reference to the strip, he tells Garibaldi that his cat and dog (i.e. Catbert and Dogbert) are planning to take over the galaxy.

Dialogue to Rewind For: 'It's good to see they're continuing the fine tradition of hiring from the shallow end of the gene pool,' Bester says, apropos of Zack Allen's security guards.

Ships That Pass in the Night: The *Pollux*, an Earthforce destroyer, wipes out a number of ships full of refugees.

Other Worlds: The name of the Pak'ma'ra homeworld is Pak'ma (although the *Babylon 5* CD-Rom lists it as Melat).

Proxima III, Beta Durani and the MacArthur Mid-Range Colony all get a mention.

Culture Shock: In the past, the Minbari Grey Council has comprised three from each caste. Delenn now re-forms it with two from the Religious caste, two from the Warrior caste and four from the Worker caste, to ensure that the other two are kept in check.

Literary, Mythological and Historical References: Bester quotes Marley's ghost from Dickens's *A Christmas Carol*.

I've Seen That Face Before: Efrem Zimbalist Jnr is one of the great survivors of American television. He was the star of the action series *The FBI* in the early 1970s ('A Quinn Martin Production') and more recently has found gainful employment as the voice of Alfred in the animated *Batman* TV series.

'No Surrender, No Retreat'

Transmission Number: 415
Production Number: 415

Written by: J Michael Straczynski
Directed by: Mike Vejar

Captain Edward MacDougan: Richard Gant
Captain Trevor Hall: Ken Jenkins
Commander Sandra Levitt: Marcia Mitzman Gaven
Commander Robert Philby: Neil Bradley

Plot: Events suddenly shift into a higher gear as conflict is joined. It's a great story, with drama and action to spare.

The 'A' Plot: Sheridan calls a surprise meeting of the League of Non-Aligned Worlds and tells them about the price tag for his help in protecting them from Raiders – he wants them to declare null and void the mutual defence treaties their governments had signed with Earth. He also wants each race to contribute at least one destroyer-class vessel to the defence of Babylon 5.

Marcus and the White Star fleet are sent to Proxima III, and Sheridan joins them later. They emerge from hyperspace and demand that the Earthforce ships guarding the colony free it immediately. Captain Hall of the *Heracles* fires on Sheridan's forces, and conflict is joined. Captain MacDougan is persuaded to keep the *Vesta* out of the conflict, despite the rebellion of his Executive Officer; the *Fury* remains noncombatant; the *Juno* withdraws from combat; the *Pollux* is destroyed when a White Star ship crashes into it; the *Nemesis* takes severe damage and surrenders. The *Heracles* surrenders after its Executive Officer, Commander Levitt, relieves Captain Hall of command. Sheridan offers the captains of the *Heracles*, the *Vesta*, the *Fury* and the *Nemesis* three options – stay loyal to President Clark and return to Earth, remain and guard Proxima III or join the rebellion. None of them stay loyal to Clark.

The 'B' Plot: Londo goes to visit G'Kar in his quarters and tries to make peace. G'Kar refuses to respond, but later joins Londo at the bar for a drink and agrees to sign, with Londo, a joint declaration of support for Sheridan's rebellion..

The 'C' Plot: Vir tells Garibaldi that Sheridan is moving against Earth. Garibaldi is so disgusted at Sheridan's action that he leaves Babylon 5. He does not expect ever to return.

The Arc: A pivotal point in the series here, marked by the fact that the season itself takes its overall title from this episode. After almost three seasons of increasing problems on Earth, Sheridan decides to lance the boil.

Sheridan asks Franklin to get as many Shadow-enhanced telepaths available as possible, although he doesn't say why. We discover the terrible truth about his plans for the telepaths in episode 420 ('Endgame').

Observations: This episode begins on 2 September 2261.

'Before war broke out between our two governments, you bought me a drink,' Londo reminds G'Kar. He's referring to the events of episode 209 ('The Coming of Shadows').

Ivanova's Life Lessons: 'Trust Ivanova, trust yourself; anyone else – shoot 'em.'

Dialogue to Rewind For: Sheridan: 'From now on, Earth stands alone. We're taking back Proxima III. We're taking back Mars. Then we're going to take back our home – or die trying.'

Vir: 'I don't always like the way Londo does things – me and most civilised worlds – but, you know, sometimes he's right, so I force myself to give him the benefit of the doubt.'

Ships That Pass in the Night: The *Heracles*, the *Juno*, the *Pollux*, the *Nemesis*, the *Vesta* and the *Fury* are all guarding Proxima III at the start of the episode. The *Alexander* is loyal to Sheridan. White Stars 2 (Sheridan's vessel), 7, 12, 14 and 18. Marcus is in White Star Prime.

Literary, Mythological and Historical References: Lieutenant Corwin says to Ivanova, 'So from now on I guess the operational phrase is, "trust no one".' This may well be a reference to the cult American TV series *The X Files*, whose motto this phrase is.

'Exercise of Vital Powers'

Transmission Number: 416
Production Number: 416

Written by: J Michael Straczynski
Directed by: John Lafia

Lise Hampton: Denise Gentile   **Wade:** Mark Schneider
William Edgars: Efrem Zimbalist Jnr
Ms Constance: Shelley Robertson

Plot: There is a certain sense here of the writer taking an active role in moving the characters to where he needs them on the board. It's all terribly talky, and all it would take to make it risible is a couple of 'As you well know . . .' comments from the cast, but Efrem Zimbalist gives it a much-needed gravitas.

The 'A' Plot: Mr Garibaldi is on Mars, visiting his new employer – William Edgars. Garibaldi wants to know why he has been smuggling drugs through Babylon 5's customs, and he also wants to do something about Sheridan's crusade. He cannot turn Sheridan over to Clark, but he can turn Sheridan over to Edgars.

Edgars has Garibaldi questioned under duress and in the presence of a telepath. Garibaldi passes the questioning, and Edgars decides to trust him further, but Edgars has Wade kill the telepath afterwards.

Edgars takes Garibaldi at least partially into his confidence: he is terrified that telepaths will attempt to take over human society, and he intends stopping them. Edgars is worried that if Sheridan presses Clark then Clark will release the final checks holding Psi Corps back. Garibaldi decides to collaborate with Edgars and betray Sheridan to him, but what Garibaldi doesn't know is that Edgars has a group of telepaths in a medical unit in his house on Mars, infected with some kind of disease.

The 'B' Plot: Franklin is attempting to revive the Shadow-enhanced telepaths, but he cannot remove the implants without killing the patients. Lyta Alexander discovers by accident that she can revive them by temporarily 'pushing away' the Shadow influence.

One of the telepaths remembers being operated on by the Shadows, and attempts to kill himself, but Lyta prevents him.

Franklin confronts Sheridan and asks what he intends doing with the telepaths; Sheridan tells him, and Franklin is shocked.

The 'C' Plot: Sheridan's forces are moving forward, and more of President Clark's forces are defecting by the day.

The Arc: 'I said I would ask you to come when the time is right,' says Edgars to Garibaldi. If there's a catchphrase for this series, it's 'when the time is right'.

The awoken telepath remembers being operated on by alien surgeons. The scenes are very similar to those seen in episodes 314 ('Ship of Tears') and later in 517 ('Movements of Fire and Shadow') – in fact, the alien surgeons are identical.

According to Edgars, Morgan Clark had President Santiago killed because Santiago disagreed with Clark's policy of running loyalty checks on his staff.

Observations: Babylon 5 is eighteen light years away from Earth.

Dialogue to Rewind For: 'Everything is illusion, Mr Garibaldi – concepts of language, light, metaphor – nothing is real' – Wade.

'Do you know how the ancient Greeks defined happiness?' William Edgars asks Garibaldi. 'Happiness, they said, was the exercise of vital powers along lines of excellence in a life affording them scope.'

Literary, Mythological and Historical References: Edgars refers to President Clark's 'night of the long knives'. This refers to the night of 30 June 1934, during which the elite German paramilitary force of the *Schutzstaffel* (the SS), acting on the orders of Adolf Hitler, murdered the leaders of their rivals in the *Shturmabteilung* (the SA) in order to secure Hitler's power base.

Accidents Will Happen: 'Its rising foretold the death of kings, the collapse of empires,' says Wade talking about Mars, but surely Mars rises every night. Venus certainly does – that's why it's called the Evening Star.

Edgars says that the Germans handed power to the Nazis in 1939, but the elections that brought them to power were actually in 1932.

'The Face of the Enemy'

Transmission Number: 417
Production Number: 417

Written by: J Michael Straczynski
Directed by: Mike Vejar

William Edgars: Efrem Zimbalist Jnr
Captain Edward MacDougan: Richard Gant
Lise Hampton-Edgars: Denise Gentile
Captain Leo Frank: Ricco Ross
Number One: Marjorie Monaghan
Alison Higgins (ISN Reporter): Diana Morgan

Captain James: David Purdham
Wade: Mark Schneider   **Bester:** Walter Koenig
Psi Corp Member: Harlan Ellison

Plot: An episode of answers rather than questions – what Edgars is really up to, why Garibaldi has been acting so oddly – and it's all pretty stunning.

The 'A' Plot: The war against Clark continues, but it's getting more intense as Sheridan's forces get closer to Earth. President Clark's forces have been told that, if they are captured, Sheridan will have them killed, and Sheridan has to persuade them otherwise. Ships are joining up left, right and centre, and even Sheridan's old command, the *Agamemnon*, changes sides.

On Earth, Sheridan's father is taken into custody. Mr Garibaldi sends a message to Sheridan, telling him this, with the aim of luring him to Mars where he too can be taken into custody. Garibaldi tells Sheridan that he has some people who can help spring his father, but they want a personal meeting with Sheridan. Ivanova recommends strongly that Sheridan ignore such an obvious trap, but he heads for Mars anyway, where Garibaldi drugs him and takes him prisoner.

The 'B' Plot: On Mars, William Edgars tells Mr Garibaldi that President Clark isn't the real problem – it's Psi Corps. Edgars believes that the telepaths are the greatest threat to freedom that humanity has ever seen. He tells Garibaldi that the vial of drugs he had Garibaldi smuggle through B5 customs is the antidote to a disease that his own people created – a disease that will attack only telepaths. If the telepaths are not given regular doses of the antidote, they will die, and Edgars is within a month of defeating the telepaths for ever.

Using a transmitter hidden in a tooth, Garibaldi sends a secret message to Bester and his Psi Corps troops. As a result, Psi Corps attack Edgars's base, killing him and Wade and taking both the disease and the antidote away.

Bester mentally 'debriefs' Garibaldi, and tells him that he had implanted a secondary personality inside Garibaldi's head which would infiltrate Edgars's organisation and discover his plans. Removing this personality, Bester leaves Garibaldi to come to terms with the full extent of his betrayal.

The 'C' Plot: Franklin and Lyta arrive on Mars, along with a cargo of frozen telepaths with Shadow implants. Number One is not happy about a telepath arriving on Mars, given their record operating against the Resistance.

The Arc: The virus that kills telepaths is probably based on Shadow technology, according to Bester. The Shadows are pretty good with organic technology – the virus that devastates the Earth in the setup for *Crusade* is a Shadow special.

Lyta Alexander tells Stephen Franklin, 'Some day there's going to be a war between telepaths and mundanes, Stephen. I just hope I don't live to see it.' This prediction partly comes true in the first half of season 5, but its effects will be felt some time between *Babylon 5* and *Crusade* in the planned and scripted movie intended for theatrical release.

Observations: This episode contains the first reference to Psi Corps's new Bloodhound units – elite telepaths assigned to military units who have few scruples about how they use their powers. They will take a bigger role in the first half of season 5.

We see clips in this episode from episode 322 ('Z'ha'dum'), 402 ('Whatever Happened to Mr Garibaldi?') and 407 ('Epiphanies'). There are also references to Wade smuggling an object through Babylon 5 security (episode 414 – 'Moments of Transition') and to Garibaldi sacking Lyta Alexander (also episode 414).

During the filming of the scene where Garibaldi is forced to remember everything that has been done to him and everything he has done, the actor Jerry Doyle originally played it much more aggressively. 'I remember doing the scene, slamming my head against the wall and doing a primal scream,' he says. 'I think they cut that out. That was the only thing I didn't like. But that's their choice – they do it for whatever reason. I just thought at some point when all that piss-and-vinegar stuff is coming back into your veins, and you're conscious of all the things that people have done to you, you wouldn't be silent – but Joe wrote it as the silent scream, because it was overloading the system. I thought it would be cool to have a shot of me doing the scene, then the shuttlecar tracking where it was going, and then a CG [computer-generated] pullaway on that car disappearing into the distance with that scream fading. That's not the way they cut it. That's their decision.'

Ivanova's Life Lessons: 'What's going on? You all look like a Pak'ma'ra just ate your cat.'

Dialogue to Rewind For: Bester: 'Whatever you think of me, Mr Garibaldi, I'm not capricious or cruel.' Yeah, right.

Ships That Pass in the Night: The *Hydra* and the *Delphi* are Clark's ships and are taken out of commission by Sheridan's action. The *Cadmus*, the *Vesta* and the *Agamemnon* are three of Clark's ships that come over to Sheridan. The *Agamemnon* was previously seen in episode 308 ('Messages From Earth'). White Star 20 is also mentioned.

Questions Raised: Why is Sheridan so damn stupid as to walk into an obvious trap? His father wasn't dead: he was in custody. Why not just wait until Clark was defeated and Earth was free?

If Hitler's face was well known to everyone in Britain in the 1940s, why did it not occur to Sheridan that *his* face would be known on Mars?

How does Bester know the content of the conversation between Sheridan and Justin in episode 322 ('Z'ha'dum')?

'Intersections in Real Time'

Transmission Number: 418
Production Number: 418

Written by: J Michael Straczynski
Directed by: John Lafia

William: Raye Birk   **Drazi:** Wayne Alexander
Interrogator: Bruce Gray   **Minister:** Peter Brown

Plot: It seems churlish, if not perverse, to criticise an episode that takes such an uncompromising antitorture stance, but I'm going to anyway. Political prisoners are tortured around the world in ways that no sane person can even imagine, and this episode does them no service at all. It makes physical abuse look like something a person with sufficient strength of will can resist. That's wishful thinking. If a little vomiting and a little mental confusion was the worst that could happen to a political prisoner then perhaps Straczynski's polemicising would be acceptable, but where were the electrodes on the testicles? Where was the repeated rape? Where was the complete physical degradation and humiliation? It's a safe, cosy form of abuse that Straczynski shows us: one that, I hate to say, affects the audience less than the equivalent *Star Trek: The Next Generation* episodes, 'Chain of Command' Parts One and Two. Better not to show any torture at all than show the watered-down version on display here.

The 'A' Plot: Following his betrayal by Michael Garibaldi, Sheridan is imprisoned on Mars. President Clark wants him to sign a statement repudiating everything he has done and confessing his sins, and to that end assigns an interrogator to break Sheridan's will by any means necessary. They cannot fake it, as Sheridan's confession has to stand up to a telepathic scan. The interrogator does this by inflicting pain (using Narn paingivers), by confusing Sheridan's sense of time (altering the lighting outside the cell arbitrarily), by humiliating him (giving him a poison that causes severe vomiting) and by confusing his mental faculties (using invalid dialectical arguments).

The interrogator brings a Drazi prisoner into Sheridan's cell and, as Sheridan watches, the prisoner confesses that he was part of a conspiracy to influence Sheridan's mind. Sheridan persuades the Drazi to recant his confession, but is shocked when the Drazi is strapped to a gurney and taken to Room 17, where he is apparently electrocuted.

Sheridan is on the verge of breaking when a vision of Delenn gives him strength to carry on resisting. He refuses categorically to sign the confession, and is strapped to a gurney and taken to Room 17 – apparently to be electrocuted. In fact, in Room 17 he is strapped to a chair and a different interrogator begins the same litany as the previous one did, days before. The cycle has started again, with the difference that the Drazi whom Sheridan thought dead is standing behind the interrogator, very much alive.

Observations: This episode contains clips from episode 417 ('The Face of the Enemy').

Sheridan makes a coded reference to his interrogation by Jack the Ripper in episode 221 ('Comes the Inquisitor').

A character named 'Minister' is credited at the end of the episode, but never appears in the transmitted version.

The actor Dakin Matthews dropped out as William the Interrogator shortly before filming started, and was replaced by Raye Birk (who had originally auditioned for the part). The last-minute change necessitated some simplifications in the way the director approached the episode.

A scene on Mars in which a repentant Garibaldi is almost killed by Number One was originally filmed for this episode, but was shifted to episode 419 ('Between the Darkness and the Light') when this episode ran seven or eight minutes too long, and 419 ran eight minutes short.

Dialogue to Rewind For: William the Interrogator: 'Do you have any allergies or illnesses I should be aware of? Are you currently taking any medication? Have you had any trouble with your heart?'

Sheridan: 'You just have to say "No, I won't" one more time than they can say, "Yes, you will".'

I've Seen That Face Before: The man playing the Drazi prisoner is Wayne Alexander, who previously played Jack the Ripper in episode 221 ('Comes the Inquisitor'), a Narn in episode 320 ('And the Rock Cried Out, No Hiding Place') and Lorien in the first four episodes of season 4, and subsequently appeared as a Drakh in the last few episodes of season 5.

'Between the Darkness and the Light'

Transmission Number: 419
Production Number: 419

Written by: J Michael Straczynski
Directed by: David J Eagle

Number One: Marjorie Monaghan
Captain James: David Purdham
David Eisensen: Marc Gomes **Interrogator:** Bruce Gray

Plot: Stunning.

The 'A' Plot: Susan Ivanova leads the White Star fleet
further towards Earth, confronting Clark's forces as she goes
and absorbing those who wish to convert to the cause, but not
everyone who has defected to Ivanova's side is being truth-
ful. Some are agents for Clark, and they have told him
that a rendezvous is planned between Ivanova's forces and
Delenn's ships. Ivanova discovers this, and also discovers
that destroyers of a new, advanced design will be waiting for
them.

During the conflict with Clark's new destroyers – ships that
combine human and Shadow technology – the ship that
Ivanova is commanding is badly damaged, and Ivanova herself is injured. A rescued Sheridan then takes command of the
fleet for the final assault on Earth.

The 'B' Plot: Sheridan is still being questioned by the
forces of President Clark, who are using drugs to disorientate
him. Meanwhile, a guilty Garibaldi makes contact with the
Mars Resistance, who then kidnap him and systematically
beat him up. Garibaldi manages to convince Stephen Franklin
that he has been used by Psi Corps by requesting that Lyta
Alexander scan him to determine whether he is telling the
truth. He tells Franklin and the Resistance that he knows
where Sheridan is being held.

Franklin, Lyta and Garibaldi sneak through a series of
access tunnels towards the staging area where Sheridan is
being kept. Despite Garibaldi being stabbed during an encounter with security guards they find Sheridan. They then

manage to escape, having to shoot their way past the security forces, and get Sheridan off Mars so that he can rejoin the fleet.

The 'C' Plot: Londo Mollari calls a meeting of the League of Non-Aligned Worlds without Delenn knowing about it. She turns up and gatecrashes, to find a vote going on. The vote is passed, and Londo tells Delenn that they have all agreed to provide League ships to support Ivanova's fleet.

Observations: This episode contains clips from episodes 322 ('Z'ha'dum'), 402 ('Whatever Happened to Mr Garibaldi?') and 417 ('The Face of the Enemy').

Ivanova and Marcus refer to a conversation they had in episode 321 ('Shadow Dancing').

The scene in which Garibaldi is almost killed by Number One was originally filmed for episode 418 ('Intersections in Real Time'). It was moved over to this episode when 418 ran seven or eight minutes long, and 419 ran eight minutes short.

Ivanova's Life Lessons: 'Who am I? I am Susan Ivanova, Commander, daughter of Andrei and Sophie Ivanov. I am the right hand of vengeance, and the boot that is going to kick your sorry ass all the way back to Earth. I am death incarnate, and the last living thing that you are *ever* going to see. God sent me.'

Dialogue to Rewind For: Mr Garibaldi after having Lyta Alexander scan him: 'I just realised I need a lot more fibre in my diet.'

An Earthforce security guard: 'I don't watch TV. It's a cultural wasteland filled with inappropriate metaphors and an unrealistic portrayal of life created by the liberal media elite.'

Ships That Pass in the Night: The *Damocles* and the *Orion*, both loyal to President Clark, are wrecked by Ivanova's forces, White Stars 4 and 9 are named. And, of course, we get our first sight of President Clark's Earthforce destroyers with integrated Shadow technology – the Warlock Class, as we later discover.

Questions Raised: What did Ivanova do when she discovered that some of the ships in her fleet were actually loyal to President Clark? Did she challenge them, or just leave them where they were?

'Endgame'

Transmission Number: 420
Production Number: 420

Written by: J Michael Straczynski
Directed by: John Copeland

Earthforce NCO: Ungela Brockman
General Robert Lefcourt: J Patrick McCormack
Number One: Marjorie Monaghan
Captain James: David Purdham
Senator Crosby: Carolyn Seymour
Captain Mitchell: Julian Stone
ISN Anchor: Maggie Egan
President Clark: Gary McGurk

Plot: If there's one triumphal moment that affects me more than any other in this series, it's the sight of the *Agamemnon* appearing through the fiery demise of the last planetary defence platform. It's a simple special effect but its emotional punch is dependent upon some quite complex audience investment in the characters – most particularly the fact that Sheridan would willingly sacrifice his life for others by ramming the platform before it can fire on the Earth, the fact that his crew love and respect him so much that they will follow him without question when he gives the order to ram, and the fact that the man who trained Sheridan and then was prepared to kill him is the one who saves his life by blowing up the platform before the *Agamemnon* hits it. All unstated, all in the background, and yet all brought to bear on a few seconds of CGI.

The 'A' Plot: Sheridan's fleet is almost at Mars, on its way to Earth. Sheridan, leading from the *Agamemnon*, is aware that he must deal with the Earthforce destroyers in Mars orbit (led by the *Apollo*) before moving on to his final goal, lest they attack him from the rear. Having introduced Shadow-enhanced telepaths on to the Earthforce ships in order to disrupt their computers, he orders his vessels to jump to Earth.

On Earth, a panicking President Clark kills himself. Senator Crosby, who appears to lead the opposition against Clark, informs Sheridan that Clark has turned the planetary defence grid against Earth. The planet is within a few minutes of 40 per cent destruction. The systems cannot be overridden. Sheridan's forces destroy most of the planetary defence platforms, but one is left operational, out of range of all ships apart from the *Agamemnon*. Sheridan orders the *Agamemnon* to ram the platform, as the ship's weapons are off line, but the *Apollo* destroys it first. Earth is free and safe.

The 'B' Plot: On Mars, Stephen Franklin and Lyta Alexander smuggle cryogenically frozen telepaths on to Earthforce destroyers with the aid of a Resistance agent who works in the Earthforce shipping area. Meanwhile, another section of the Mars resistance, led by Garibaldi, takes control of various ground stations around the landing and take-off area. From there, Lyta Alexander transmits a telepathic signal to the frozen telepaths. They wake up and disrupt the computer systems on the ships.

The 'C' Plot: A fatally wounded Susan Ivanova is shipped back to Babylon 5. Marcus Cole discovers that an alien device on the station can possibly save her life – at the expense of his own – and so leaves the fight for Earth and heads for Babylon 5, where he places Ivanova in the machine and switches it on.

The Arc: Marcus realises from something that Lennier lets slip halfway through the episode that the alien machine confiscated by Stephen Franklin in episode 121 ('The Quality of Mercy') is capable of saving Ivanova's life. Watch Delenn's face in the pre-title sequence when she and Sheridan are standing over Ivanova's inert body: that's when *she* realises the same thing.

The Shadow-enhanced telepaths that Sheridan uses (or abuses) in order to paralyse the ships in orbit around Mars were set up as early as season 3. Bester's girlfriend is one of the telepaths, as seen in episode 314 ('Ship of Tears'), but she is not one of those Sheridan uses.

President Clark arranges for the Earth defence system to turn against the planet, in an attempt to destroy it as a viable entity. Clark then leaves a coded message telling people what he has done. This is reminiscent, surely, of Captain Jack in episode 410 ('Racing Mars'), who laced his conversation with small clues that he was not acting of his own volition. Had President Clark been fitted with a Shadow controller, and was he attempting to break free of its influence?

Finally, after nearly three seasons of President Clark's overt and covert influence, Earth is free.

Observations: This episode starts on 1 November 2261.

There is a reference to Dr Hobbs, Franklin's second in command. She was previously seen in episodes 315 ('Interludes and Examinations') and 318 ('Walkabout'). There is also a reference to the death of Franklin's one-time lover Cailyn (we knew she was seriously ill in episode 318 – 'Walkabout').

When President Clark kills himself, he leaves a message on his desk on which the words 'The ascension of the ordinary man' are written sixteen times. Certain letters are circled, spelling out the message 'Scorched Earth'. This tips Senator Crosby off that Clark has ordered the planetary defence system to attack the Earth itself. The note was the Director John Copeland's tip of the hat to the Stanley Kubrick film *Doctor Strangelove*.

We get a clip from episode 202 ('Revelations').

The Director, John Copeland, is also the series Producer.

Dialogue to Rewind For: Franklin to Garibaldi: 'I assume you worked out that whole longitude/latitude thing – I know you get confused sometimes.'

Sheridan: 'We have come home.'

Sheridan: 'All power to engines. Give me ramming speed.'

Ships That Pass in the Night: The *Apollo* is still loyal to President Clark, and is in orbit around Mars. It's commanded by General Lefcourt, who taught Sheridan at the academy.

The *Aegean*, the *Theseus* and the *Artemis* have switched loyalties to Sheridan.

I've Seen That Face Before: Carolyn Seymour is a British actress who may be remembered for her starring role in Terry Nation's drama about the destruction of most of the world's population: *Survivors*. More recently she has appeared in *Star Trek: The Next Generation*, among other things.

Welcome back Rance Howard as David Sheridan. Howard previously appeared in episodes 310 ('Severed Dreams') and 315 ('Interludes and Examinations').

Questions Raised: What exactly is ramming speed? Does Earthforce Academy give special training in how to ram a vastly expensive piece of hardware into alien ships, just in case all weapons are inactive and there's no other choice? If they do, why is there a ramming speed? What happens if you ram too slowly, or too fast?

'Rising Star'

Transmission Number: 421
Production Number: 421

Written by: J Michael Straczynski
Directed by: Tony Dow

Luko: Joey Dente   **Lise Hampton:** Denise Gentile
David Sheridan: Rance Howard
General Foote: Michael Potter
President Susanna Luchenko: Beata Pozniak
Bester: Walter Koenig   **ISN Anchor:** Maggie Egan

Plot: We're into what, at the time, was intended to be the last but one episode of *Babylon 5*, and for that reason it's difficult to treat it as anything but an episode that ties up loose ends and sets up a possible feature film (the Telepath Wars), but ties them up in a very neat and watchable way.

The 'A' Plot: Sheridan has surrendered to Earthforce following President Clark's suicide and the destruction of the rogue planetary defence system.

Bester visits Sheridan in his comfortable holding cell, wanting to know whether Sheridan used Bester's lover, Carolyn Sanderson, as one of his telepathic weapons in the war against President Clark's forces. Sheridan tells Bester that he chose the telepaths carefully, looking for the ones who had no family and whose condition was irreversible. Carolyn was not one of them.

President Luchenko, who has taken over from President Clark, tells Sheridan that, although he did the right thing, he is guilty of insurrection at best and treason at worst. His presence in Earthforce is inconvenient and embarrassing, and she forcefully suggests that he resign his commission. To sweeten the deal she offers amnesty for him and for his people.

Sheridan announces his resignation live on ISN, but shortly afterwards is offered, and accepts, the presidency of the new Interstellar Alliance that has been born out of the ashes of the League of Non-Aligned Worlds. Shortly after that, he and Delenn marry.

The 'B' Plot: Delenn presents Londo and G'Kar with a proposal for the formation of an Interstellar Alliance, prior to presenting the same proposal to the various members of the League of Non-Aligned Worlds. Shortly afterwards, Delenn announces live on ISN that the League of Non-Aligned Worlds is being dissolved and replaced with an Interstellar Alliance, which will help developing worlds and enforce the peace. Earth is invited to join, and accepts. The colony worlds such as Mars will be allowed to vote for their freedom.

The 'C' Plot: Susan Ivanova has recovered from her fatal injuries, thanks to Marcus Cole's use of the alien healing device. Marcus is, however, dead, and Ivanova decides to leave Babylon 5 and explore the galaxy as captain of a new Warlock-class Earthforce ship.

The 'D' Plot: Garibaldi locates Lise Hampton (-Edgars) in the clutches of the Mars Mafia. They had kidnapped her and were holding her to ransom, and so Garibaldi frees her. They become lovers again.

The Arc: Well, it's all over bar the shouting. Now that Clark is dead and the war with Earth is over, Sheridan and

Delenn have taken control of the new Interstellar Alliance. In a very real sense, Sheridan is now the *de facto* ruler of the galaxy.

Back on Centauri Prime the Regent is ill, possibly dying, and the Centarum have decided to make Londo the new Emperor. He's not too happy about the prospect: although it's everything he dreamt about back when he first arrived on Babylon 5, now he knows it's just another step along the road to his death – an event he's seen in his dreams (episode 101 – 'Midnight on the Firing Line') and which we've seen in the future (episode 317 – 'War Without End' Part Two).

Bester has destroyed the telepath virus developed by Edgars Industries, but has kept the antidote, just in case.

'I know you,' Sheridan tells Bester. 'Even with Clark gone you'll keep moving your telepaths into positions of power, and then, when the time is right, you'll try and take over the government . . . Oh you'll wait a few years until things quiet down, and then you'll start a war between the telepaths and the normals.' Quite perceptive, and probably the basis for the first cinematic *Babylon 5* movie (assuming it ever gets made).

Observations: Alternative versions of certain scenes were filmed such that Marcus Cole could either have been dead or almost dead. In the end, it was decided that the character should die. Referring to the suddenness of his death and the lack of reaction from anyone apart from the (departed) Ivanova, J Michael Straczynski said that the characters would have more time to grieve down the road, and the repercussions of his life and death would be felt long after his passing and echo through parts of the fifth season. None of this actually happened, of course.

Dialogue to Rewind For: A tearful Susan Ivanova, talking about the deceased Marcus Cole: 'At least I should have boffed him just once.'

Ivanova: 'All love is unrequited Stephen . . . all of it.' (To which Delenn later adds, 'She's wrong, of course.')

John Sheridan to Bester: 'Death? Been there, done that.'

Londo: 'Delenn has a fascinating proposal for you all. I

hope you have brought a change of underwear – you will need it after you have read this.'

G'Kar: 'You do not make history, you can only hope to survive it.'

Delenn's voice-over at the end: 'It was the end of the Earth year 2261, and it was the dawn of a new age for all of us. It was the end of one chapter and the beginning of another. The next twenty years would see great changes: great joy and great sorrow, the Telepath War and the Drakh War. The new Alliance would waver and crack, but in the end it would hold, because what is built endures, and what is loved endures, and Babylon 5 . . . Babylon 5 endures.'

I've Seen That Face Before: Walter Koenig gets one scene as Bester (remember, it would have been his last if there had been no season 5) and it's nice to see Rance Howard back as John Sheridan's dad. He previously appeared in episodes 310 ('Severed Dreams') and 315 ('Interludes and Examinations').

Accidents Will Happen: 'You will be dishonourably discharged, court-martialled and brought to trial,' President Luchenko tells Sheridan. Impossible on two counts: first, Sheridan can't be dishonourably discharged until *after* a court martial (according to current military rules) and, secondly, a court martial *is* a trial: you can't have both.

Questions Raised: The League members to whom Delenn presents her proposal for an Interstellar Alliance are the Centauri, the Narn, the Brakiri, the Drazi, the Gaim, the Llort and the Pak'ma'ra. We know, from the dialogue in the next episode (422 – 'The Deconstruction of Falling Stars') that a dozen or so races have joined the Alliance. Adding humanity and the Minbari, that makes nine races we can name, so there are a lot more races who haven't yet been asked. Will they be?

Who the hell is Luko? He's mentioned in the credits, but I'm damned if I can work out why.

'The Deconstruction of Falling Stars'

Transmission Number: 422
Production Number: 422

Written by: J Michael Straczynski
Directed by: Stephen Furst

Brother Alwyn Macomber: Roy Brocksmith
Brother Michael: Neil Roberts
Latimere: Alastair Duncan   **Daniel:** Eric Pierpoint

Plot: Very disconcerting on first viewing, but the more one watches this the better it gets. It's *real* science fiction, as opposed to television science fiction. The episode comprises a series of views of the future, each one related to the legacy left behind by Sheridan and Delenn. What it shows, very clearly, is that, although the details of their lives and their actions have faded and been rewritten, they did change the course of history, perhaps even for the better.

2 January 2262: A late-night discussion programme on ISN shortly after the initiation of the Interstellar Alliance questions Sheridan's ability to run the Alliance.

2 January 2362: A university tutorial addresses the question of whether Sheridan and Delenn were personally responsible for the events around the formation of the Interstellar Alliance, or whether they were merely figureheads for the force of history. An elderly Delenn appears in front of the historians and psychologists conducting the tutorial and sets them right.

2 January 2762: Changes in Earth policy require the reputation of the Interstellar Alliance to be blackened so that Earth can break away, and so intelligent holographic representations of John Sheridan, Stephen Franklin, Delenn and Michael Garibaldi, complete with all their memories, are created in order to fake events which will be released to the 'proles'. Earth wants to expand, to invade other worlds, and the Rangers are preventing this. Some kind of civil war is just about to occur on Earth: the government is split, and the colony worlds have declared independence (again). The Garibaldi hologram inveigles their controller to reveal strategic facts about the coming attacks on the outer colonies, and then broadcasts all the details to the colonies, who attack and wipe out the EarthGov base.

2 January 3262: In a devastated world a thousand years after the formation of the Interstellar Alliance, an order of monks (not recognised by the Catholic Church) are responsible for keeping alive the knowledge of the past. Space is closed to the inhabitants of Earth. Sheridan, Delenn and Ivanova are mere legends, the truth of which is lost, and the myth that the Rangers will return to help Earth is just that – a myth. The Rangers are, however, working in secret to gradually reintroduce knowledge to human society.

A million years in the future: Earth's sun is about to go nova and the race that humanity has evolved into – a race of energy beings who cloak themselves in encounter suits – are transferring everything they know about their home to a storage facility on New Earth.

The Arc: There is a brief reference to some events concerning Sheridan and Delenn's son. The implication is that he was concerned with some great loss of life. There are more hints of this in episode 521 ('Objects at Rest').

There are references a hundred years in the future to the establishment of a colony of telepaths on Babylon 5. This occurs between episodes 501 and 511 ('No Compromises' and 'Phoenix Rising'), and was mentioned in episode 421 ('Rising Star').

The 'official' story is that Sheridan died on Minbar, twenty years after the formation of the Alliance, but stories denying this have apparently sprung up. We get to see the truth in episode 522 ('Sleeping in Light').

The Alliance is still going a hundred years after its formation.

Babylon 5 was apparently destroyed in 2282, twenty years after the formation of the Interstellar Alliance. This would correspond to around the time of the death of John Sheridan as predicted in episode 404 ('Falling Toward Apotheosis') and seen later in episode 522 ('Sleeping in Light').

About 500 years after the formation of the Alliance, Earth

is again turning in on itself, becoming insular and aggressive towards other alien races. There is disagreement between different factions on Earth, resulting in a civil war which lays waste to the planet: a period known later as 'the Great Burn'. The Rangers blockade Earth, refusing to allow any aid in or any of the inhabitants out. They do, however, attempt to surreptitiously aid the redevelopment of humanity, guiding them towards elementary scientific discoveries without allowing them to develop too fast.

Brother Michael refers to Sheridan's death, resurrection and eventual ascension into Heaven. The death occurred in episode 322 ('Z'ha'dum'), the resurrection in episode 403 ('The Summoning') and the ascension into heaven is a religious interpretation of what happens in episode 522 ('Sleeping in Light').

A million years in the future, humanity has become a kind of proto-Vorlon: having evolved into beings of pure energy who still like to use their human form and who travel around in encounter suits. The latter fact indicates that humanity is acting *in loco parentis* to younger races in the same way that the Vorlons were to us. Episode 518 ('The Fall of Centauri Prime') implies that humankind is moving *en masse* to the Vorlon homeworld.

Observations: J Michael Straczynski came in for some sustained criticism from some fans over this episode. They expressed in strong terms their belief that he had betrayed the spirit of *Babylon 5* by indicating that there would be more wars, more killing, and that nothing Sheridan or Delenn had done had made any difference. These accusations have more to do with betrayed expectations of a happy ending than with any serious criticism of the episode's dramatic validity, and Straczynski's response was characteristically robust.

'The Deconstruction of Falling Stars' was actually filmed as the first episode of season 5, but was moved to the end of season 4 to replace 'Sleeping in Light'. 'Sleeping in Light' had, of course, been filmed as the last episode of season 4, but when TNT picked up the option for season 5, J Michael

Straczynski took the decision to hold 'Sleeping in Light' over to the end of that season.

The episode ends with the caption, 'Dedicated to all the people who predicted that the Babylon Project would fail in its mission. Faith manages.' It's a not particularly subtle jibe at the many people who knocked the series during production, predicting its failure.

Just before the title sequence, the picture breaks up as 'temporal distortion' affects what the mysterious observer is watching. A rapid image flashes past: they are all taken from later in the episode.

Brother Michael refers to 'the Blessed Lorien', the First One who appeared in the first four episodes of season 4.

Yes, those early photographs are of a young Bruce Boxleitner.

The wedding of Sheridan and Delenn – an event for which some fans have been waiting for three entire seasons – occurs off screen.

All of the regular cast get their usual season credits in the title sequence, whether they appear in the episode or not, with the exception of Claudia Christian. Her name has been removed from the credits. This triggered some speculation among fans that Straczynski was taking his revenge upon her for walking off the series; rewriting history to expunge her name. The truth is somewhat less lurid. The gist of the argument, for those unfamiliar with the labyrinthine complexities of American television, is that Claudia Christian's contract specified that she would appear in 22 episodes and be paid for the same. That term 'appear' is the crux of the issue: Claudia Christian did not appear in all the episodes of season 4 but, for contractual reasons, was credited as if she had. If she were to be credited for 23 episodes (all of season 4 and the last episode of season 5) that 23rd episode would count as a one-off guest-starring role and attract an appropriate payment.

Dialogue to Rewind For: 'Perhaps it is something I said,' Londo muses when Garibaldi and Franklin give him a very odd look. 'Perhaps it is everything you say,' G'Kar responds.

Culture Shock: The Centauri celebrate deaths with elaborate parties, but treat weddings as sombre affairs.

Literary, Mythological and Historical References: One of the subplots of this episode – a religious order attempting to fight a new Dark Age by preserving scientific knowledge – is similar in scope and theme to the novel *A Canticle for Liebowitz*, written as a series of novellas by Walter M. Miller between 1955 and 1957 and published as a novel in 1960. The resemblance is unintentional, but J Michael Straczynski has stated that he realised while he was writing the script that he was in familiar territory.

Questions Raised: How was Delenn able to travel from Minbar to the tutorial (which is certainly not being held on Minbar) in time to interrupt its progress? Did she start out several days, if not weeks, before it started, just so she could burst in and say very little? Or was she already there on other business and, if so, why did the people holding the tutorial say she hadn't been seen for so long?

Season 5:
'Wheel of Fire'

'And so it begins.'

'There is a hole in your mind.'

'What do you want?'

'No one here is exactly what he appears.'

'Nothing's the same any more.'

'Commander Sinclair is being reassigned.'

'Why don't you eliminate the entire Narn Homeworld while you're at it?'

'I see a great hand, reaching out of the stars.'

'Who are you?'

'President Clark has signed a decree today declaring martial law.'

'These orders have forced us to declare independence.'

'Why don't these people get off their encounter-suited butts and do something?'

'You are the one.'

'If you go to Z'ha'dum you will die.'

'Why are you here? Do you have anything worth living for?'

'I think of my beautiful city in flames . . .'

'. . . giants in the playground . . .'

'Now get the hell out of our galaxy!'

'We are here to place President Clark under arrest.'

   – Kosh, Minbari Assassin, Sinclair, G'Kar, Sinclair, General Hague, Londo, Elric the Technomage, Sebastian, ISN Newsreader, Sheridan, Sheridan, Kosh, Lorien, Delenn, Sheridan, Sheridan, Sheridan

Regular and Semi-Regular Cast:

President John Sheridan: Bruce Boxleitner
Captain Elizabeth Lochley: Tracy Scoggins
Michael Garibaldi: Jerry Doyle
Delenn: Mira Furlan
Londo Mollari: Peter Jurasik
G'Kar: Andreas Katsulas
Dr Stephen Franklin: Richard Biggs
Vir Cotto: Stephen Furst
Lennier: Bill Mumy
Zack Allen: Jeff Conaway
Lyta Alexander: Patricia Tallman
Byron: Robin Atkin Downes

Observations: Season 5 came about thanks to the intervention of the cable channel TNT. Having already purchased all of seasons 1 to 4 for syndication (i.e. showing at the same time every night of the week), they also provided a home for the continuation of the series. While Warner Brothers would still own the show and take the profits, TNT would undertake to buy the rights to show the new episodes first (in practice, co-financing the episodes). The arrangement appeared ideal – TNT was staffed with fans of the show, and they supported it without interfering.

One change to the filming of the season that was a direct result of the switch to TNT was the reduction in the preparation and filming time for each episode. 'The pace at which we are doing them is slightly more frenetic,' John Copeland has said, 'because we're shooting on a six-day schedule. That means there are two less days per episode as far as Joe [Straczynski] and I are concerned. A day less of prep and a day less of shoot means that everything starts compressing.' Copeland's careful choice of words does not disguise the fact that moving from an eight-day schedule to a six-day schedule means that each episode in season 5 was made in three-quarters the time of the episodes in seasons 1 to 4. There are two ways of looking at this: either production time had been wasted in seasons 1 to 4 or the quality of the episodes in season 5 was going to suffer. It seems obvious to most fans which of those views was the more likely to be true.

The loss of 25 per cent of the schedule per episode, allied to the fact that the actors were making less money per episode (for complicated financial reasons that are explained more fully in an appended essay to this book: 'There's Always a "Boom" Tomorrow') indicates very strongly that the budget TNT were assigning to every episode was significantly smaller than the budget Warner Brothers had assigned. Straczynski has been very quiet on this subject, even going so far as to claim that the actors were making the same amount of money per episode for season 5 as the previous seasons (a claim denied by the actors), but the results were obvious on screen. Season 5 looks ... well, dowdy compared with the rest of the series.

The major changes to the cast for season 5 were, of course, the loss of Jason Carter (Marcus Cole) and of Claudia Christian (Susan Ivanova). As with the Foundation Imaging/Netter Digital Imaging switch between seasons 3 and 4, it is unlikely that the full set of reasons why either actor left will ever be made public. Jason Carter appears to have vanished with little fanfare, but the aftershocks of Claudia Christian's departure, including claim and counter-claim by Claudia Christian and J Michael Straczynski themselves, rippled through the fan base for months afterwards. All that's in the public domain are the statements that have been publicly made by the two of them, and these statements contain enough contradictions to suggest that events have occurred that one or the other is (or both are) unaware of. One is irresistibly reminded of the reasons why Pat Tallman did not return for season 1 after appearing in the pilot movie. A fuller discussion of both Straczynski's and Christian's publicly stated reasons is given in the essay I mention above.

Straczynski sensibly did not recast the role of Ivanova, preferring instead to alter a few words of a voice-over in episode 421 ('Rising Star') to explain the absence of her character, Susan Ivanova, and then to create the new character of Captain Elizabeth Lochley to satisfy the now vacant plot functions (although Claudia Christian has indicated that it was to have been Ivanova, not Lyta, who would have become involved with Byron in season 5). Tracy Scoggins and Catherine Oxenberg were running neck and neck for the part until the final audition: Scoggins got it. 'I read for the Movie of the Week that Shari Belafonte got,' Scoggins recalls, referring to the second *Babylon 5* TV movie (*Thirdspace*), 'and I told my agent at the time, "That's OK, because I'm going to be a regular on the show!" And my agent was thinking I was sadly delusional.'

Co-producer George Johnsen did not return for season 5. He has since stated that he wanted to reduce his workload and spend more time with his family.

Given the problems over whether season 4 was to be the last ever season of *Babylon 5* or not, and J Michael Straczynski's consequent pulling of the major events of the beginning of season 5 – the conclusion of the War to Retake Earth – into season 4, season 5 became in many people's minds little more than an inconsequential add-on to the rest of the story, a build-up of throwaway episodes leading up to the held-over 'Sleeping in Light'. Straczynski's later decision also to move the destruction of the Drakh homeworld out of season 5 and into a stand-alone TV movie (setting up the *Babylon 5* spin-off show, *Crusade*) didn't help matters either. Straczynski himself was publicly unrepentant. He claimed that season 5 was concerned with empire building and was a natural outgrowth of season 4.

As if the problems over losing a lead actress and also having already farmed plot material to season 4 weren't bad enough, Straczynski lost several weeks' worth of work when staff at a hotel at which he was staying for a convention threw out his handwritten outlines for the first few episodes.

The title sequence for season 5 was, as usual, created according to Straczynski's detailed instructions. The music was written by Christopher Franke, based on an original theme he had introduced on to the second *Babylon 5* soundtrack album (on the track 'Voices of Authority', although not from that episode); the visual clips are, of course, from previous episodes; but the lines of dialogue are this time taken from previous episodes as well, telling the story of the station so far.

Or are they? In fact, from episode 507 onwards the voices have been re-recorded and the theme music rebalanced.

As it has turned out, Straczynski has written all but one of the episodes of season 5 himself (albeit one of the episodes he wrote was co-plotted with Harlan Ellison). This was not, however, the initial plan. He explained before the season started that he planned to bring in about five scripts by outsiders. Only one freelance script actually made it into the finished season, however – the one written by Neil Gaiman – and Straczynksi was forced to fill in the gaps. One in particular that will be missed is a script by Peter David and Bill Mumy (Lennier) called 'Dying to Be Heard', which would probably have gone out as 508. It concerned Londo's replacement arriving on the station, and various acts of terrorism occurring elsewhere.

'No Compromises'

Transmission Number: 501
Production Number: 502

Written by: J Michael Straczynski
Directed by: Janet Greek

John Clemens: Anthony Crivello
Simon: Timothy Eyester

Plot: A welcome return to the style and pace of the second season.

The 'A' Plot: A Ranger is shot on Mars by a man named John Clemens, who then travels to Babylon 5 with the body. He leaves the body floating outside the station with a sign around its neck – 'Special Delivery for Babylon 5' – then sends a message to Sheridan's quarters saying, 'Dear Mr President, as of this date you are officially a dead man. Have a nice day.'

Clemens's intention is to assassinate Sheridan during the presidential inauguration ceremony, and to that end he kills the new Gaim Ambassador and uses the Gaim's encounter suit to infiltrate the inauguration. Detected by one of the rogue telepaths who have arrived on the station, he misses with his shot and escapes.

Sheridan continues with the inauguration, but Clemens steals a Starfury and tries to kill Sheridan from outside the station. Garibaldi pulls Clemens's Starfury away using the grapple of his own Starfury, and Clemens is killed by the station's weaponry. The inauguration goes ahead.

The 'B' Plot: A telepath named Byron asks for refuge on the station – refuge for him and his people. They are all rogue telepaths who refused to join Psi Corps but who also disagreed with the Resistance. An independent Babylon 5 is the closest thing they can find to a home, until they have enough people to form a colony of their own. Lochley refuses, but Sheridan says yes – partly because one of Byron's telepaths saved his life, but mostly because he knows a telepath war is coming, and he's building up his weapons.

The 'C' Plot: Captain Lochley arrives on the station as the replacement for Susan Ivanova. She's firm, independent and seems to want to do things by the book.

The Arc: Sheridan is finally inaugurated as President of the Alliance. One of his first acts is to make Garibaldi his Head of Covert Intelligence (hmm, very democratic, assigning his friends to positions of authority – the Labour Party would be proud). The Alliance will be based temporarily on Babylon 5, but will eventually relocate to Minbar. Wouldn't an uninhabited planet be more tactful – something like Epsilon 3?

Sheridan refers to the telepath war that they all know is coming. This war was back-referenced in episode 422 – 'The Deconstruction of Falling Stars' – and may eventually turn up as a cinematic *Babylon 5* outing.

Observations: Sheridan asks G'Kar to write an oath of office and a declaration of principles for the new alliance. G'Kar's literary skills have been set up over the past two seasons or so.

Sheridan and Lochley have met before. He asked for her in particular as the new commander of Babylon 5.

President Kyoshi of the Eastern Bloc was (at least partly)

responsible for the War of the Shining Star, which engulfed the Earth Alliance fifty years ago.

Mike Manzoni – the series' Facilities Manager – is the man hanging the sign on Lochley's wall when Garibaldi confronts her. It's probably a union thing.

Dialogue to Rewind For: G'kar: 'You want to be President?' Sheridan: 'I do.' G'Kar: 'Put your hand on the book and say "I do".' Sheridan: 'I do.' G'Kar: 'Fine. Done. Let's eat.'

Dialogue to Fast-Forward Past: Byron to Lochley: 'The geometries that circumscribe your waking life draw narrower until nothing fits inside them any more.' Which is a pretentious way of saying, 'You're not happy, are you?'

Ships That Pass in the Night: Earth Alliance Destroyer *Acheron*.

Other Worlds: Beta IX is an Earth colony (but in episode 101 – 'Midnight on the Firing Line' – we were told that the Centauri invaded the entire Beta system).

Culture Shock: A new Gaim ambassador arrives on the station. The Gaim, we finally discover, are an insectoid race who are ruled by a number of Queens. The *Babylon 5* CD-ROM released in late 1997 states that the Gaim who are sent away as ambassadors are specially bred bipeds, and the *real* Gaim are different in form.

It is a Narn tradition that, for the first ten years of their lives, they have temporary names. After they are ten, they can choose the faith they wish to follow and the name they wish to use.

Station Keeping: Zack Allen is still head of security.

Babylon 5 is still an independent state until the Alliance formally buy it from Earth. Earthforce are still running it partly because of tradition and partly to calm everyone after the civil war on Earth.

I've Seen That Face Before: Welcome back Joshua Cox as David Corwin, and Robin Atkin Downes (previously seen as the Minbari Morann in episode 409 – 'Atonement' – and later to be seen in the TV Movie *In the Beginning*) as Byron.

Accidents Will Happen: The security files in Garibaldi's office keep cycling through the same fourteen faces. That makes about one known evildoer per 20,000 members of the station's population – nice to see that Zack has been tough on crime in Garibaldi's absence.

'Captain, you'd better get down to Bay 3,' someone tells Lochley. 'There's something here you should see.' Why don't they tell her what it is? Alternatively, why doesn't she ask?

The Principles of the Alliance contain the first page of every religious book of every race in the Alliance. What about atheists – don't they get represented? What about religions without holy books?

Clemens's message to Sheridan said that John Wilkes Booth was in the Confederate army. He never was. Additionally, Clemens said on the message, 'I know you're a fan of history,' and, 'Did you know that President Lincoln was sure he would die in office?' When Garibaldi is listening to the same message later, Clemens says 'I know you're a fan of Lincoln.'

When Clemens is rushing out to conduct his assassination, the door of his quarters manages to open while he has his back turned.

Questions Raised: What happened to Simon to traumatise him so?

What is it with John Clemens and that bloody music box?

'The Very Long Night of Londo Mollari'

Transmissions Number: 502
Production Number: 503

Written by: J Michael Straczynski
Directed by: David J Eagle

Ruell: Ross Kettle
Med Tech: Akiko Ann Morison

Plot: Slow and rather repetitive, but fun to watch.

The 'A' Plot: Londo Mollari collapses while taking a drink of the Centauri spirit *brivari*. It is initially thought that he has been poisoned, but tests in medlab show that he has had a heart attack. Dr Franklin does his best to keep him alive, but even he admits that Londo will die unless he has the will to live. To everyone's relief, Londo pulls through.

The 'B' Plot: In a hallucinatory state, Londo's mind is desperately trying to prevent his body from dying. He tells himself, through the iconic figures of Delenn, Sheridan, Vir and G'Kar, that his heart can no longer stand the weight of the guilt he feels over the destruction of the Narn Homeworld and the consequent effect on his own people. In the end, he realises that it is only by apologising to G'Kar that he can bear to live. This he does – both in his hallucination and in reality.

The 'C' Plot: Heartsick, owing to his love for Delenn and his jealousy of Sheridan, Lennier leaves Babylon 5 in order to join the Rangers. There he hopes to become a better man.

The Arc: Sheridan appears in Londo's vision dressed in various sets of clothing, reflecting various phases of his life since he arrived on the station. The last set of clothing he wears appears to be a shroud of some kind. This may refer to the fact that his life has been cut short following his actions against the Vorlons in episode 404 ('Falling Toward Apotheosis'), or to his eventually 'passing beyond the Rim' in episode 522 ('Sleeping in Light').

Observations: Hydromorphazine is a stimulant for Centauri hearts.

There is a dialogue reference back to episode 306 ('Dust to Dust') to G'Kar's temporary telepathic link with Londo.

Flashbacks occur to episodes 209 ('The Coming of Shadows', where we first see G'Kar strangle Londo twenty years in the future), 220 ('The Long, Twilight Struggle', where Londo and Refa go to the Narn Homeworld) and 403 ('The Summoning', where G'Kar gets whipped).

We get Andreas Katsulas giving a pretty good Cartagia impression.

We also get to see Londo's genitalia (again).

Lennier has been to Earth before.

Londo mentions his first wife – a dancer whom he was forced to divorce. This wife came before the ones seen in episode 207 ('Soul Mates').

This script uses a similar title to that of a script planned but never made for season 2 – 'The Very Long Night of Susan Ivanova'. J Michael Straczynski has said that it is not a rewrite. He just liked the title.

Dialogue to Rewind For: Vir: 'What is wrong with you people? Don't you have anything else better to do? Why don't you get a hobby, read a book or something?'

Lennier, speaking for all of us: 'It's been a hell of a five years.'

Londo, also speaking for all of us: 'The metaphor's getting a bit thick, don't you think?'

Vir: 'Prophecy is a guess that comes true. When it doesn't, it's a metaphor.'

Londo, echoing a question that used to be asked quite a bit in this series: 'Who are you?'

Other Worlds: The planet (or race) of Khefti is mentioned.

Culture Shock: We're told again that Centauri have two hearts – one pumps blood and the other acts more like a kidney.

Accidents Will Happen: Londo sees Sheridan in a whole range of past and present costumes, but always with the same beard.

Londo says he's never said sorry before, but he did so in episode 101 ('Midnight on the Firing Line'). Perhaps he means he's never said sorry and meant it.

Dr Franklin refers to Londo's bipulmonary system – that means two lungs. He means his bicardiac system – two hearts.

'The Paragon of Animals'

Transmissions Number: 503
Production Number: 504

Written by: J Michael Straczynski
Directed by: Mike Vejar

Ranger: Bart Johnson
Verchan: Tony Abatemarco
Drazi Ambassador: Kim Strauss

Plot: The Enphili are a bit of a disposable alien race – I would be surprised to see them turning up in the Alliance conference chamber – but the subplots are fun. Garibaldi is already managing to subvert the moral foundations of the Alliance by manipulating and using people, and Byron is looking increasingly sinister.

The 'A' Plot: An alien race known as the Enphili are being attacked by Raiders. The Raiders have been exploiting their planet for ten years or so, systematically gutting it of mineral resources, but the Enphili have finally decided to fight back, precipitating bombing raids by the Raiders.

The Enphili planet is on the edge of Drazi space, but the Drazi have never claimed it. The Enphili ask a passing Ranger to help them: he makes it to Babylon 5 with their request to join the Alliance, but his White Star ship has been attacked on the way and he is badly injured.

At Sheridan's request, Lyta Alexander telepathically scans the Ranger in order to find out what has happened. He dies, but not before she finds out from him about the Enphili and the Raiders. A White Star fleet is sent to stop the Raiders and save the Enphili, but Sheridan is told that they are heading into a trap – the Drazi are in league with the Raiders and are splitting the profits. Sheridan shames the Drazi Ambassador into pulling the Drazi fleet back, and the Raiders are wiped out.

The 'B' Plot: Garibaldi asks Byron's group of renegade telepaths to gather information for the Alliance. Byron refuses, citing their reluctance to be used by 'mundanes', so

Garibaldi asks Lyta Alexander to approach him instead, the idea being that one telepath ought to be able to talk straight to another one. Taken with Lyta, Byron agrees to release two telepaths to help Garibaldi. In addition, he tells her that he has discovered that the Drazi are in cahoots with the Raiders – they are allowing the Raiders to exploit worlds on the edges of their space in return for half the profits.

The 'C' Plot: Most races – led by the Drazi – are refusing to sign the Declaration of Principles of the new Alliance. President Sheridan uses the involvement of the Drazi in the Enphili/Raiders situation to shame the members of the Alliance into signing.

Observations: There is a mention of the Abbai in this episode – apparently they are thinking of joining the Alliance. We saw them during various first-season episodes, especially 109 ('Deathwalker').

We get a mention of that well-known telepath Bester – Lyta Alexander says that he has scanned several people on the edge of death, gone too deep and seen more than any human being should see. When Lyta herself scans the Ranger at the moment of his own death she sees him moving along a tunnel of light, although whether this is the literal truth of what is happening to him or a vision from his oxygen-starved brain is unclear.

Dialogue to Rewind For: 'You cannot legislate morality,' says the Drazi Ambassador, and he should know.

G'Kar to Londo: 'Oh, go away. Repress someone else.'

G'Kar's Declaration of Principles for the new Interstellar Alliance is worth repeating in full:

> The Universe speaks in many languages, but only one voice.
> The language is not Narn, or Human, or Centauri, or Gaim or Minbari.
> It speaks in the language of hope,
> It speaks in the language of trust,
> It speaks in the language of strength and the language of compassion.

It is the language of the heart and the language of the soul.
But always, it is the same voice.
It is the voice of our ancestors, speaking through us,
And the voice of our inheritors, waiting to be born.
It is the small, still voice that says:
We are one
    No matter the blood
    No matter the skin
    No matter the world
    No matter the star;
We are one
    No matter the pain
    No matter the darkness
    No matter the loss
    No matter the fear;
We are one.
Here, gathered together in common cause, we agree to
    recognise this singular truth and this singular rule:
That we must be kind to one another
Because each voice enriches us and ennobles us and each
    voice lost diminishes us.
We are the voice of the Universe, the soul of creation, the
    fire that will light the way to a better future.
We are one.
We are one.

Dialogue to Fast-Forward Past: That said, G'Kar's '. . . We must be kind to one another' makes me remember Bill and Ted's 'Be excellent to one another': something I have been trying to forget for some time.

'His ship was shot to hell,' according to Franklin. Well, it'll be in good company considering the number of other things from this series that have preceded it.

Literary, Mythological and Historical References: Byron quotes from William Shakespeare's *Hamlet*, which is where the title comes from.

131

'The View From the Gallery'

Transmission Number: 504
Production Number: 505

Story by: Harlan Ellison and J Michael Straczynski
Written by: J Michael Straczynski
Directed by: Janet Greek

Mack: Raymond O'Connor
Bo: Lawrence LeJohn

Plot: It's a story that serves the same function as episode 215 ('And Now For a Word') and 408 ('The Illusion of Truth') in that it shows our heroes from the outside, viewed by strangers, rather than from the inside, but it's by far the best example. It's clumsy, but at least it's not preachy.

The 'A' Plot: Long-range sensors have been deployed in hyperspace to pick up the approach of an alien fleet. The Gaim have warned Sheridan of them: they test the defences of planets or Alliances, looking for weaknesses they can exploit during an invasion. They send in scouts to test Babylon 5, but the station's defences and its Starfuries manage to repulse them and the fleet moves on.

The 'B' Plot: Mack and Bo, two maintenance workers, move back and forth throughout the station, keeping vital systems running, and crossing the paths of the regular actors as they do so.

Observations: There is a reference to the events of episode 311 ('Ceremonies of Light and Dark').

People who die leave an ephemeral telepathic trace on their surroundings and their clothes.

The Enphili from the previous episode (503 – 'The Paragon of Animals') are mentioned.

Sheridan tells Delenn that he will see her again '. . . in a place where no shadows fall'. This was originally said by Delenn to Sheridan in episode 218 ('Confessions and Lamentations').

Spoo (a type of basic staple food favoured by many races

around the galaxy) is the butt of a few jokes in this episode. It was first mentioned in episode 101 ('Midnight on the Firing Line').

Byron seems to have a fetish about people really believing what they say. It arose with Lyta Alexander in episode 503 ('The Paragon of Animals') and again with Mack and Bo here.

Mack says that there is a rumour that Ivanova 'quit because she wasn't getting paid enough money'. This is almost certainly a dig at the fans (and the magazine writers, let's be fair) who claimed that Claudia Christian left the series for that very reason.

'I thought Del Rey was working Brown Sector.' This is a coded reference to Del Rey books, who have taken over the *Babylon 5* novel licence from Dell.

Nice to see Harlan Ellison's name on an episode. It doesn't make up for not having 'Demon on the Run' or 'Midnight in the Sunken Cathedral' or even *The Last Dangerous Visions*, but it's nice.

Dialogue to Rewind For: 'I wasn't talking to you,' Londo tells G'Kar. 'I was talking to the universe.'

Ships That Pass in the Night: The *Ares* was an Earthforce ship shot down during an intercolony war when Stephen Franklin was a child. His father was on board, but survived.

Other Worlds: The Narn day has 31 hours (Narn hours or human hours?).

Culture Shock: Note that these unnamed aliens who temporarily invade Babylon 5 come in two varieties – some have tall, domed helmets and some have helmets with flatter tops and flared sides. They wear the helmets because they breathe a different atmosphere from that on Babylon 5.

Literary, Mythological and Historical References: Byron quotes from *Hamlet* again (as in episode 503 – 'The Paragon of Animals'). It's probably the only play he knows.

Accidents Will Happen: Early on, Mack says that spoo goes for ten credits an ounce. Towards the end, he says it goes for fifteen credits an ounce. Mistake or joke: who knows? Who cares?

Questions Raised: Who are these aliens, and why do they wear such crap costumes?

'Learning Curve'

Transmissions Number: 505
Production Number: 506

Written by: J Michael Straczynski
Directed by: David J Eagle

Turval: Turhan Bey
Durhan: Brian McDermott
Rastenn: Nathan Anderson
Tannier: Brendan Ford
Trace: Trevor Goddard

Plot: Hmm – the Rangers as a fascist organisation who can ignore the entire judicial process in order to take their own personal revenge on those who hurt them. I hope to God this is the prelude to Straczynski's subversion of the Rangers, rather than his idea of how the perfect police force should operate. There is something terribly American about a force of do-gooders with executive authority to do anything they wish.

The 'A' Plot: Four Minbari Rangers leave the Minbari homeworld and arrive on Babylon 5. Two are senior members of the order, who wish to confer with Delenn; the other two are junior acolytes who are acting as aides to their masters.

During an exploration of Downbelow, the acolytes witness an attack on a woman: one of them does not wish to become involved, while the other rescues the woman but is attacked and badly beaten by the man who initiated the attack – a criminal named Trace.

Zack Allen sets out to bring Trace to justice, but Delenn and the Rangers overrule him. The injured Minbari leaves medlab and is allowed to regain his self-confidence by fighting and beating Trace in a gladiatorial contest supervised by the senior Minbari.

The 'B' Plot: A new crime lord has set himself up in the Downbelow area of Babylon 5 – a human named Trace. He is killing his rivals and those who will not submit to his authority, and Zack Allen wants him brought to justice. Trace is aware of this, and decides to kill Zack before Zack can capture him. Trace is beaten up by a visiting Minbari, and his reign of terror brought to an end.

The 'C' Plot: Garibaldi does not trust Lochley, and gets her to admit that she fought for President Clark during the civil war.

Observations: The insectoid crime lord N'Grath is no more, having been replaced by the rather more human Trace. We last saw N'Grath in episode 111 ('Survivors').

Talking about Garibaldi, Lochley tells Sheridan she never expected to find a *second* man as stubborn as she is. The first was Sheridan himself, as we discover in episode 506 ('Strange Relations').

Turval mentions Marcus, and the death of his brother. This is a reference to the events shown in the ninth *Babylon 5* novel – *To Dream in the City of Sorrows*.

Garibaldi asks Zack Allen to let him see Captain Lochley's personal file – he did the same to Sheridan at the beginning of season 2, you will recall. He also makes reference to Delenn's attack on the Drakh in episode 411 ('Lines of Communication').

The characters of *Turv*al and Dur*han* may have been named to reflect the actor Turhan Bey (who actually plays the character of Turval). Durhan has been mentioned before: most notably in episode 319 ('Grey 17 is Missing').

The first UK showing of this episode was cut by Channel 4: the fight scene at the end is a lot nastier than Channel 4 would have us believe.

Dialogue to Fast-Forward Past: 'We leave for Babylon 5!' You and everyone else, mate.

Other Worlds: Beta VII gets a name check.

Culture Shock: An alien race known as the Yolu get a mention: they were seen in episode 114 ('TKO') – it was a Yolu who was in charge of the fight.

I've Seen That Face Before: Turhan Bey previously played the Centauri Emperor Turhan (yes, same name) in episode 209 ('The Coming of Shadows').

Accidents Will Happen: The *Babylon 5* novel *To Dream in the City of Sorrows* describes Durhan as tall and imposing. In this episode he's short and stout.

Questions Raised: Are the Rangers really as out of control as this episode suggests?

'Strange Relations'

Transmission Number: 506
Production Number: 507

Written by: J Michael Straczynski
Directed by: John C Flinn III

Bester: Walter Koenig
Byron: Robin Atkin Downes

Plot: It's fun, and it all hangs together, but Bester's appearances are getting rather tedious. He turns up with some evil scheme, his scheme is thwarted and he strides off, muttering darkly. For Heaven's sake, give the man something else to do!

The 'A' Plot: Bester arrives on Babylon 5 with a group of telepaths who specialise in hunting down telepaths – Bloodhound Units. His aim is to bring Byron's people into custody by whatever means are necessary. Sheridan is unhappy, given what Bester has done to him and his friends over the years, but Captain Lochley points out that Bester is acting completely within the law. Sheridan reluctantly accepts the situation.

Lochley cooperates with Bester to a point, but a stray comment by Dr Franklin about cross-species infection gives her the reason she has been looking for to delay him. Claiming that the telepaths may have been exposed to alien diseases, she tells Bester that they have to be kept in quarantine on Babylon 5 for sixty days before she can let him take them to Earth. Reluctantly, Bester agrees, and leaves.

The 'B' Plot: Summoned back to Centauri Prime, Londo Mollari is all set to board a Centauri liner when a docking-bay accident prevents him from leaving the station. The liner departs without him, but as soon as it sets its homing beacon for Centauri Prime it explodes, killing everyone aboard. The liner has been sabotaged, almost certainly in an attempt to kill Londo himself.

The 'C' Plot: G'Kar and Delenn offer Dr Franklin a job collating a database of alien medical information in an attempt to prevent cross-species infections occurring – a source of great concern given that the aim of the Alliance is to foster greater cooperation between alien races. Franklin, pleased to be asked but rather daunted at the prospect, agrees. Maintaining her role as coordinator of difficult and unlikely jobs, Delenn asks G'Kar to act as Londo's bodyguard when he returns to Centauri Prime: an important job now that it's clear someone is trying to kill Londo. Pleased to be asked but daunted by the prospect, G'Kar agrees.

Observations: Captain Lochley has encountered Bester before. She claims not to like him. She also confesses to Garibaldi that she and John Sheridan were married once, for three months or so. Realising they had made a drastic mistake, they divorced.

Zack Allen used to be based on Io (his job – not his character).

There are hints that Bester and Byron knew each other. These hints will be explained further in episode 511 ('Phoenix Rising').

References are made to Neeoma Connelly (previously seen in episode 112 – 'By Any Means Necessary') and Dr Lilian Hobbs (previously seen in episodes 315 – 'Interludes and Examinations' – and 318 – 'Walkabout').

Dialogue to Rewind For: Londo: 'This is where it begins to go badly for all of us.'

Captain Lochley: 'I've just decided – if you can't join 'em, beat 'em.'

Dialogue to Fast-Forward Past: The whole of Byron's 'willow tree' speech, which is frankly too twee and too tedious to reprint here, is suspect, starting from 'It was three . . . no, four lifetimes ago', and trudging on for far too long.

Ships That Pass in the Night: Transport 11719 gets a name check (a number check?), as does Earth Transport *Marx* (and wouldn't it be nice to think that it had been named after Groucho, rather than Karl?).

Culture Shock: Londo makes reference to the fact that his people have a limited precognitive ability. We see this a number of times in the series, most notably in episodes 113 ('Signs and Portents') and 309 ('Point of No Return').

'Secrets of the Soul'

Transmissions Number: 507
Production Number: 508

Written by: J Michael Straczynski
Directed by: Tony Dow

Ambassador Tal: Jana Robbins
Kirrin: Fiona Dwyer
Peter: Jack Hannibal
Carl Townsend: Stuart McLean

Plot: It's bitty, it's badly thought out and it's weak. Franklin is never at risk, although we are made to think he is; the Hyach/Hyach-'Doh!' plot seems to have sprung out of the previous Centauri/Xon material in episode 105 ('The Parliament of Dreams'); and Byron just wanders around spouting platitudes. Oh dear.

The 'A' Plot: Dr Franklin is taking his duties as adviser on potential medical threats to the Alliance seriously. He asks all of the alien ambassadors on the station to provide him with their medical records, but he finds the Hyach particularly reluctant. Eventually their Ambassador – Tal – capitulates but Kirrin, Tal's aide, is suspicious of Franklin's motives.

Franklin soon realises that the Hyach medical records are incomplete – they date back only some eight hundred years. When Kirrin refuses to release any more, Franklin delves into the historical records of other species, looking for some reference to the Hyach that dates back further than two hundred years. What he finds indicates that another, more primitive race used to share the Hyach homeworld – the Hyach-do – but they no longer exist.

When Kirrin realises what Franklin has discovered about the Hyach-do she prepares to kill him, but Ambassador Tal intervenes. Tal admits to Franklin that the Hyach wiped out this other race in a massive act of genocide, but that act proved their own undoing. The genetic material introduced into the Hyach race during intermarriages with the Hyach-do was somehow keeping them fertile. With the Hyach-do dead, the Hyach are dying out as well.

Franklin is appalled, and Ambassador Tal tells Franklin that the elders of the Hyach race wanted the help of the Alliance in reversing the degeneration of their species but could never admit what they had done. They hoped, however, that Franklin would uncover the truth. Now he has, he undertakes to kick off a programme of research aimed at helping them.

The 'B' Plot: More telepaths are arriving on the station to join Byron's group. Zack Allen isn't happy, but he can't see any way around it. One of the telepaths – Peter – has some telekinetic skills as well. He becomes separated from his friends in Downbelow, and falls foul of Carl, a local thug. Carl beats Peter up and, against Byron's advice, the telepaths take their revenge on Carl and his people.

The 'C' Plot: Lyta and Byron become emotionally and physically close. During their lovemaking, Lyta's telepathic barriers are broken down and the telepaths are made aware of how the Vorlons had created them as a weapon to use against the Shadows. Furious at how they had been used and then discarded, they resolve to demand a homeworld of their own, where they can live their own lives free of abuse and control.

The Arc: This episode contains two important moments: the one where the telepaths realise they have been created by the Vorlons, and the one where they go against Byron's wishes. The one links back to numerous previous events in the series, the other links forward, prefiguring the telepaths' end. And we get to see Vorlons as well, and the Vorlon homeworld. Truly an episode of wonders.

Observations: The killing of Carl by the telepaths is the first real sign that Byron's control over them is not absolute – some of them disagree with his teachings. This will reach its head in episode 511 ('Phoenix Rising').

Lyta makes reference back to a symbolic (and rather tedious) story Byron told her in episode 506 ('Strange Relations').

Several cuts were made by the UK's Channel 4 for the first UK transmission of this episode, primarily of one of Carl's thugs covered in flames, and of Carl being abused by the telepaths.

Dialogue to Rewind For: 'The Vorlons ... changed me,' Lyta admits. That's the understatement of the year.

Dialogue to Fast-Forward Past: 'Do you know what you are?' Byron asks Lyta. 'A BCFMO – a brightly coloured, fast moving object.' If that's his idea of a chat-up line he should get out more.

Other Worlds: For the first, and perhaps only, time we get to see the Vorlon homeworld. But only the inside of a big room.

Culture Shock: The Pak'ma'ra appear to be a religious race who believe themselves to be the chosen of God. They can digest almost anything apart from fish.

The Hyach have been civilised for some seven thousand years – that's a good few thousand longer than humanity. Their political system is a gerontocracy – government by the eldest members of the society. In a similar manner to *Homo sapiens* and *Homo neanderthalis*, the Hyach evolved alongside a more primitive race known as the Hyach-do. The two races were close enough genetically for interbreeding to take place – in fact, it was the genetic input from the Hyach-do that kept the Hyach race fertile. The Hyach-do were discriminated against by the Hyach and, several hundred years ago, the Hyach had the Hyach-do completely wiped out.

Accidents Will Happen: 'No tyranny has ever really lasted,' Franklin tells the Hyach. 'No government based on violence has ever endured.' Well, to be honest, no government based on any system at all has ever really endured. They all get replaced by something else.

'Day of the Dead'

Transmission Number: 508
Production Number: 511

Written by: Neil Gaiman
Directed by: Doug Lefler

Rebo: Penn Jillette
Zooty: Teller
Voice of Zooty: Harlan Ellison
Zoe: Bridget Flanery
Dodger: Marie Marshall
Morden: Ed Wasser
Adira Tyree: Fabiana Udenio
Brakiri Ambassador: Jonathan Chapman

Plot: A rather poetic interlude in an otherwise rather dire set of episodes.

The 'A' Plot: The Brakiri have asked Captain Lochley to sell them a part of Babylon 5 for one night so they can conduct a religious ceremony. The ceremony has to be carried out on Brakiri territory, and for that reason they cannot rent the station – they must buy it for a short period.

As the station passes into Brakiri hands an energy barrier cuts off this territory from the rest of the station and the corridors and rooms take on the characteristics of the Brakiri homeworld. The quarters of Londo, Garibaldi, Lennier and Lochley are in Brakiri territory, and each of them receives a visitation from someone from their past – someone who has since died. Londo sees Adira Tyree, the slave he freed and fell in love with. Garibaldi sees 'Dodger' Derman, a Marine private with whom he was emotionally involved. Lochley sees Zoe, an old friend who died of a drugs overdose in the days when Lochley was the wild child of a military father. Lennier, unexpectedly, sees Morden: the man who worked for the Shadows. Come sunrise on the Brakiri homeworld the revenants vanish, leaving behind them only confusion, some emotional resolution and a few words of wisdom.

The 'B' Plot: The famed human comedy double act Rebo and Zooty – whose comedy crosses species barriers to many of the known races – arrive on Babylon 5. They want to give up comedy and go into politics.

The Arc: Morden tells Lennier that he will betray the Anla'shok. This prediction, which Lennier does not believe, comes true in episode 521 ('Objects at Rest').

Zoe gives Lochley a message for Sheridan, a message from Kosh. The message is: 'When the long night comes, return to the end of the beginning.' The relevance of this becomes clear in episode 522 ('Sleeping in Light').

Observations: In the first few moments of the episode it might seem as if Rebo (Penn Jillette) has been carrying round a case with Zooty (Teller) inside, but there's an almost invisible cut between his swinging the suitcase up and his opening it. The cut is hidden by a passing character.

Garibaldi tells Sheridan and Lochley that the Brakiri believe comets to be symbols of death and destruction. This was referred to in episode 303 ('A Day in the Strife').

Adira Tyree first appeared in episode 103 ('Born to the Purple'), and died in episode 315 ('Interludes and Examinations'). 'Dodger' appeared in episode 210 ('GROPOS').

This episode was originally intended to be set after episode 511 ('Phoenix Rising') but was moved to create more variety of tone.

The writer, Neil Gaiman, is a British comics writer best known for his radical reinterpretation of DC's character the Sandman. Straczynski has long had a wish to bring Gaiman on to the series: the Gaim are named after him, and their proboscis-like helmets are modelled on the helmet worn by Gaiman's Sandman character.

The conceit whereby the character of Zooty allows his machine to speak for him was introduced so that the guest star Teller did not have to speak on camera – a personal foible of his and Penn Jillette's magic act.

The script for this episode has been published by Dreamhaven Books.

Dialogue to Rewind For: Rebo to Zooty: 'For you, fifty thousand years of human evolution was something that happened to other people, wasn't it?' (This line, Gaiman acknowledges, was based on one in the UK TV comedy *Blackadder*.)

Londo: 'If Vir can be Emperor, a small Earth cat can be Emperor.'

Morden: 'Looking back on it, though, I think I just tried to make people happy.'

Other Worlds: The Brakiri homeworld is known as Brakir. It's 27 light years from Babylon 5.

Culture Shock: The Brakiri ceremony has certain resonances to Mexican celebrations, down to the skull decorations. It occurs every 200 years or so.

Literary, Mythological and Historical References: Rebo and Zooty's film, *Sons of the New Desert*, is probably either a remake of or a sequel to the Laurel and Hardy film *Sons of the Desert*.

Rebo's line in the Babylon 5 customs area, 'I have nothing to declare, my dear man, except my genius,' is a steal from Oscar Wilde's famous line when he was going through the New York Custom House.

'Dodger' half quotes Mark Twain's 'The report of my death was an exaggeration.'

Dodger and Garibaldi can both quote the American poet Emily Dickinson.

I've Seen That Face Before: Penn Jillette and Teller (other name unknown) are magicians. Penn Jillette is *not* an actor, despite his various film credits and frequent appearances in *Sabrina: Teenage Witch*.

Accidents Will Happen: Not so much an accident, more a regret: it's a shame about Morden's new hairstyle. Obviously they have hairdressers in hell.

The poem 'Dodger' recited wasn't by Emily Dickinson, despite her claim to the contrary. It's 'A Few Figs from Thistles', by Edna St Vincent Millay. Garibaldi, however, got it right, with Dickinson's 'Because I could not stop for Death.'

'In the Kingdom of the Blind'

Transmission Number: 509
Production Number: 509

Written by: J Michael Straczynski
Directed by: David J Eagle

Regent: Damien London
Byron: Robin Atkin Downes
Minister Vitali: Neil Hunt
Minister Jano: Ian Ogilvy
Telepath: Victor Love
Minister Vole: Francis X McCarthy

Plot: Great stuff from the primary plot here, with the wonderful Damien London and the disgracefully underused Ian Ogilvy, along with a good few shocks. Shame about the telepaths, however: Byron is so wet and so stupid that he brings all his problems on himself and gets no sympathy from the viewer.

The 'A' Plot: Londo Mollari and G'Kar arrive on Centauri Prime, to some disquiet on the part of the Centauri court. Londo's friend, Minister Jano, tells Londo that the Regent has been acting oddly, talking to himself, muttering strange things, getting drunk and secluding himself away from the court. This surprises Londo, primarily because he thought the Regent didn't drink. Jano also tells Londo that certain inconsequential matters concerning Centauri supplies and ships have been reclassified as state secrets.

When Jano returns to his rooms, he is killed by agents of the Regent. Londo and G'Kar are also attacked, this time by agents of Centauri Minister Vole (in conjunction with Minister Vitali), but are saved by mysterious aliens with telekinetic powers.

The Regent tells Londo that he is dying, and that his mysterious alien allies wish Londo to stop asking questions about Centauri affairs.

The 'B' Plot: Byron and his fellow telepaths are enraged at the fact that the Vorlons created them as a weapon against the Shadows. They use their powers to siphon information from the various Alliance ambassadors when passing them in corridors or standing with them in lifts, and then trick Garibaldi into letting Byron speak to the Alliance members. Byron asks for a homeworld for telepaths, and threatens to reveal the secret information gleaned from the minds of the ambassadors if his demands are not met.

Byron has miscalculated, however. Feelings on the station turn against the telepaths, and some of them are attacked when they go for supplies. Sheridan withdraws his protection from them, so Byron decides to make a stand: going on hunger strike to raise public sympathy. Some of the telepaths disagree with his decision, and split from the group, deciding to take up arms instead.

The 'C' Plot: There has been a major increase in attacks on Alliance shipping, but the cargoes have been left in place so it's obviously not Raiders. The attacks have hit each race equally, so it's difficult to see who might be responsible. It becomes clear to us by the end of the episode – but not to anyone else – that Centauri ships are carrying out the attacks.

The Arc: The legacy of the Shadow War begins to bite, with alien infiltrators influencing events on Centauri Prime through the Regent and (we later discover) attacking Alliance ships for their own mysterious purposes. This plot strand will echo through the rest of the season and into the follow-on series: *Crusade*.

Observations: This episode takes place the day after episode 507 ('Secrets of the Soul').

Channel 4 cut various shots during the first UK transmission, including a shot of Minister Jano hanging from the ceiling of his room (dead, not doing aerobics) and another of Minister Vole with a knife in his chest.

Zack Allen estimates there are between 50 and 150 telepaths on the station.

'We will speak one more time before the end,' the Regent tells Londo. That happens in episode 517 ('Movements of Fire and Shadow').

'There will come a moment when I ask you to leave me behind,' Byron tells Lyta. That moment occurs in episode 511 ('Phoenix Rising').

Dialogue to Rewind For: The Regent: 'Once I would have thought "pastels" for the curtains, but I think we're well beyond pastels now.' This refers back to episode 407 ('Epiphanies').

Culture Shock: There's a new race in the Alliance conference room. They're sitting to the left of the Abbai, are basically humanoid and have piglike snouts.

We get our first real sight in this episode of the Drakh: the satanic aliens who are in the process of taking over from the Shadows as villains of the piece. It is a Drakh who confronts the Regent in his throne room at the end of the episode, and we see it (or another remarkably like it) in episode 517 ('Movements of Fire and Shadow'). Note, by the way, that the creature seen in episode 411 ('Lines of Communication') was a Speaker for the Drakh, not one of the Drakh themselves.

Literary, Mythological and Historical References: The title misquotes the Victorian writer HG Wells, who wrote (in his short story 'The Country of the Blind'), 'In the Country of the Blind, the One-eyed man is King.' The meaning is obvious – a minority with an advantage will always rule a majority without that advantage. Wells's aphorism was already well known as a saying, and derived from similar maxims in writings by Desiderius Erasmus (*c.* 1466–1536), and John Skelton (*c.* 1460–1529), among others.

I've Seen That Face Before: Ian Ogilvy, who plays Lord Jano, is a well-known British actor who once auditioned for the part of James Bond and is best known (at least to people of my age) as the next television incarnation of the Saint after Roger Moore.

Damien London has appeared as the Minister (now the Regent) in various episodes from the first season onwards.

Questions Raised: Why does Byron confront the Alliance in his demand for a homeworld? All other alien races seem to treat their telepaths well apart from humanity. Shouldn't he be petitioning Earth – or, at least, Captain Lochley as representative of Earth? I can't imagine the Centauri or the Minbari feeling terribly guilty, considering the way telepaths are fêted in their societies.

'A Tragedy of Telepaths'

Transmission Number: 510
Production Number: 510

Written by: J Michael Straczynski
Directed by: Tony Dow

Na'Toth: Julie Caitlin Brown
Byron: Robin Atkin Downes
Thomas: Leigh McClosky
Drazi Ambassador: Kim Strauss
Brakiri Ambassador: Jonathan Chapman
Lara: Caroline Ambrose
Bester: Walter Koenig

Plot: It's all rather bitty – none of the plots have much resolution – but, for all that, it's good solid drama.

The 'A' Plot: On the Centauri homeworld, Londo realises that production of war material has increased, rather than decreased.

G'Kar intercepts a consignment of fresh spoo – which no Centauri would be seen dead eating – and realises that a Narn must be held captive somewhere in the palace. He and Londo track down the cell in which G'Kar's old aide – Na'Toth – is being held prisoner, having been forgotten by everyone except the guard who feeds her. Londo cannot countermand the order of the late Emperor that put her there, so he and G'Kar disguise her in the clothes of a Centauri female and get her to a ship, from where she is transferred to a Narn ship that will return her to the Narn Homeworld.

The 'B' Plot: Following the problems with Byron and his telepaths, Lochley sends a message to Bester asking for his help. She then receives a surreptitious message from the telepaths asking for a meeting, but, when she manages to get into the sector where they have sealed themselves in, all they want to do is say goodbye.

Meanwhile, the telepaths who refused to be sealed up with Byron break into a weapons store and arm themselves. They attack Lochley, Zack Allen and Bester, but fail to achieve much. Bester's Bloodhound Units arrive, ready to take the telepaths back into custody.

The 'C' Plot: At the site of the latest attack on Alliance shipping, where the victims were Drazi, a chunk of metal from a Brakiri spaceship is found. Sheridan is unconvinced that the Brakiri are behind the attacks. The Gaim, however, have discovered fragments of Drazi spacecraft amid the wreckage of their own. The Drazi threaten to attack the Brakiri, and so Sheridan threatens retaliation from the White Star fleet if they do so.

The Arc: All three plots are tied into the arc, but if this episode vanished from space and time then the series would have lost nothing.

Observations: Captain Lochley speaks a little Centauri.

Spoo, the clue that triggers Londo and G'Kar into realising that there is a Narn prisoner in the palace, has been mentioned several times previously in this series, most notably in episodes 101 ('Midnight on the Firing Line') and 203 ('The Geometry of Shadows').

Brief clips of the Centauri bombing the Narn Homeworld and of Londo looking on are used here from episode 220 ('The Long, Twilight Struggle').

There has been a World War Three. The War of the Shining

Star (previously referred to in episode 501 – 'No Compromises') also gets a mention.

The late, unlamented Emperor Cartagia liked to dress in women's clothing. And why not?

The title of the episode suggests an apposite collective noun for a group of telepaths, similar to 'an unkindness of ravens' or 'a murder of crows'. In fact, the originally announced title was 'Cat and Mouse', but this seems to have been a mechanism for keeping the contents of the episode secret rather than because it was ever under serious consideration.

I've Seen That Face Before: Welcome back (Julie) Caitlin Brown as Na'Toth. The character last appeared in episode 212 ('Acts of Sacrifice'), although this particular actress last played her in episode 117 ('Legacies'). Julie Caitlin Brown also played the part of Guinevere Corey in episode 214 ('There All the Honor Lies').

Accidents Will Happen: There's a shot, late on in the episode, of several ships close to the station. One of them is an Earth ship similar to the *Asimov*. It seems horribly out of scale, given its size (based on previous episodes) and the ships around it.

Questions Raised: Who on Earth (or indeed Babylon 5) sleeps in a sports bra? Well, Captain Lochley does.

Why does Zack keep having to wait half an hour for another maintenance man to come down to Brown sector after the last one is spooked by the telepaths? Why can't he just have them lined up round the corner?

What plot function does Lochley's visit to the telepaths serve? She learns nothing, they learn nothing, nobody changes their opinion. It seems like a delaying tactic on the part of the writer (no, surely not).

Why are the Centauri putting fragments of metal from a range of different races amid the wreckage of Alliance ships? If they concentrated on one race, their plan might work more quickly. Evidence pointing to many races looks more like a mistake on their part.

'Phoenix Rising'

Transmission Number: 511
Production Number: 512

Written by: J Michael Straczynski
Directed by: David J Eagle

Bester: Walter Koenig
Byron: Robin Atkin Downes
Thomas: Leigh J McCloskey
Peter: Jack Hannibal
Telepath: Victor Love

Plot: Very weak, and too reliant on people doing stupid things to be convincing. Nobody gets anything more than functional, plot-derived dialogue. Still, thank heaven this telepath thing's all over, eh? Back to some *real* drama now.

The 'A' Plot: A Psi Corps shuttle arrives on Babylon 5 (again), disgorging Bester's people. He wants the telepaths in custody by the next morning at the latest.

While Byron's people hold out within their sealed area of Downbelow, the armed renegades take over Medlab One and make hostages of Franklin, Garibaldi and the various medics and patients. They demand safe passage off Babylon 5 and the commencement of negotiations designed to lead to the establishment of a telepath homeworld.

Bester and Lyta make their way secretly from Downbelow to Medlab One and prevent the renegades from killing the hostages. Byron assures Sheridan that he can bring the situation to a peaceful close, and asks permission to gather his people together in Downbelow. Sheridan grants permission, but Bester and his people intervene before Byron and his people can hand themselves over into Sheridan's protective custody.

During the ensuing mêlée, Byron deliberately kills himself and many of his followers. Before his death he gives Lyta the information he has collected on safe houses and contacts, and Lyta passes that information on to the few remaining telepaths.

The 'B' Plot: Byron tells Lyta that he was a Psi Cop, Bester's protégé, and an Omega Squadron pilot. During a simple operation to intercept a covert, rogue-telepath smuggling ring, the 'blips' were recovered, but Bester ordered the destruction of the transport and all its crew as a message to the other smugglers. Byron reluctantly killed the people – the 'mundanes', as he called them – and then left Psi Corps.

The 'C' Plot: Mr Garibaldi tries to kill Bester, but fails. Bester tells Garibaldi that, during the period when he had Garibaldi in captivity, he implanted various injunctions in Garibaldi's mind against killing him or allowing him to come to harm. This information pushes Garibaldi over the edge, and he starts drinking again.

The Arc: This episode marks the long-awaited end to the telepath plot strand. However, given the title of the episode, one can foresee a later plot strand arising from the ashes of this one . . .

Observations: Channel 4 made their usual selection of cuts to the first UK transmission of this episode. The primary cut occurs at the end of the pre-title sequence, and excises a line from Captain Lochley while she and Bester are staring at a crucified telepath in a lift.

As well as being a telepath, Lyta can sense things at long range – things such as objects, passages and clear routes. This is presumably a legacy of the Vorlons.

The scene when the telepaths are preparing to kill Garibaldi in Medlab One was prefigured in episode 422 ('The Deconstruction of Falling Stars'), where a group of academics in the future are watching it and criticising Sheridan's policy. Much of the footage for this scene was filmed for and shown in that episode, and repeated inside this episode.

Byron refers back to conversations Lyta and he had in episodes 506 ('Strange Relations') and 509 ('In the Kingdom of the Blind') and sings a song he first sang in episode 506.

Dialogue to Rewind For: 'We may not be pretty,' Bester tells Lochley, 'but we're a hell of a lot better than the alternatives.' What a load of rubbish. Almost every other race we know in the *Babylon 5* universe treats its telepaths better than humanity does.

Dialogue to Fast-Forward Past: Bester's dialogue in the pre-title sequence and later with Garibaldi gives the phrase 'exposition' an entirely new gloss.

Byron: 'We are no longer who we were. We are what we have become.' Er . . . aren't we all?

Culture Shock: There has been a ban on Earth for many years on the development of robots. The people who carried out this work before the ban were known as Cybertechs.

Literary, Mythological and Historical References: Bester refers to the injunctions in Garibaldi's mind as 'Asimovs', referring to the Three Laws of Robotics defined by the SF writer Isaac Asimov in various short stories during the 1950s and 1960s. The laws are: (1) a robot may not injure a human being or, through inaction, allow a human being to come to harm; (2) a robot must obey the orders given to it by human beings, except where such orders would conflict with the First Law; (3) a robot must protect its own existence, as long as such protection does not conflict with the First or Second Law. Time will tell whether Bester has programmed Garibaldi with all of the laws, or just a modified version of the first one.

I've Seen That Face Before: Walter Koening as Bester and a clutch of background teeps and teeks (but not geeks).

Questions Raised: Why has Earth banned the use or development of robots?

If there were a crawlspace leading into or out of the sealed area of Downbelow, surely Zack Allen and his people would know about it. After all, they have access to all the plans of the station.

Zack Allen and his troops are armed with PPGs when they try to regain Medlab One, but they are beaten off by a man who can throw things at them. Is this convincing?

'The Ragged Edge'

Transmission Number: 512
Production Number: 513

Written by: J Michael Straczynski
Directed by: John Copeland

Ta'Lon: Marshall Teague
Tafiq Azir: John Castellanos
Brannagan: Mirron E Willis
Narn Acolyte: Mark Hendrickson

Plot: Getting off the station is a good idea – this is one of the few times this season, ignoring the occasional spacecraft cockpit – but the story seems more like an extended excuse for trying out the virtual sets for *Crusade* than a decent plot-driven addition to the series.

The 'A' Plot: Members of Alliance have voted to boycott all further Council meetings until the Alliance can guarantee the safety of their shipping.

During an attack on a human transport near Drazi space, a lone survivor manages to get to the Drazi homeworld in an escape pod. During their search of the wreckage, the Rangers discover this and report it back to Delenn and Sheridan. The assumption is that the Drazi government may not cooperate over finding this man, as he was almost certainly a smuggler.

Garibaldi has a friend in the Drazi capital, and travels to the Drazi homeworld to find the survivor. Garibaldi's friend has heard that the man is still alive, but that the criminal organisation who were paying him for smuggling items to them are looking to take the payment out of his hide. Garibaldi's friend is killed – either by this organisation or by some third party – and Garibaldi is attacked. With various Drazi forces after him, Garibaldi finds the pilot – also dead – and returns to Babylon 5 with a clue: a button pulled off the clothes of one of the people who killed the survivor. Londo identifies the button (without knowing where it came from) as coming from the uniform of a Centauri Imperial guard.

The 'B' Plot: Londo and G'Kar return to Babylon 5 after

less than a month away, but there has been a huge change in the way G'Kar is treated by the other Narn on the station. They are deferential and respectful. Ta'Lon, a Narn warrior, admits that when G'Kar left for the Centauri homeworld the Kha'Ri were worried that G'Kar might be killed and that his book would be lost, so they 'liberated' it from his quarters. By now, four or five hundred thousand copies are in circulation, and G'Kar is a renowned religious figure. G'Kar is not best pleased.

The 'C' Plot: (a) Garibaldi's drinking is beginning to interfere with his work. He's missing meetings, and his drunkenness probably led to the loss of a critical witness to the mysterious attacks on Alliance shipping. (b) Doctor Franklin decides to leave Babylon 5 to take over the position of Head of Xenobiology in EarthDome, effective 1 January 2261.

The Arc: Sheridan, Delenn and Garibaldi are now aware that the Centauri are involved in the attacks on Alliance shipping, although they do not believe that Londo is actually aware of that involvement.

Observations: Garibaldi used to work on Europa.

The surviving pilot is never named in the episode, but in the credits he is called Brannagan.

The UK's Channel 4 did their usual hack job on the first showing of this episode, trimming scenes of Garibaldi fighting the people who killed the pilot.

Garibaldi tells Delenn that the mission is totally 'fubar'. That's an American military acronym that stands for 'fucked up beyond all repair'.

Dr Benjamin Kyle is currently Head of Xenobiology at EarthDome. Dr Kyle was Babylon 5's first doctor, in the pilot episode 'The Gathering'.

This episode was directed by the show's Producer, John Copeland.

Dialogue to Rewind For: 'Well, there you have the key to your popularity,' Londo tells G'Kar in a classic monologue: 'your absence. Go away for a month and they bow. Go away for six months, they will tear the place apart when you come back. Perhaps you should go away and never come back again – then your popularity would be so overwhelming it would blacken the stars ... I have always said this about you – nothing so improves your company like the lack of it. The less they see of you, the more they like you ... Perhaps you could make some money from this. Ten credits for you not to be there for an hour; a hundred credits for you not to be there for the day; and for you not to be there for the rest of your life ... well, they could never afford it.'

Dialogue to Fast-Forward Past: In response to G'Kar's question 'Ta'Lon, is it you?', Ta'Lon says, with classic J Michael Straczynski sensitivity for dialogue: 'It's me most days, except for those days when I don't feel quite like myself and I suppose that I am someone else, but for now yes, it's me.'

Ships That Pass in the Night: *Redstar 9*, a transport vessel that's been involved in smuggling to the Drazi, is destroyed by the Centauri.

Other Worlds: We see the Drazi homeworld for the first time: a hot, reddish-brown place.

Garibaldi used to work on Europa – probably the Europa that's a moon of Saturn.

Culture Shock: Having a human bodyguard is a status symbol to the Drazi. The Drazi used to be an outdoor race who came indoors only for sleeping (that probably explains why they are so ratty all the time).

I've Seen That Face Before: Marshall Teague returns as the Narn warrior Ta'Lon. He previously appeared in a number of episodes.

Questions Raised: Why does Ta'Lon keep insisting on unsheathing his sword and then cutting his hand with it? Why not just ... not unsheath it?

'The Corps is Mother, the Corps is Father'

Transmission Number: 513
Production Number: 514

Written by: J Michael Straczynski
Directed by: Stephen Furst

Bester: Walter Koenig
Johnathan Harris: Dex Elliott Sanders
Lauren Ashley: Dana Barron
Drake: Mike Genovese
Chen Hikaru: Reggie Lee
Gordon Bryce: Brendan Ford

Plot: There's long been a debate about whether it's possible to write sympathetically about a Nazi character. Nazis are human beings, naturally, but they have an accrued reputation that colours everything that's thought or written about them. This episode neatly answers the question, by making Bester into the hero without whitewashing his faults. Sheridan has done things that are just as bad as Bester, the Alliance has done things that are just as bad as Psi Corps, but they believe they are justified because they believe they are in the right. But Bester and Psi Corps also believe they are in the right, as this episode shows. So who are the villains now?

The 'A' Plot: Johnathan Harris, a schizophrenic telepath studying with Psi Corps on Earth, murders his roommate and heads for Babylon 5. His roommate was a student of Alfred Bester, and so Bester is assigned to bring him in. Harris is a 'mind shredder' – trained in invasive telepathic techniques – and Bester is warned by his superior, Drake, to be careful.

Bester arrives on Babylon 5 along with two trainees – Chen Hikaru and Lauren Ashley – and track Harris through two murders. An accomplice of Harris murders Hikaru, but Zack Allen and station security track them down. Bester tries to interfere in the confrontation, but Harris is killed.

Bester and Ashley take Harris's nontelepathic accomplice back to Earth, but throw him out of an airlock along the way.

The 'B' Plot: On Babylon 5, the murdering telepath

Johnathan Harris takes to gambling in order to raise enough money to leave. He rips the knowledge of how to play cards out of the mind of a small-time gambler, killing him afterwards, and then uses his telepathic powers to win at the Babylon 5 casino. He falls in with an accomplice, but is killed by Babylon 5's security forces.

The 'C' Plot: Assigned to look after two trainee Psi Cops, Bester realises that one of them is falling in love with him. He takes them both to Babylon 5, where the other one is killed. By the time he and the surviving trainee leave the station, he knows she is tough enough to become a Psi Cop.

The Arc: Little arc connection here, apart from a general raising of paranoia leading up to the telepath war, and the setting up of the Psi Corps motherships floating in hyperspace. One might expect these motherships to become important in the telepath war, which we know is coming up.

Observations: Psi Corps headquarters has various 'improving' signs dotted around – OBEY; THE CORPS IS MOTHER; THE CORPS IS FATHER; MATERNIS, PATERNIS; PROTECT THE FAMILY; TRUST THE CORPS. The signs are in a similar typeface to that used in the 1960s cult series *The Prisoner*. Previous references to this series and linking it to Psi Corps have occurred in episodes 106 ('Mind War') and 202 ('Revelations').

Psi Corps have a number of motherships that spend most of their time in hyperspace, ferrying Psi Corps shuttles and Black Omega squadrons to where they are needed. Nobody outside Psi Corps is aware of these ships.

Bester refers in passing to his lover, Carolyn Sanderson, who is in suspended animation in medlab. She was first seen in episode 314 ('Ship of Tears'), and was mentioned in passing in episode 421 ('Rising Star').

The series title in the title sequence has been removed for this episode, and replaced with the Psi Corps logo and the phrase 'Trust the Corps'. The title has actually been placed at the end of the title sequence, as if painted on the end of the station (where 'created by J Michael Straczynski' usually appears).

Note that only one of the regular characters – Zack Allen – appears in this episode.

Stephen Furst, who directed this episode, normally plays Vir in the series.

During the first UK showing of this episode Channel 4 cut shots of a man bleeding from the eyes when attacked by Johnathan Harris on Babylon 5, and also a stabbing.

'Johnathan Harris' was the actor who played Doctor Zachary Smith in the 1960s TV series *Lost in Space*. Nice to see a reference to him here. We presume that 'Lauren Ashley' is no relation to Laura Ashley, who designs frilly, floral clothing for upper-middle-class ladies.

Dialogue to Fast-Forward Past: 'A field agent has to be able to hold his own for at least an hour,' says Bester. Nice work if you can get it.

Ships That Pass in the Night: Starliner *Asimov* docks at Babylon 5 just as Bester appears. It's appeared at the station several times before.

Culture Shock: A barman tells Chen that he recently saw an insectoid alien with eight compound eyes and a transparent stomach. He also claims that the hump on the back of the Pak'ma'ra isn't a hump at all, but he never actually says what it is. J Michael Straczynski has suggested elsewhere that the hump is actually the female of the Pak'ma'ra species, symbiotically attached to her 'mate'.

I've Seen That Face Before: Walter Koenig, of course.

'Meditations on the Abyss'

Transmission Number: 514
Production Number: 515

Written by: J Michael Straczynski
Directed by: Mike Vejar

Drazi Ambassador: Ron Campbell
Drazi Vendor: Carl Ciarfalio
Findell: Martin East

Captain Montoya: Richard Yniguez
Narn Acolyte: Mark Hendrickson

Plot: An interesting little episode which gives us a long-overdue insight into Lennier's character as part of what is essentially a two-episode story.

The 'A' Plot: Lennier is assigned to White Star 27 with secret instructions to monitor Centauri activity around their borders. During an exercise in which he and a young Ranger named Findell are flying in Minbari fighters, White Star 27 vanishes, leaving them with only a few hours of air left and no way to get to an inhabited world before that air runs out. Lennier places himself in a trance to conserve his air supply, but Findell panics and has problems in keeping going. When White Star 27 reappears, Captain Montoya tells them it was a test – one that Lennier passed and Findell failed. A subsequent test takes the form of a scavenger hunt for homing beacons in an asteroid field, and during it Lennier has to prevent Findell from committing suicide by flying his spaceship into an asteroid. During a confrontation back on White Star 27, Captain Montoya sends Findell back to Minbar to act as a recruiter for the Anla'shok with special responsibility for weeding out unsuitable recruits.

The 'B' Plot: Lennier arrives secretly on Babylon 5 and contacts Delenn. She has summoned him to the station because she wants to send him on a mission to the borders of Centauri space in order to investigate the full extent of their activities against the other Alliance races. Lennier is the best choice among the Rangers because he knows the most about the Centauri.

The 'C' Plot: Londo has decided to promote Vir to the status of full Ambassador. Initially worried that Vir isn't yet up to the job, he finally realises he has made the right decision when Vir confronts a Drazi spy and threatens him with a sword.

The 'D' Plot: Dr Franklin has created an artificial eye for G'Kar that matches his real eye colour (the previous one was a modified human artificial eye and was blue). As recompense for fitting it, he asks G'Kar to allow him to attend G'Kar's discussions on religious matters with the other Narn. G'Kar agrees, and Franklin finds himself captivated by what G'Kar says.

The Arc: Lennier's training – especially his decision to put himself into an oxygen-conserving trance – sets up the abilities he is called upon to display in the next episode, without which he would never be able to obtain the clinching evidence that the Centauri are behind the attacks on Alliance shipping.

Observations: A small cut was made by Channel 4 in the first UK transmission of this episode to the scene where Delenn breaks a man's finger.

Delenn refers to Garibaldi's adventures during episode 512 ('The Ragged Edge'), to the Brakiri Day of the Dead in episode 508 ('Day of the Dead') and to the death of Marcus in episode 421 ('Rising Star').

'He believes the only way to get pertinent information is to ask impertinent questions,' Findell says of Captain Montoya. That's one of J Michael Straczynski's favourite sayings, and a version of it appears as the keynote quotation in Volume 1 of this book.

Lennier refers to the Minbari teacher Turval, who appeared in episode 505 ('Learning Curve') and the *Babylon 5* novel *To Dream in the City of Sorrows*.

Dialogue to Rewind For: Londo: 'It's politics, Vir. Never take it personally.'

Ships That Pass in the Night: White Star 27, referred to as the *Maria* by its captain.

Culture Shock: The Drazi marry in what appears to be the same manner as humans. Londo refers to sexual relations between Drazi and the insectoid Gaim in a manner that suggests it is possible.

Questions Raised: Why is it that Sheridan thinks he can hide the Centauri's warlike operations from the rest of the Alliance when he keeps holding meetings and not inviting Londo?

How can Findell 'debrief' new recruits? They haven't done anything to be debriefed of yet.

'Darkness Ascending'

Transmission Number: 515
Production Number: 513

Written by: J Michael Straczynski
Directed by: Janet Greek

Lise Hampton-Edgars: Denise Gentile
Centauri Minister: Thomas MacGreevy
Maitre D': Wesley Mask
Captain Montoya: Richard Yniguez

Plot: Solid drama here, with all four of the parallel plots advancing the overall story arc and all three involving the characters we have come to know and love being involved in difficult, life-changing events.

The 'A' Plot: Lennier reports to Delenn that three more attacks have taken place on Alliance shipping, and that he has intercepted coded Centauri signals before each attack, which might be orders to Centauri ships. He suspects that the Centauri have a hidden base somewhere, and manages to build a device to track the signals back to their source.

Meanwhile, Sheridan discovers that Delenn has assigned White Star 27 to a position where Lennier can spy on the Centauri, and has it recalled.

Lennier disobeys orders and takes a Minbari fighter out to search for the Centauri base. Detecting a Centauri warship, he attaches his fighter to it and goes with it to its base – a space station – and then on to an attack on Brakiri ships. He detaches his fighter after the attack, with a full record of what occurred, and sends a distress signal. Picked up, he returns to Babylon 5 and gives President Sheridan the proof that the Centauri are behind the attacks.

The 'B' Plot: Lyta Alexander is trying to raise funds for the telepath refugees, but no businessmen will deal with her. She makes an appointment with Ambassador G'Kar and makes him an offer – she will provide him with telepath genetic material if he will provide them with money and ships. G'Kar tests Lyta's moral resolve and, after she passes, he accepts her offer.

The 'C' Plot: Lise Hampton-Edgars arrives on Babylon 5, worried about where Michael Garibaldi has been. Pretty soon she discovers he has started drinking again.

The 'D' Plot: Londo is worried that no other Ambassadors will associate with him. He receives a message from the Centauri homeworld indicating that the other Alliance members are on the verge of accusing the Centauri of carrying out the recent attacks. The Centauri claim to believe the Narn to be at the root of the attacks.

The Arc: There are indications that Lyta Alexander is testing her Vorlon-given powers.

The Centauri are proved to Sheridan's satisfaction as being the power behind the attacks on Alliance shipping. How he deals with this information will affect the rest of this series, and the follow-on series as well.

Observations: Garibaldi refers to his being brainwashed by Psi Corps, being taken by the Resistance and being within a hair's-breadth of being executed. These events occurred in episodes 402 ('Whatever Happened to Mr Garibaldi?') and 419 ('Between the Darkness and the Light'). Sheridan refers to Delenn's orders to Lennier – orders she gave in episode 514 ('Meditations on the Abyss'). He also refers to the deaths of Marcus and Neroon, which occurred in episodes 420 ('Endgame') and 414 ('Moments of Transition'). Lennier's meditative state, which he uses to conserve oxygen in his Minbari fighter, was set up in episode 514 ('Meditations on the Abyss').

Lyta Alexander refers to Ambassador Kosh's arrival in summer 2257, and to a conversation she and G'Kar had around that time.

Garibaldi refers to the last time he was in the Fresh Air restaurant – when Jeffrey Sinclair got engaged shortly before President Santiago was assassinated. Those events occurred in episode 122 ('Chrysalis'). He seems to be lying, because the maitre d' assumes he wants to drink alcohol with the meal, and his drink problems have only recently resurfaced.

Dialogue to Rewind For: 'No one really trusts anyone, Vir – it is the natural order of things' – Londo Mollari.

Ships That Pass in the Night: White Stars 7, 12, 14 and 27.

'And All My Dreams, Torn Asunder'

Transmission Number: 516
Production Number: 517

Written by: J Michael Straczynski
Directed by: Goran Gajic

Minister Chelini: Thomas MacGreevy
Drazi Ambassador: Kim Strauss
Brakiri Ambassador: Jonathan Chapman

Plot: Directed more like an art movie than a television episode, with judicious use of light, shadow and slow motion, this is *Babylon 5* at its absolute best.

The 'A' Plot: At a meeting of the Alliance Council, Sheridan and Delenn present the evidence that the Centauri are behind the attacks on Alliance shipping. Stephen Franklin testifies that the weaponry used by the attackers is of Centauri manufacture; Michael Garibaldi presents the Centauri button he discovered on the Drazi homeworld; Lennier presents the recordings of the attack on Brakiri shipping he made. Londo rejects the evidence, claiming that his race are being set up by other forces, but President Sheridan imposes a blockade on the Centauri.

Londo passes the evidence back to Centauri Prime, where the ruling forces claim that the attacks are being staged by the Narn. The Centauri withdraw from the Alliance and state that if any shots are fired on their shipping it will be considered an act of war. Londo leaves the station under the threat that he may never be able to return.

A Centauri transport accompanied by Centauri warships is intercepted by Drazi warships. Shots are fired and the Drazi ships destroyed. A state of war now exists between the Interstellar Alliance and the Centauri Republic.

The 'B' Plot: Londo leaves the station in order to return to Centauri Prime. G'Kar is still his bodyguard, because the Alliance leaders are sure Londo is not aware that his government are responsible and feel he should be protected. When war breaks out between the Alliance and the Centauri, G'Kar is arrested by the Centauri Royal Guard. When Londo protests, he is arrested too.

The 'C' Plot: Mr Garibaldi is still drinking heavily, to the point where he is missing important meetings as a result. Sheridan places him in charge of coordinating the White Star fleet response to Centauri aggression, but he is drunk when a critical message comes in and fails to send the fleet to the right place.

The Arc: The imagery of the lone candle is something that's occurred throughout the series, and Delenn here explains its meaning. 'What does the candle represent?' Sheridan asks. 'Life,' Delenn replies. 'Whose life?' he asks. 'All life,' she responds, 'every life. We are all born as molecules in the hearts of a billion stars – molecules that do not understand politics, policies, differences. Over a billion years we foolish molecules forget who we are and where we came from. In desperate acts of ego we give ourselves names, fight over lines on maps and pretend that our light is better than everyone else's. The flame reminds us of the piece of those stars that lives on inside us, the spark that tells us, "You should know better." The flame also reminds us that life is precious, as each flame is unique. When it goes out it is gone for ever, and there will never be another quite like it.'

Observations: Mr Garibaldi refers to the events of episode 512 ('The Ragged Edge').

Director Goran Gajic is the husband of Mira Furlan, who plays Delenn.

The scene where Londo stares up into the sky of Centauri Prime and watches the Centauri warships fly overhead is a deliberate echo of episodes 209 ('The Coming of Shadows') and 301 ('Matters of Honor'), in which he saw Shadow ships flying in the same manner. The scene is referred to again in episode 517 ('Movements of Fire and Shadow'), but it's neither Centauri nor Shadow ships he sees then.

'When the time is right, you will see the Regent,' says the Minister. If Christopher Franke ever writes lyrics for the Babylon 5 theme, I would suggest that the chorus should start: 'When the time is right . . .' (it would have to be the season 5 theme: the words don't scan for the season 4 theme).

For anyone worried by the sign on the desk in front of Delenn about eighteen minutes in – the one that looks like it says NOGAFSGER IFAENIM, it actually says MINBARI FEDERATION in reverse. We're seeing the sign from the back, and the font used in the series makes the letters look like other letters from the back.

Dialogue to Rewind For: Sheridan: 'We gave you a promise and we are bound by that promise, and damn you for asking for it, and damn me for agreeing to it, and damn all of us to hell because that's exactly where we're going. We talked about peace – you didn't want peace. We talked about cooperation – you didn't want cooperation. You want war. Is that it? You want a war – well you've got a war.'

Centauri Minister: 'We are now officially at war with the Alliance.'

Dialogue to Fast-Forward Past: Delenn: 'So many candles will go out tonight – I wonder sometimes we can see anything at all.' How to get so far inside a metaphor that it's difficult to see your way clear to getting out again.

Culture Shock: All races who are members of the Alliance have eyes that work in the same way (with rod and cone cells). How likely is this?

'Movements of Fire and Shadow'

Transmission Number: 517
Production Number: 518

Written by: J Michael Straczynski
Directed by: John C Flinn III

Drakh: Wayne Alexander
Regent: Damien London
Minister Chelini: Thomas MacGreevy
Kulomani: Josh Clark
Daro: Bart McCarthy
Na'Tok: Robin Sachs
Doctor Literana Varda: Neil Bradley

Plot: We're back to the kind of intensity we were getting at the end of season 3, and just as some of us were beginning to think the series had lost itself.

The 'A' Plot: The war is spiralling out of control, and on Babylon 5 the Centauri are under threat from the rest of the station's inhabitants.

Reports arrive that Centauri forces have begun targeting enemy jumpgates – something that nobody else has ever done before in interstellar conflict. There is also a risk that the station itself might come under attack: a Centauri vessel is detected approaching Babylon 5, unmanned and with its jump engines set to explode in order to take out Babylon 5's jumpgate, but Alpha Squadron manage to destroy the ship just before it emerges from the jumpgate.

Sheridan orders the White Star fleet to join the conflict, authorised to fire on any Centauri vessel in conflict with Alliance ships, and calls a Council of War, but discovers to his surprise that there is no consolidation of forces between the different races. The Drazi are fighting separately from the Narn; the Narn are fighting separately from the Brakiri.

Garibaldi has determined that there are two separate Centauri fleets – one operating defensively, the other operating offensively – and Sheridan realises that there is no obvious Centauri strategy; nobody actually knows what they want.

The Narn suggest a frontal attack on the Centauri, but Sheridan disagrees. The Narn and Drazi decide to attack Centauri Prime itself without the assistance of humanity. Sheridan discovers their plans and races to stop them, but before he can arrive the ships emerge from hyperspace above Centauri Prime and begin to attack a strangely defenceless world . . .

The 'B' Plot: Vir tells Stephen Franklin and Lyta Alexander that the Drazi are not returning the bodies of Centauri killed in conflict. As Franklin points out, it's one of the key Principles of the Alliance that bodies should be returned. Vir asks Franklin and Lyta to go to the Drazi homeworld and investigate. Franklin agrees; Lyta asks for a 500,000-credit fee.

When they arrive on the Drazi homeworld they make contact with a Drazi doctor, who claims that no Centauri bodies are on the planet. He also claims that the Centauri bodies were in such disarray that they could not be recovered from their destroyed craft, but Lyta knows he is lying and confronts him. Drazi forces attack them all, but Lyta and Franklin defeat them.

Lyta detects a location in the doctor's mind, and together they force him to take them there. He takes them to a large, warehouse-like building where organic components are being kept. Lyta recognises them as leftover Shadow technology: control devices for starships.

The 'C' Plot: On Centauri Prime, Londo and G'Kar are incapacitated in their cells. Londo is kidnapped by mysterious aliens, and a surgical procedure carried out on him. Returned to his cell and awakened without any knowledge of what has occurred, he gains his release and discovers that the Regent has disabled the planetary defence systems and sent away all the ships guarding Centauri Prime. As Londo watches, helpless, the forces of the Narn and the Drazi appear in their skies . . .

The 'D' Plot: Sheridan worries that the Alliance might run out of White Star ships – they lost many of them during the war with the Shadows and more still during the War to retake Earth. He proposes a new class of ship: the Minbari are to provide design specifications and material; Earth is to fund construction. Sheridan asks Delenn to travel to Minbar to arrange the details, but on the way she and Lennier are attacked by Centauri warships and their ship is disabled, leaving them stranded and drifting in hyperspace with most of their crew dead . . .

The Arc: The war between the Centauri and the Alliance hots up in this episode. Sheridan discovers that the Centauri ships are actually being controlled by leftover Shadow technology – implying that the Centauri have had some contact with one of the Shadow vassal races – but it is too late. As the episode closes, Centauri Prime is on the verge of destruction by breakaway Alliance forces.

Londo is captured and a surgical procedure is carried out on him that seems designed to test his fitness for something. We cannot help but suspect that he is being measured for a Shadow Controller, similar to that found on Captain Jack in episode 410 ('Racing Mars') and on the Regent in episode 509 ('In the Kingdom of the Blind'). We know that Londo eventually ends up with one of these Controllers, because we see a future flash of him with one in episode 317 ('War Without End' Part Two). We can be fairly sure that this future is unavoidable because Londo is seen in the same circumstances in the first *Babylon 5* TV movie, *In the Beginning*.

The alien surgeons who carry out the procedure on Londo are very similar to the ones Lyta Alexander saw in the mind of the Shadow-enhanced telepath in episode 416 ('Exercise of Vital Powers') and Carolyn Sanderson recalled as having operated on her in episode 314 ('Ship of Tears'). The surgeons are obviously one of the Shadow vassal races who perhaps specialise in maintaining and attaching the Keepers. An alien of a different type, who appears to be in authority, pronounces Londo 'suitable'. We have seen an alien of this type before on Centauri Prime, in episode 509 ('In the Kingdom of the Blind'), and, although it has not yet been identified in the series, we know from the opening credits that it is a Drakh. The Drakh, of course, were Shadow servants who were sniping away at League of Non-Aligned Worlds ships in the middle of season 4 (finally being revealed in episode 411 – 'Lines of Communication').

Sheridan's plans for a new class of ship may well come to fruition just in time for the follow-on TV series *Crusade*. My guess is that the first ship will be called . . . the *Excalibur*.

Observations: The Vree are declared neutral in the war.

The Regent says that he had told Londo they would talk once more before the Regent died. That conversation was held in episode 509 ('In the Kingdom of the Blind').

Londo's horrified glance up into the sky, only to see the Narn and Drazi jump points forming, echoes a series of previous shots: primarily in episodes 209 ('The Coming of Shadows') and 301 ('Matters of Honor'), where he was having a precognitive dream of seeing Shadow ships in the sky of Centauri Prime; 402 ('Whatever Happened to Mr Garibaldi'), where that dream came true, and 516 ('And All My Dreams, Torn Asunder') where the sky was filled with Centauri warships.

Dialogue to Rewind For: Regent: 'I'm glad I won't live to see what follows.'

Vir: 'Our biggest losses have been in the Drazi space. They are real good fighters – not terrific conversationalists, and their table manners can make you go blind in one eye – but really tough behind the weapons consoles.'

Other Worlds: The Draxis Colony is on the border of Drazi space.

Culture Shock: We see a new alien race on the Drazi homeworld – they are humanoid, with what appear to be gills where mouth and nose are on a human.

I've Seen That Face Before: Robin Sachs, who plays General Na'Tok, previously played the same part in the episodes 222 ('The Fall of Night') and 318 ('Walkabout'). A familiar face on Babylon 5, he also appeared as the Minbari Hedronn in episode 201 ('Points of Departure') and 211 ('All Alone in the Night') and as the Minbari Copelann in the first TV movie *In the Beginning*.

Damien London (the Regent) and Thomas MacGreevy (Minister Chelini) are both returning Centauri faces.

Wayne Alexander (Drakh) previously played Jack the Ripper in episode 221 ('Comes the Inquisitor') and Lorien (the first few episodes of season 4), as well as a Narn and a Drazi in various episodes.

Bart McCarthy, who plays Daro here, previously played the

leader of the Minbari Warrior caste, Shakiri, in episode 414 ('Moments of Transition').

'The Fall of Centauri Prime'

Transmission Number: 518
Production Number: 519

Written by: J Michael Straczynski
Directed by: Douglas E. Wise

Drakh: Wayne Alexander
Ranger: Simon Billig
Regent: Damien London
Na'kal: Robin Sachs

The Plot: This one is up there with the best of them: a plot that grows naturally out of everything that has gone before and a performance of awesome tragic power from Peter Jurasik as Londo Mollari. Sadly, whichever way you look from this point in the season, it's downhill.

The 'A' Plot: The surface of Centauri Prime is being bombed and blasted by the Narn and Drazi fleets, taking their revenge for the attacks on Alliance shipping and, in the case of the Narn, for two separate invasions of their Homeworld and enslavements of their people.

On the planet itself, Londo Mollari rescues G'Kar from the cell he is being held in: G'Kar appears to have broken some ribs (if Narn have ribs). Londo leaves G'Kar in a place of safety and confronts the Regent, who tells Londo that his actions in sending the home fleet away and arranging for the planetary defences to be turned off were dictated by others – a mysterious race known as the Drakh. The Drakh reveal themselves to Londo and, through the Regent, tell him that not only are they taking their revenge on his race for his destruction of their ships, they also want a homeworld of their own after the destruction of Z'ha'dum. The Drakh say that they have planted fusion bombs throughout Centauri Prime: if Londo refuses to help them they will detonate the bombs. Millions of Centauri will die, and the Alliance will be blamed. The Regent points out that he is actually Londo's alibi: when he is dead, Londo will be made Emperor and can call off the retaliation by the returning Centauri fleet, blaming the Regent for starting the war. The Regent also reveals that he is being controlled by a Drakh creature called a Keeper that has attached itself to his neck.

The Keeper detaches itself from the Regent, who promptly dies. A separate Keeper is attached to Londo. It permits him to prevent any further bloodshed by surrendering to the Alliance, and to tell Sheridan that the Regent arranged the attacks on Alliance shipping using left-over Shadow technology bought on the open market, but forces him, during his inaugural address to the Centauri people, to stir up anti-Alliance feeling and a stern patriotism. The Centauri people, bitter at their treatment, secede from the Alliance and decide to forge their own path: exactly what the Drakh want.

The 'B' Plot: Sheridan and his White Star fleet head at great speed for Centauri Prime to stop the bombing. On the way, Garibaldi tells Sheridan that Delenn's White Star is feared lost, having run into a Centauri fleet in hyperspace.

When Sheridan's fleet finally arrive at Centauri Prime he calls for the Narn and Drakh fleets to cease fire. Na'kal, the Narn in charge, points out that the Centauri ships that were sent away will be returning soon. They will attack the Alliance fleet with every weapon they have, and Sheridan can either join the Narn and Drakh against the fleet or stand by and watch the battle commence. Sheridan refuses to open fire on the oncoming Centauri fleet: instead he opens communications with the Centauri homeworld just in time for Londo to surrender to him.

The 'C' Plot: On their crippled White Star, Delenn and Lennier prepare to face the end. Lennier tells Delenn that he loves her, just before they are rescued by a Centauri fleet acting on orders from Londo Mollari.

The Arc: We've been building up to this moment for many seasons now. The Centauri wrecked the Narn Homeworld at the end of season two; the Narn have just returned the favour. The Centauri are now a broken, beaten people; ripe for conquest by the Drakh, and Londo has been manipulated into accepting the position that he always wanted but at a price too terrible to contemplate.

Lyta Alexander, or a remnant of the Vorlon programming inside her, tells Sheridan and friends that the Vorlon Homeworld is off-limits for the next million years or so, until humanity is ready. That would tie in nicely with the future events we saw in episode 422 ('The Deconstruction of Falling Stars') in which humanity was evolving into Vorlon-like form in a million years and was moving to a new home world when the Earth was about to be destroyed by solar flares. Were they moving to the Vorlon Homeworld?

Observations: This episode contains flashbacks from episodes 103 ('Born to the Purple'), 105 ('The Parliament of Dreams'), 209 ('The Coming of Shadows'), 220 ('The Long, Twilight Struggle'), 317 ('War Without End' Part Two), 406 ('Into the Fire'), 407 ('Epiphanies'), and 517 ('Movements of Fire and Shadow').

The episode gets that rarity: a 'previously, on *Babylon 5*' reminder to viewers of what happened in the last episode. Those actual words are said by Jerry Doyle.

Londo's first official act as Emperor is to appoint Vir as Ambassador to Babylon 5. He wants to get Vir to safety, away from the Drakh and from what will happen to Centauri Prime. Quite right too.

Dialogue to Rewind For: The Regent: 'They say they do not want your life, Mollari – at least, not yet.'

The Drakh: 'You are now what we need you to be – a beaten, resentful people who will have to rebuild, who will have to rely on our good graces, who can be used and guided as we wish to guide you. Perfect ground for us to do our work. Quietly. Quietly.'

The Drakh again: 'What we want from you – is you.'

The Regent: 'I have to go now, Londo. I have been many things in my life, Mollari. I have been silly, I have been quiet when I should have spoken, I have been foolish, and I have wasted far too much time, but I am still Centauri, and I am not afraid.'

Londo Mollari to G'Kar: 'In the months and the years to come you may hear many strange things about me – my behaviour.'

Londo Mollari: 'Isn't it strange, G'kar: when we first met I had no power and all the choices I could ever want, and now I have all the power I could ever want and no choice at all.'

Dialogue to Fast-Forward Past: Sheridan, getting this season's 'As You Well Know' award: 'So – this is the Shadow technology they used to control the Centauri warships.' To which the only rational answer is: 'No, Mr President, that's your birthday present.'

Culture Shock: The Drakh seem to grow the Keepers as part of their flesh: or perhaps they just suckle them.

Both the Regent and Londo appears to be able to pick up telepathic messages from the Drakh via their Keeper.

There is a suggestion that the Drakh can communicate over long distances – many light years and into hyperspace.

I've Seen That Face Before: Wayne Alexander has been in so many episodes as so many different characters that it's hardly worth listing them. He played Lorien – but you know that. Farewell, alas, to the amazing Damien London, an actor whose part grew to fit him, and farewell too to Robin Sachs, another multi-part actor and one woefully underused in this episode.

'The Wheel of Fire'

Transmission Number: 519
Production Number: 520

Written by: J Michael Straczynski
Directed by: Janet Greek

Lise Hampton-Edgars: Denise Gentile
Officer: Monique Edwards

Plot: Some beautiful acting here from Tracy Scoggins and from Jerry Doyle – possibly the finest acting either of them has shown in the series to date. It's also nice to see Lyta

Alexander getting a decent storyline to end on: Patricia Tallman has been one of the two or three most consistently interesting things about this series. What we see here is consistent with the way her character has been heading since the third season, and illustrates a basic truth that sometimes your worst enemy is the friend you turned away.

The 'A' Plot: Attacks on Psi Corps property on Earth are on the increase, and all the clues point to Lyta Alexander as being the head of the rogue telepath terrorists. Zack Allen and Captain Lochley attempt to arrest her, but she resists, using her telepathic powers to prevent the security guards from taking her into custody. Sheridan intervenes – due to his experiences with Kosh, he is immune from her control – and she is incarcerated.

Garibaldi offers Lyta a deal: if she takes out the neural block Bester placed in Garibaldi's head – the one Garibaldi believes is causing his alcoholism – he will have Edgars Industries intercede with EarthGov on her behalf. Lyta makes a counter proposal: she will agree to stop funding terrorist activities and will leave the station if Garibaldi will use Edgars Industries to secretly disburse funds for the terrorist underground. If Garibaldi manages to do that for two years then she will remove the telepathic block imposed by Bester. Garibaldi reluctantly agrees.

The 'B' Plot: Garibaldi's drinking is now so far out of control that he is missing important meetings and failing in his duties as Head of Security. President Sheridan realises that Garibaldi is out of control and suspends him from his duties until he sorts himself out.

Captain Lochley stops by Garibaldi's quarters and gives him a pep talk, admitting that her father was an alcoholic and she has that tendency herself. Lochley also sends a message to Lise Hampton-Edgars on Earth, purportedly from Garibaldi, asking her to come to Babylon 5. Lise does, and asks Garibaldi to come back to Mars with her, marry her and help run Edgars Industries. Garibaldi agrees, seeing in her offer a chance for a new life for himself.

The 'C' Plot: G'Kar has resumed to Babylon 5, where it is apparent that the cult of personality directed against him has only got worse. Back on the Narn Homeworld the Narn are split: some want G'Kar to take control of the planet and the other half want him to vanish, after first giving them his blessing. G'Kar decides to leave the station and explore the universe, and he offers to take Lyta Alexander with him.

The 'D' Plot: Delenn passes out while talking to Sheridan. Doctor Franklin tells Sheridan that Delenn is pregnant.

The Arc: Lyta's fate completes the arc her character has followed since the first season: that of well-meaning dupe. She has always been a tool of others; now she is taking control herself. Who can blame her? 'In a war you have a certain number of small weapons,' she tells Franklin: 'a certain number of medium-sized weapons, and one or two big ones – the kind of weapons you drop when you are out of small weapons and the medium weapons and you have nothing left to use.' She is the big weapon: the doomsday device. It's as yet unclear what the Vorlons actually expected her to be able to do: perhaps there are still some buried instructions from the Vorlons in her mind, as already shown in the second TV movie: *Thirdspace*.

Delenn's pregnancy was foreshadowed in episode 317 ('War Without End' Part Two), in which we discover that in the future she and Sheridan will have a child named David, and also by episode 422 ('The Deconstruction of Falling Stars') in which future academics make passing reference to their child.

Observations: Sheridan refers back to Stephen Franklin's 'problem'. This is a reference to his abuse of stimulants which coloured much of the last half of season three. Lochley tells Garibaldi that her father was an alcoholic and that she has a tendency to alcoholism herself: events first touched on in episode 508 ('Day of the Dead').

'Garibaldi was always going to fall back into the bottle,' J Michael Straczynski has said, 'and initially it was going to be Sheridan or someone else helping him out of it. So who helped him out of it was a movable feast. It could have been virtually anybody. But by having Lochley in this position, and showing that if she hadn't been from a similar background, suddenly there's more of a connection there. So that should work nicely because they start off with an antagonism with each other because they each recognise in each other, subliminally almost, the same problem, and you almost hate in the other person what you see in yourself. So anyone could have helped him out, and that arc would have been exactly the same, but to create a character with that specific background, enabled me to give that thread more strength than it would have had otherwise.'

Speaking about the resolution of the Lyta Alexander plot, J Michael Straczynski has also said: 'This is, of course, the key to the whole reason for the Byron thing. If it had not gone on as long as it had, had not had the impact it had on her, she would not be where she is now in the storyline. You really needed something *major* to bring her to this point, and that was it.' This is a little difficult to swallow considering the fact that everything that happened between Byron and Lyta Alexander was originally going to be done between Byron and Ivanova. Given everything that had happened to Lyta in season four, one or two episodes would have been enough to push her over the edge. Seven or eight seems like overkill.

The title is, amongst other things, a reference to William Shakespeare's *King Lear* Act 4, Scene 7, where Lear lies on his sickbed:

> 'You do me wrong to take me out o' the grave:
> Thou art a soul in bliss; but I am bound
> Upon a wheel of fire, that mine own tears
> Do scald like molten lead.'

One 'pissed' from Franklin and two 'bastards!' from Delenn. They're going all out this season, aren't they?

Edgars Industries bribes influential senators. Garibaldi seems to see nothing wrong in this. And he's a lawman?

The shot of Londo at the end of the episode was almost certainly shot for the previous episode and edited into this one. It's unlikely they would have got Peter Jurasek back into the studio and into make-up just for a few seconds of silence.

Dialogue to Rewind For: Lyta Alexander to Captain Lochley: 'You cannot stop someone who has been touched by Vorlons.'

Lise Hampton-Edgars to Michael Garibaldi: 'There is no normal life, Michael – there's just life.'

Dialogue to Fast-Forward Past: Well, we'll count Franklin's entire discussion concerning whether or not God can create a rock so big that even He cannot lift it.

'You're not the only one that's been touched by the Vorlons!' Sheridan says, making the Vorlons sound like abusive parents.

Garibaldi: 'It turns out that G'Kar is leaving too. You know, it's funny – with him leaving and taking Lyta with him, and Franklin taking a job back on Earth, and me leaving soon, Londo gone, hell, even Sheridan's heading off to Minbar with Delenn as soon as he gets the new facilities for the Alliance in order . . . I don't know, it just doesn't seem like this place is going to be the same any more.' Could there *be* a clumsier piece of exposition?

Questions Raised: Why is Lyta Alexander in a straitjacket when she is incarcerated in the security area? Does Zack think her powers depend on her being able to wave her hands?

'Objects in Motion'

Transmission Number: 520
Production Number: 521

Story by: J Michael Straczynski and Harlan Ellison
Written by: J Michael Straczynski
Directed by: Jésus Treviño

Casey: James Hornbeck
Lise Hampton-Edgars: Denise Gentile
Number One: Marjorie Monaghan
Guard: Jeffrey James Castillo
Paretti: Walter Williams
Narn: Neil Bradley

Plot: We're in the end game now, with any potentially interesting plot developments interrupted by characters getting long goodbye speeches. It's hard to see why Harlan Ellison gets a co-story credit on this episode: the story as filmed is hardly big enough to fill the back of an envelope.

The 'A' Plot: Theresa Halloran – formerly Number One of the Martian Resistance – arrives on Babylon 5 with a message for Michael Garibaldi. Someone is going to try and kill both him and Lise Hampton-Edgars within the next couple of days. Halloran also tells Lise that, according to one of her spies, the company Lise inherited has a number of 'black' projects on the go that Lise does not know about, projects similar to William Edgars's plot to develop a virus to be used against telepaths. People within the company are concerned that Lise and/or Garibaldi might discover and cancel those projects, which is why an assassin has been hired.

Zack Allen suggests keeping Garibaldi and Lise out of sight so that the assassin cannot find them, and then holding a farewell ceremony for G'Kar at which they will be present. That way the killer will have only one opportunity to kill them – and Zack's people will be ready.

The killer (Casey) arrives on Babylon 5, kills a security guard, replaces the guard's communicator link with a fake and uses the stolen one to tap into security channel communications. He makes his attempt on Garibaldi and Lise at G'Kar's farewell party, but Zack has managed to identify him and takes him captive before he can fire. Lise, however, is wounded by mistake when a second assassin attempts to kill G'Kar. Worried, Garibaldi arranges for he and Lise to be married, then uses Lyta Alexander's telepathic skill to discover that the first assassin was hired by the entire Board of Directors of Edgars Industries. He confronts the Board, and blackmails them into resigning *en masse*.

The 'B' Plot: A fanatical follower of G'Kar becomes distressed when it becomes public knowledge that G'Kar is leaving the station. He attempts to shoot G'Kar at a farewell party but hits Lise Hampton-Edgars by mistake. She is wounded, but survives.

The 'C' Plot: G'Kar talks to Lyta Alexander, and asks her whether she is willing to leave the station and travel with him. She agrees. They leave together.

The Arc: Everything is winding down now. This episode marks the moment when G'Kar, Lyta Alexander and Michael Garibaldi leave the station – possibly for ever.

Observations: Despite the change of President and the granting of Mars's freedom, Martian currency and documentation are still not recognised by Earth.

Series documentation reveals the name of the Narn who attempts to kill G'Kar as being Tru'Nil, although this is never made clear in the episode.

Without approval or permission, a fanatical fan creates and sells something to honour the object of their fanaticism. Does this ring any bells? Not with me. No sir.

This episode was originally announced as 'Objects in Motion' then briefly changed to 'The Alien Within' before changing back to 'Objects in Motion' again.

Dialogue to Rewind For: Sheridan's moment of self-revelation: 'I've had an idea – and you know how dangerous that can be!'

G'Kar, talking about leaving to explore the universe: 'Perhaps we will find something extraordinary. Perhaps something extraordinary will find us.'

Franklin, talking about Babylon 5: 'When this place was built I think irony was one of the primary materials used in construction.'

Delenn to Sheridan: ' "Now" is all we have.'

Dialogue to Fast-Forward Past: The entire scene with Delenn arriving on the station just as Garibaldi and Lise are about to leave screams 'contrived!' at the top of its voice, and none of the actors seem quite sure how to play it.

Ships That Pass in the Night: Mars Starliner *Kafka* (or *Kaafka*, as the tannoy voice says) takes Garibaldi and Delenn away from Babylon 5. G'Kar's new ship is pretty nifty, by the way.

I've Seen That Face Before: Marjorie Monaghan returns to play Theresa Halloran (previously known as Number One) again. She previously appeared in various season four episodes starting with 410 ('Racing Mars') and ending with 420 ('Endgame').

'Objects at Rest'

Transmission Number: 521
Production Number: 522

Written by: J Michael Straczynski
Directed by: John Copeland

Ta'lon: Marshall Teague
Dr Lilian Hobbes: Jennifer Balgobin
Ranger: Simon Billig
Number One: Marjorie Monaghan
ISN Reporter: Maggie Egan
Employee: Mike Manzoni

Plot: This was the last ever episode of *Babylon 5* to have been filmed, and in many ways it says the goodbyes better than the final transmitted episode, primarily because it has inherited less baggage from the episodes that have gone before. Shame that the main plot driver (the coolant leak) is such a plot *device*.

The 'A' Plot: Lennier returns to Babylon 5 in order to help Delenn and Sheridan move their belongings to Minbar. Sheridan and Delenn attempt to leave the station without any undue fuss, but ISN have already found out that they are leaving and the station crew give them a warm, emotional send-off.

On board a White Star ship, heading through hyperspace for Minbar, Sheridan is taking a late night stroll when he discovers a coolant leak in a weapons system. Trapped behind a safety screen and at risk from being overcome by the fumes he asks Lennier to release the screen and let him out – but Lennier refuses and leaves. Within moments Lennier regrets his decision and returns, but by that time Sheridan has freed himself. Lennier takes a fighter and leaves the White Star, heading off into hyperspace in a state of bitter recrimination. In his quarters in Tuzanor on Minbar, a diary is found in which he makes clear that he considers Sheridan and Delenn's marriage to have been a mistake. He is obviously deeply obsessed with Delenn.

Lennier communicates with Delenn, telling her that he is terribly sorry about what he almost did and that he cannot return to Minbar until he has come to terms with it himself. He does say, however, that he is sure they will meet again.

The 'B' Plot: Arriving on Minbar, Sheridan and Delenn find Emperor Londo Mollari waiting for them. They have dinner and talk about old times, but Londo has his own agenda. Knowing that Delenn is pregnant, he gives them a gift to be passed to their child when he reaches his eighteenth birthday. The gift is an ancient Centauri vase, but neither Sheridan nor Delenn know that there is a Drakh Keeper hidden inside in a state of suspended animation. When David Sheridan comes of age and is given the vase, the Keeper will take him over.

The 'C' Plot: Ta'Lon – the Narn warrior who befriended G'Kar and Sheridan – arrives on the station looking for G'Kar. He is surprised to find that G'Kar has left, but discovers that G'Kar has left a message for him in which G'Kar asks Ta'Lon to be the representative on Babylon 5 of the Narn. Doctor Franklin hands over the reins of power in Medlab to Doctor Lillian Hobbes.

The Arc: At this stage in the proceedings plot strands are being closed off but with enough threads left hanging that future spin-offs (televisual and literary) don't have to start from scratch. The Drakh's attempt to take control of David Sheridan fits in with their way of operating (although their choice of victim is a bit odd – see **Questions Raised** below), and Lennier's betrayal of the Rangers was set up previously in episode 508 ('Day of the Dead'). His love of Delenn has been implicit in many episodes, but was first made plain in episode 311 ('Ceremonies of Light and Dark').

Observations: This episode takes place the day after the previous episode ends (Delenn has just returned from

Minbar) and almost a year since episode 501 ('No Compromises').

Doctor Hemandez gets a name-check as someone qualified to run Medlab. She appeared in episode 110 ('Believers').

Many of the production team make an appearance in this episode. Designer John Iacovelli is one of the new Edgars Industries' board members, while the crowd that sees Sheridan and Delenn off is comprised mainly of people who work on the series in one capacity or another. Mike Manzoni, the series' Facility Manager, is one of the new Edgars Industries' board of directors.

Other Worlds: Vermini VII lies on the border of Brakiri and Drazi space.

I've Seen That Face Before: Simon Billig returns as a Ranger for no particularly good reason, having previously appeared in episode 518 ('The Fall of Centauri Prime'). He was probably just hanging around the studio at the time. Marjorie Monaghan makes her second appearance in a row as Theresa Halloran. Marshall Teague reappears as Ta'lon (he first appeared in episode 211 – 'All Alone in the Night' – and last appeared in episode 512 – 'The Ragged Edge'). Jennifer Balgobin also reappears as Dr Lilian Hobbes (she previously appeared in episodes 315 – 'Interludes and Examinations' – and 318 – 'Walkabout').

Accidents Will Happen: G'Kar arranged things such that as soon as Ta'Lon accesses the message G'Kar had left for him, the one asking him to become the Narn's new representative on Babylon 5, a copy would be sent to President Sheridan 'and the others'. That would work if he turned up the day after G'Kar left – as he did – but not if he turned up 6 months later. By that time the Kha'ri would have settled on someone else as their representative.

Let's understand this – the Keeper is on Londo's right shoulder. From the Keeper's point of view, when Delenn appears to get some indication that something is amiss she is staring off to the Keeper's right. This means she was staring several feet to the right of Londo's head. What was she staring at?

Questions Raised: Whatever happened to Major Atumbe? He was Babylon 5's third in command, after Sinclair/Sheridan and Ivanova in the first two seasons. Perhaps something drastic happened to him, something so terrible that nobody wants to talk about it. There's a trilogy of novels there, I have no doubt.

Operating under the instructions, if not the control, of the Drakh, Londo arranges for Sheridan and Delenn's son to be taken over by the Drakh in eighteen years' time. Why? The Presidency of the Interstellar Alliance is not (as far as we know) an inherited post. Sheridan isn't an Emperor, just a President. David Sheridan might decide to be an artist, or a street cleaner, or a dealer in kevas and trillium, rather than go into politics. What's in it for the Drakh?

If there had been alcohol on the dinner table in Truzenor, would Londo have been able to evade the control of his Keeper and tell Sheridan and Delenn the truth?

'Sleeping in Light'

Transmission Number: 522
Production Number: Made as 422, but renumbered 523

Written by: J Michael Straczynski
Directed by: J Michael Straczynski

Lorien: Wayne Alexander
Earthforce Publicist: Romy Rosemont
Commander Nils: David Wells
Mary: Sharon Annett
Aide: Dan Sachoff
Ranger: Lair Torrant
Captain of the Guard: Kent Minault

Plot: There should have been fireworks. There should have been parties to rival the millennial celebrations. And yet what we get is only television. It's good television, and it raises a tear or two, but it also raises some disturbing questions. We waited this long, and we still don't see Sheridan and Delenn's son? We get no explanation for the flash forward to both of them in prison on Centauri Prime from 'War Without End'? If we'd been told all along that there would be loose threads it wouldn't have been so bad. If we'd been told nothing at all about the last episode, it wouldn't have been so bad. But we were told, specifically, by the big cheese himself, that everything would be explained. Everything. And it wasn't. It's not this ending that let's us down, it's the absence of the one we were promised.

The 'A' Plot: Sheridan is having dreams about Lorien – remembrances of things that happened twenty years ago. He suspects that he is on the verge of dying, having lived out the twenty years that Lorien promised him. He sends out invitations to his old friends – Michael Garibaldi, Stephen Franklin, Susan Ivanova, Vir Cotto, Zack Allen – and they immediately make their way to Minbar for one final meeting, and one final party (all except for Zack, who couldn't be tracked down by the Rangers). They remember old stories, and old friends who are no longer alive – Londo Mollari, G'Kar, Lennier, Marcus Cole. They laugh, and they cry, and they try not to talk about Sheridan's imminent demise.

Sheridan leaves the next day, taking a one-man White Star ship and heading out into hyperspace. He makes for Babylon 5, where the station is about to be blown up, and meets up with Zack Allen again, but does not stay for the closing ceremony.

Sheridan travels to the Coriana system, where the Shadows and Vorlons were finally defeated. As he is on the verge of dying, he meets up with Lorien again. Lorien takes Sheridan out of the ship and beyond the Rim, to where the First Ones have gone.

The 'B' Plot: Delenn, aware that Susan Ivanova is dissatisfied with her life, offers her the job of Ranger One.

The 'C' Plot: Babylon 5 reverted to Earth control a few years before, but as much of the Alliance business is now done from Minbar nobody visits the station any more. It is now not only surplus to requirements, but also a danger to navigation. As a visiting Garibaldi, Franklin, Ivanova, Zack

Allen, Vir and Delenn make their farewells and leave, the station is deliberately blown up.

The Arc: Sheridan was President of the Interstellar Alliance for seventeen years. He was re-elected on a regular basis. Delenn followed him as President.

Ivanova has become a General in Earthforce, and is bitter and disappointed.

Vir is now Emperor of Centauri Prime (the planet appears to have recovered somewhat from its problems, and is on speaking terms with the Alliance).

Garibaldi and Lise are still in charge of Edgars(-Garibaldi) Industries.

Franklin is still Chief of the Insterstellar Alliance's Xenobiological Research programme after twenty years.

David Sheridan is still alive, despite Londo's plans, and is a Ranger. We don't know, however, whether he's controlled by a Keeper or not.

Babylon 5 blows up. Well, it had to, really. We saw it blowing up in episodes 113 ('Signs and Portents'), 120 ('Babylon Squared') and 326 ('War Without End' Part One) – the first two being visions of the future, the other a transmission from the future. The strong implication in all three episodes was that the station was destroyed during an attack by some unspecified enemy. In 'Babylon Squared' a future version of Garibaldi claims to have set the fusion reactors to explode. Whether that's the future that J Michael Straczynski was aiming for when he first started planning the series, or whether he always knew he was going to have it blown up in a calm, controlled way as a hazard to shipping, will remain forever a moot point. But it's gone, whatever way you look at it.

Observations: This episode has no title sequence: it just begins and keeps going. The episode title flashes up shortly after the beginning.

The episode contains flashbacks from episode 402 ('Whatever Happened to Mr Garibaldi?'), 403 ('The Summoning') and 404 ('Falling Toward Apotheosis').

'This is the new question for this season, in "Sleeping in

Light",' J Michael Straczynski has said. 'There's the questions of "Who are you?", "What do you want?", "Why are you here?" and the fourth question is "Where are you going?" Now we see where they're all going.'

The Hugo award that J Michael Straczynski won for episode 209 ('The Coming of Shadows') is sitting on Ivanova's desk.

This episode was filmed at the end of season four, when it was suspected that there would be no season five. When season five was commissioned, a new episode was filmed to go at the end of season four and 'Sleeping in Light' was held back for a year.

As with episode 521 ('Objects at Rest') several *Babylon 5* staff members make cameo appearances in this episode, including Producer John Copeland and co-Producer (at the time) George Johnsen. J Michael Straczynski is, appropriately enough, the maintenance worker who shuts off the station's lights and blows the place up. The question is – does he make it off the station in time?

Dialogue to Rewind For: Sheridan: 'I'm almost out of time, Delenn.'

Susan Ivanova: 'Babylon 5 was the last of the Babylon stations. There would never be another. It changed the future, and it changed us. It taught us that we have to create the future, or others will do it for us. It showed us that we have to care for one another, because if we don't, who will? And that true strength sometimes comes from the most unlikely places. Mostly though I think it gave us hope that there can always be new beginnings, even for people like us.'

Dialogue to Fast-Forward Past: 'Where are the others?' Delenn asks. 'They're putting Vir to bed,' Sheridan replies, 'which is where we should be.' What, the audience choruses, all of you in bed with Vir?

Please God, not another interminable story from Sheridan about how wonderful his dad was.

Ships That Pass in the Night: There's a new type of White

Star ship around, 20 years in the future. We also get to see the *Talos* – an Earthforce ship.

Culture Shock: Vir Cotto says that there are forty-nine gods in the Centauri pantheon. This matches perfectly with episode 122 ('Chrysalis'), where we were told that there were fifty gods in the Centauri pantheon but Vir wasn't sure whether one of them should be included or not. Presumably now, as Emperor, he has the power to enforce his decision.

I've Seen That Face Before: Wayne Alexander as Lorien, of course. From villain to hero in three episodes: a good trick if you can do it.

Accidents Will Happen: In the scene with Garibaldi and Franklin talking on Mars, just after Garibaldi's daughter leaves, watch the doorway on the side she went through. As Garibaldi says 'Stocks haven't moved up or down in over a week,' you can see the hem of the dress of the actress playing his daughter, just moving outside the doorway. She's standing around waiting for her cue to come back in with the Ranger.

THE TV MOVIES

In the Beginning

Transmission Number: Not Applicable
Production Number: TNTCF2

Written by: J Michael Straczynski
Directed by: Mike Vejar

Lenonn: Theodore Bikel
Dukhat: Reiner Schöne
Morann: Robin Atkin Downes
Coplann: Robin Sachs
General Lefcourt: J Patrick McCormack
President: Tricia O'Neil
Captain Sterns: Jason Azikiwe
Captain Jankowski: Tim Colceri

Plot: *In the Beginning* has everything that *Babylon 5* is renowned for: drama, tragedy, humour and a massive scope illuminated by small details. Everything feels *right* about this movie: even the characters who get one or two scenes in the whole thing (such as Stephen Franklin) do not feel underused. The only problem is the way the plot is wrapped up: although we see a mammoth amount of futuristic war footage we never actually see the war end, and we get to hear about the Minbari surrender only in a voice-over by Londo. This unbalances the entire thing: in our minds, because we have never seen the conclusion to the war, it is almost as if the war were still going on at the end.

The 'A' Plot: On the Minbari homeworld, Lenonn, the leader of the Anla'shok, is having problems. The Anla'shok are now little more than a historical curiosity, but they were set up a thousand years ago by the semimythical Minbari leader Valen in order to prepare for a prophesied war against a supremely powerful foe known only as the Shadows. Now, however, nobody is interested in Valen's prophecy, and Lenonn's request for more support for the Anla'shok has been rejected. Lenonn demands (as is his right) to speak to the Minbari ruling body, the Grey Council, and explains to them that Valen foretold a thousand years ago that the Shadows would return in a thousand years, but that no preparations have been made. Dukhat, the Leader of the Grey Council, decides to travel to the Shadows' former homeworld of Z'ha'dum in order to investigate for himself whether or not the Shadows are returning, taking a heavy cruiser and only a few support vessels with him. What the Grey Council is unaware of is that Dukhat has two Vorlons – ancient enemies of the Shadows – in his quarters, and is being guided by their advice.

On their way to Z'ha'dum, Dukhat is killed during a surprise attack by a previously unknown race known as 'humans'. The Minbari, spurred on by Dukhat's former aide and Grey Council member Delenn, begin a holy war to exterminate humanity.

Lenonn, concerned over the Minbari's rather precipitate actions, suggests that Delenn visit a re-creation of Dukhat's sanctuary. She does so, and finds the two Vorlons. They give her a message from Dukhat, recorded before his death, suggesting that the Minbari must ally themselves with humanity if the Shadows are to be defeated. Delenn is appalled, and sends Lenonn on a mission to discuss a cessation of hostilities with the humans, but Lenonn is killed by unknown forces (actually, the Centauri).

The Minbari prosecute their successful attacks on humanity, and Delenn finds she has no leverage to force a peace. During their final assault on Earth, when they are just a few hours away from destroying humanity completely, Delenn suggests that the Grey Council take a human aboard their ship and interrogate him as to the planet's defences. On advice from the Vorlons she chooses one particular ship from all the ones attacking them, and takes its pilot (Jeffrey Sinclair) captive. During their interrogation they discover – by accident – that he has a Minbari soul. Not only that, he has the soul of Valen – their legendary prophet and leader from a thousand years ago. The Minbari, who believe in reincarnation, assume that Valen has been reborn into human form in order to tell the Minbari that humanity will be important in the coming war, and so the Minbari surrender as the moment of their greatest victory approaches.

The 'B' Plot: It is the year 2243. On Earth, General Lefcourt attempts to assign Lieutenant Commander Sheridan to the *Prometheus* as First Officer, taking him off his current assignment on the *Lexington*. The *Prometheus* is shortly to undertake a mission to investigate the reclusive Minbari race and Lefcourt obviously considers this a plum assignment, but Sheridan refuses, citing his obligations to the *Lexington*'s commanding officer, Captain Sterns, and his belief (shared by many in Earthforce) that the commanding officer of the *Prometheus*, Captain Jankowski, is a 'loose cannon'.

Sheridan returns to his duties on the *Lexington*. His refusal to leave that ship and her captain means that he is not on the *Prometheus* when it accidentally starts a war with the Minbari by opening fire on one of their vessels.

The war escalates, and Earthforce finds it impossible to achieve even one victory against the Minbari ships. As conflict continues, the *Lexington* comes across a Minbari transport which appears to be damaged and vulnerable to attack: Captain Sterns believes it to be a trap, but still manages to fall for the Minbari ploy. The *Lexington* is attacked by a Minbari heavy cruiser – the *Black Star* – and is badly damaged. Captain Sterns is killed in the attack, and Sheridan takes command of the remainder of the ship. Knowing that the Minbari ship is still lurking in the area, and will home in on any distress call and destroy what remains of the *Lexington*, Sheridan has his crew place nuclear devices on some nearby asteroids and uses a fake distress call to lure the Minbari cruiser back. The bombs are exploded, and the ship is destroyed.

Returning to Earth as a hero, Sheridan is sent by General Lefcourt on a mission to an abandoned Earthforce listening post in order to meet with a Minbari representative who is empowered to discuss terms for peace. He is accompanied on this delicate mission by Stephen Franklin, an Earthforce doctor, and G'Kar, a Narn who has brokered the talks. The meeting comes under attack by unidentified forces (actually a Centauri ship): the Minbari representative is killed and Sheridan, Franklin and G'Kar are picked up by the Minbari. Sheridan and Franklin are to be killed, but Sheridan gains the attention of the Minbari leader by using a phrase that the dying Minbari gave him. The Minbari leader allows him and Franklin to live, and returns them to their own forces.

The war escalates, going on for another two years. Sheridan's heroic actions have failed to turn the tide, and as the Minbari approach Earth the President calls for a general evacuation, supported by every fighting ship Earthforce has left. In the midst of the final battle, however, the Minbari surrender on the verge of victory.

The 'C' Plot: Londo Mollari, a liaison to the Centauri delegation on Earth, is engaged in the purchase of artistic trinkets for his jaded people when he discovers that the humans, flushed with ambition after their victory against the Dilgar, intend expanding their area of influence. They ask his advice on sending an expedition to Minbari space to see whether they pose a threat. Londo suggests that such a course of action might invite reprisals from the Minbari, and such proves to be the case.

Later, when a war between humanity and the Minbari is in full swing, humanity asks the Centauri government, via Londo, for help. Londo refuses, saying that the Minbari would take action against the Centauri if it were known that they had supplied the humans with weapons. Rebuffed, the humans go to the Narn for weapons. As G'Kar of the Narn explains, the Narn aren't worried because most of their weapons are based on Centauri designs, and even if the Minbari discover the weapons they will blame the Centauri rather than the Narn.

When Londo discovers that G'Kar is planning an expedition with two humans he assumes that it is concerning weapon sales, and so he has the expedition attacked by a Centauri warship. What he did not know, but later discovered, was that the humans and the Narn were meeting with a Minbari representative for peace talks, and his actions have condemned both sides to another two years of war.

The 'D' Plot: Dr Stephen Franklin, an Earthforce doctor, refuses to pass details of Minbari physiology to Earthforce (he obtained those details before the war when he was 'hitch-hiking' around various alien worlds and operated on a group of them). He is imprisoned, then released to go on a mission with Lieutenant Commander Sheridan to discuss peace terms with the Minbari.

The 'E' Plot: In the future an elderly Centauri Emperor Londo II tells two small Centauri children the story of the Earth–Minbari war. Outside the palace, the Centauri world is in flames owing to some unknown catastrophe. After the children have gone, Londo calls for his two prisoners: John Sheridan and Delenn.

The Arc: The plot of *In the Beginning* was established long ago within the series proper. The knowledge that Earth and Minbar had been at war was mentioned as early as the pilot, 'The Gathering', as was Jeffrey Sinclair's capture by the Minbari. Some details of what the Minbari did to him were revealed in episode 108 ('And the Sky Full of Stars') and the remainder in episode 201 ('Points of Departure'). The latter episode also introduced John Sheridan's interaction with the *Black Star*. Valen's prophecy concerning the return of the Shadows formed a backdrop to the first three seasons, with episode 317 ('War Without End' Part Two) giving us the critical information that allowed us to realise why Jeffrey Sinclair had a Minbari soul – he travelled back in time and was transformed into a Minbari to lead the struggle against the Shadows, in a reverse of Delenn's transformation into a human. Delenn's actions during the war against the humans, especially her pivotal role in starting the war, were made explicit in episode 409 ('Atonement').

When Delenn is inducted into the Grey Council, a device is held in front of her. This device is the triluminary, an ancient instrument that was passed down from Valen and can be used to identify particular souls. When the triluminary lights up it indicates that Delenn is a descendant of Valen.

Lenonn says that the Minbari should make a *rapprochement* with the Vorlons. This implies that there was some kind of falling out – something that has not been mentioned before in the series. Still, the Vorlons appear to have annoyed a lot of people, if the reaction of the First Ones is anything to go by.

Observations: A reference is made to the war against the

Dilgar. These events are given more depth in episode 109 ('Deathwalker').

According to the Minbari, other races have moved into Z'ha'dum and made it their own in the thousand years since the last Shadow war.

This TV movie contains clips from episodes 108 ('And the Sky Full of Stars'), 313 ('A Late Delivery From Avalon'), 317 ('War Without End', Part Two) and 409 ('Atonement').

The title of this TV movie was first announced as *In the Beginning*, then as *Last of the Fallen* before being switched back to *In the Beginning*.

The Grey Council member Coplann (Robin Sachs) is named for the Producer, John Copeland.

It was originally believed that Claudia Christian would not be capable of playing Susan Ivanova aged eighteen, even though the wonders of make-up were being used to erase similar periods of time from Bruce Boxleitner (John Sheridan) and Richard Biggs (Stephen Franklin) (Londo, G'Kar and Delenn are all aliens, and so we can assume the ageing process works differently for them). Christian says, 'It was ironic, because they came up to me and said they were really having a hard time finding someone to play Ivanova at eighteen. No joke! I'd already humiliated myself by bringing in my high-school prom photos – they could see I hadn't changed much at all. I was just a little fatter. So finally Joe Straczynski said to them, "You know, she looks the same." My attitude was, if you're having one person playing their young self, then everybody has to. Otherwise it looks stupid. So now I'm playing it, with a short wig on, and looking like a tomboy with very little make-up. Hopefully the DP will light me very nicely and then no one will notice! That was the whole irony of the last-episode thing – they were happy with me playing fifty but not eighteen. I look closer to eighteen than fifty, I think! It's just one scene anyway.'

Jerry Doyle does not appear as Garibaldi in this movie. 'When they shot the movies this last summer, I wasn't in either one of them,' he says. 'That was business; I got some shitty advice from my agent.'

Although he set *In the Beginning* before the pilot 'The

Gathering', J Michael Straczynski resisted the urge to return to the original costumes and make-up that had been used before the re-envisioning that went on for the series proper.

Some criticism was made of the movie at the time it was shown for not having more Soul Hunters in (episode 102 – 'Soul Hunter' – makes it clear they attempted to get to Dukhat's body but were prevented from doing so by the Minbari).

Peter David's novelisation of *In the Beginning* (the first novelisation of any *Babylon 5* script ever to be released) is told, rather stylishly, from the point of view of Londo Mollari. David introduces a number of scenes that are not in the script, such as meetings between John Sheridan and Jeffrey Sinclair and between Sheridan and his future wife, Anna. J Michael Straczynski is debating whether to accept these meetings as being part of 'official' continuity or not.

Koshisms: Delenn: 'What are you doing here?' Kosh: 'Creating the future.'

About the humans: 'They are the key.'

'We have always been here.'

'The truth points to itself.'

Dialogue to Rewind For: Dukhat: 'When the darkness comes, if you ever have doubt about your actions, all you need do is look into the face of a Vorlon. Once you see that, all doubt is erased for ever.'

Delenn, about humans: 'In the name of Valen, and the one who is Valen's shadow in this life, we cannot kill them.'

Londo Mollari: 'The quiet ones are the ones that change the universe . . . the loud ones only take the credit.'

Londo again, about humanity: 'They changed the universe, but in doing so paid a terrible price.'

Dukhat to Delenn: 'I'm not saying anything. I didn't say anything then and I'm not saying anything now.'

Londo Mollari, about humanity's actions at the end of the war: 'When they ran out of ships, they used guns. When they ran out of guns they used knives, and sticks, and bare hands. They were magnificent.'

Londo again, musing as Emperor in the future: 'How strange, to have come so far and to want so little.'

And again: 'The story is not over yet. The story is never over.'

Ships That Pass in the Night: The *Churchill* (an Earthforce ship) is mentioned, and we get to see the Minbari war cruiser *Black Star* before Sheridan blasts it 'straight to hell'.

Culture Shock: The Omega incident is referred to as a first-contact situation for Earth.

Station Keeping: Babylon 1 is seen to be red in this story. Babylon 4, we know from episode 120 ('Babylon Squared') is green. Babylon 5 is blue, of course. This indicates that Babylon 2 was orange and Babylon 3 yellow.

I've Seen That Face Before: Tricia O'Neil, who plays the Earth President, previously played the part of M'ola in episode 110 ('Believers'). J Patrick McCormack, who appears as General Lefcourt, played the same part in episode 420 ('Endgame'), and it's nice to be able to welcome back Reiner Schöne as Dukhat (he previously appeared in episode 409 – 'Atonement') and Robin Atkin Downes as Morann (he also previously appeared in episode 409). Robin Sachs, who plays the Minbari Coplann, previously played the strangely similar Minbari Grey Council member Hedronn in episodes 201 ('Points of Departure') and 211 ('All Alone in the Night'). Theodore Bikel, who appears as Lenonn, was previously in episode 114 ('TKO') as Rabbi Koslov.

Questions Raised: Why does Dukhat insist on going to Z'ha'dum if he has two Vorlons in his quarters? His stated aim is that he wants to see whether Valen's prophecy has any truth in it or not, but the Vorlons have presumably told him that it has (they were there when Valen made the prophecy, after all) and Dukhat later indicates to Delenn that it's impossible not to believe the Vorlons.

If, as the Minbari believe, other races have colonised Z'ha'dum in the thousand years since the last Great War, how come none of them woke the Shadows up? Why did everyone have to wait for Anna Sheridan and the party from the Earth company Interplanetary Expeditions (IPX)?

Thirdspace

Transmission Number: Not applicable
Production Number: TNTCF1

Written by: J Michael Straczynski
Directed by: Jésus Salvador Treviño

Bill Morishi: Clyde Kusatsu
Dr Elizabeth Trent: Shari Belafonte
Deuce: William Sanderson
Delta 7: Judson Mills

Plot: Interestingly enough, the events in this TV movie are linear, in that there is no cutting back and forth between different but linked plots. Every scene advances the main plot, and the whole thing is fun to watch. Shame that Sheridan has to resort to big explosions to sort out the enemy, though.

The 'A' Plot: Raiders attack an Earth transport. Ivanova takes out Delta Squadron to defeat the Raiders. They call in their base ship – a larger vessel capable of forming hyperspace gateways – but Ivanova calls in the White Star fleet. The Raiders surrender.

Delta Squadron return to Babylon 5, but discover a large artefact floating in hyperspace. It's around half a mile across, and is drifting unpowered. Ivanova leads Delta Squadron on a side trip to examine the artefact, and when they have located it she calls in all available Babylon 5 ships in order to tow it to the nearest jumpgate and thence to Babylon 5.

Lyta Alexander starts getting flashes of the same large artefact floating in hyperspace and what appear to be precognitive visions of a future in which everyone on the station has been killed. Feeling ill, she falls into a fugue state and stays in her room, obsessively scribbling on the walls, 'There is danger. Remember.'

Zack Allen notices signs of weapon fire on the exterior of the object, and is suspicious it may be booby-trapped. A maintenance 'bot sent in to take a sample of the object's exterior suddenly loses all power. Later tests on the sample the 'bot managed to remove before it lost power indicates that the artefact is over a million years old.

A ship from the Earth company Interplanetary Expeditions (IPX) arrives, and the company's representative, Elizabeth Trent, tells Sheridan that they have the expertise and the resources to investigate the artefact properly. She also tells him that the company is powerful enough to defy President Clark's embargo. Sheridan agrees to give IPX access if they help resupply the station with essential items.

Acting as if she were under the control of an external force, Lyta Alexander takes control of the station's maintenance 'bots and sends them towards the artefact, their arc-welding equipment lit and ready to destroy it. The 'bots are destroyed by the patrolling Starfuries, and, when Zack Allen and his troops break into the 'bot control centre, they find Lyta, who passes out shortly afterwards. She cannot remember anything for several hours. Other people on the station also start acting oddly: some exhibiting violence, some just locking themselves in their rooms and screaming.

IPX's investigations suggest the artefact is a type of jumpgate, but one that accesses a different type of reality – different from 'normal' space or hyperspace, which would allow almost instantaneous travel. Dr Trent refers to it as 'thirdspace'. Sheridan confronts Dr Trent, who claims her team have not discovered anything significant. Sheridan has already realised that the writing on the surface of the artefact is Vorlon, and tells Trent that he knows she is keeping something from him. Back in her centre of operations, Trent makes a decision to reconnect what appears to be a large-scale power grid on the surface of their object using the largest power cells they have. Ivanova tries to countermand the order, but it's too late. The moment the cell is connected the artefact comes to life, taking over many of the personnel on the station and glowing with energy. Ivanova tries to launch the Starfuries, but a power cut has restricted them to the cobra bays. Power is restored, and they launch. The artefact begins to open up into a jumpgate.

Sheridan goes to confront Lyta Alexander, given that she has already shown some affinity with the object and also because she may be able to translate the Vorlon writing on the side. Lyta, however, has been taken over by some kind of Vorlon race memory implanted in her mind, and tells them that the object is a Vorlon-created mistake. In their pride, as a young race, the Vorlons had come to believe they were like gods. They attempted to force a connection to another dimension, a place they believed was 'the well of souls, the source of all life'. A life form in this dimension – telepathic and older even than the Vorlons – attempted to invade this dimension. The Vorlons fought them and defeated them, temporarily, but those Vorlons who had been taken over by the enemy dropped the artefact into hyperspace before it could be destroyed. Lyta – or, rather, the controlling force within Lyta – then telepathically transmits the information into Sheridan's mind that will allow him to destroy the artefact.

Alien fighters begin to emerge from the jumpgate. The Starfuries engage them, but the fighters are too powerful. Delenn calls in the nearest Minbari fleet and Ivanova calls in as many White Star ships as are available.

Sheridan, acting on information received from Lyta, gets into a spacesuit and leaves the station, taking a nuclear bomb with him. He penetrates the artefact and places his bomb, but is attacked by a resident alien. He escapes it and leaves the artefact. The bomb explodes just as the larger alien warships are emerging. The aliens are destroyed – warships, fighters and all – and all telepathic control ceases.

The Arc: Lyta's Vorlon-enhanced telepathic powers take her from a P5 to above a P9.

The Vorlons have made some significant mistakes in the past – but, then, we could have guessed that.

Observations: This TV movie is set in mid-2261, after the Shadow War but before the war to liberate Earth.

The aliens who live in the realm of thirdspace were designed by the famed SF artist Wayne D Barlowe, whose illustrations have appeared in books such as *Barlowe's Guide to Extraterrestrials* (in which he re-creates aliens from famous SF novels) and *Expedition* (a David Attenborough-type guide to a fictional future expedition to an alien planet). The design of the alien city as seen in Ivanova's dream also derives from Barlowe's illustrations.

The Director, Jésus Treviño, had some intriguing ideas about the interior of the alien artefact that were, sadly, never properly realised on screen. 'Perhaps Sheridan is not only trying to plant the bomb that will destroy the alien artefact,' he said in his production notes at the time, 'but in the process is walking through an "Escher"-like maze where the floor is underneath him in one moment and then, the next step, he is walking on the ceiling.' The reference is to Maurits Cornelius Escher, a twentieth-century Dutch artist famed for his drawings of paradoxes and puzzles.

There appear to be no jumpgates in Vorlon space – at least, none known to the races involved in Babylon 5. The nearest one is ten days away.

The scene between Zack Allen and Lyta Alexander in the lift (which lasts almost three and a half minutes) was written close to the end of filming in order to make up a shortfall discovered at the end of shooting. The irony is, of course, that what Straczynski came up with is probably the one scene people will remember the most from this episode. Necessity is, of course, the mother of invention.

The actress playing a maintenance worker named Red-Horse is actually named Valerie Red-Horse.

Shari Belafonte, who plays Elizabeth Trent, is the daughter of the actor/singer Harry Belafonte.

The character of Dr Trent was originally named Dr Quijana.

The original draft of the script for *Thirdspace* had Michael Garibaldi in it, but the actor's agent could not come to agreement on terms with Babylonian.

Tracy Scoggins, who later gained the part of Captain Elizabeth Lochley, originally auditioned for the part of Elizabeth Trent. Or Dr Quijana, depending on when she auditioned.

This movie was also novelised by Peter David.

Dialogue to Rewind For: 'If I was thirty years younger and you were a little blind in one eye, what a wonderful life we could have together' – middle-aged client to Lyta Alexander.

'Our mistake ... one of many ... so many' – Lyta Alexander.

Vir to Zack Allen: 'What am I doing here? Why are you *hitting* me?'

Dialogue to Fast-Forward Past: 'And so far, we've had ten outbreaks in the last five hours, and that's just in Down-below ...' one of Zack's men reports. 'Fights mainly. We've found some people just locked in their rooms ... screaming. We've given the worst cases to medlab ... the rest we've got in lock-up.' 'And all this started after the artefact got here?' Zack asks. 'Definitely,' his man replies, and then, making his bid for moron of the week, asks, 'You think there's a connection?'

Other Worlds: Sheridan incarcerates the Raiders in a Drazi penal colony in what he calls the Drazi Freehold.

Culture Shock: The aliens from thirdspace are bigger than humans, and can survive in a vacuum. They look rather like house mites with six legs and tentacles. They are older even than the Vorlons.

There's a new alien on Babylon 5 – one that's not appeared in any episodes before and since. It's red-skinned and bald-headed, and its eyes appear to be on stalks projecting from its cheeks.

Literary, Mythological and Historical References: Sheridan's password for getting access to the nuclear weapons is Abraxas 79713. Abraxas is a mystical word used by various second-century sects of Christian origin to denote the Supreme Being (and the name of the third album by the 70s rock legend Carlos Santana). You learn something every day, don't you?

I've Seen That Face Before: The character of Deuce has appeared before in the series, in episode 115 ('Grail'), as well as the *Babylon 5* novel *Voices*. Then, as now, he was played by William Sanderson. Interplanetary Expeditions (IPX) were previously mentioned in episodes 104 ('Infection'), 215 ('And Now For a Word) and 322 ('Z'ha'dum') as well as in the *Babylon 5* novel *The Shadow Within*. They are generally not to be trusted.

Questions Raised: With all those sensors IPC are aiming at the artefact, does nobody spot the flickers of light crossing its surface?

Sheridan realises Dr Trent is hiding things from him, and gives her 24 hours to give him her report. Why 24 hours? Why not immediately?

The River of Souls

Transmission Number: Not applicable
Production Number: TNTCF3

Written by: J Michael Straczynski
Directed by: Janet Greek

Dr Robert Bryson: Ian McShane
First Soul Hunter: Martin Sheen
Jacob Mayhew: Joel Brooks
James Riley: Stuart Pankin
Mr Clute: Jeff Silverman
Soul One: Wayne Alexander

Plot: It's a dog's dinner: scripted and directed in haste. The plot might have worked as a 45-minute episode, but stretched out to 90 minutes it drags. Ian McShane and Martin Sheen seemed like good bets on paper, but McShane slurs his way through his part and Sheen has to wrestle with large chunks of dialogue in which all he is doing is advancing the plot. Rather the series had died completely than this mess had ever been committed to celluloid.

The 'A' Plot: Dr Robert Bryson, an archaeologist, discovers a huge chamber on a ruined world. The chamber contains millions of spheres, each of which contains the soul of a living being. His party are attacked by an unknown alien craft, and many are killed. Bryson escapes with one sphere – larger than the rest. As he escapes, it begins to talk to him.

Bryson travels to Babylon 5 in order to see Mr Garibaldi. Bryson has been working for Edgars Industries, and wants more funds, and Mr Garibaldi now runs the company on a day-to-day basis. Bryson tells Garibaldi that he has been seeking the secret of eternal life in the archaeological remains of other races.

While working to access the sphere, and the souls inside, Bryson accidentally manages to connect the sphere to Babylon 5's power grid. Some of the souls escape.

A Soul Hunter arrives on the station, alerted to the presence of the Soul Sphere that has been stolen from them, and Bryson goes on the run. Captain Lochley is badly injured during an attack by the souls that have escaped from the Soul Sphere. Her own soul enters the sphere for a brief period, and a soul inside tells her that their race are divided in two: sane souls and insane souls. Their race were on the verge of evolving into a higher form of life, and were about to leave their bodies behind when the Soul Hunters (alerted by the imminent death of so many bodies) arrived to take them. They have been trapped inside the sphere ever since.

Lochley's soul returns to its body and, shortly afterwards, thousands of Soul Hunter ships arrive. Through their representative already on the station, they give Captain Lochley an ultimatum: return the Soul Sphere or they will take it by force. Bryson, meanwhile, has holed up near the reactors, where the souls take control and set the station to explode. They will die, but they will have the satisfaction of taking large numbers of Soul Hunters with them.

Lochley, Garibaldi and the Soul Hunter locate Bryson and the Soul Sphere near the reactors. Attempts to reason with him and to kill him fail, and so the Soul Hunter offers the souls a bargain: his people will seek a way of releasing the souls from their torment if they will cease attempting to blow up the station. He offers to act as a bridge between the souls and the Soul Hunters by abandoning his body and allowing his soul to live inside the sphere. The souls agree, and relinquish their grip on the reactor. The Soul Hunters take the

Soul Sphere back to their own world, with their brother inside.

The 'B' Plot: A holo-brothel has opened up in Babylon 5: an environment in which punters dressed in special 'interactive' suits can experience sex with whoever they wish, courtesy of holographic technology. Captain Lochley discovers its existence from a dissatisfied customer and sets Zack to close it down, but the brothel owner's lawyer serves various legal papers and restraining orders on Lochley, accusing her of harassment and restraint of trade. The brothel is blown up by Lochley during the battle against the souls.

The Arc: None whatsoever.

Observations: Mr Garibaldi has taken over the day-to-day running of Edgars Industries, is sober and is based on Mars. Captain Lochley now commands Babylon 5. Sheridan and Delenn are on Minbar.

Martin Sheen was originally asked to play Dr Bryson, but asked if he could play the Soul Hunter when he read the script.

The script was originally titled 'The Well of Souls'.

The end theme has been replaced with a piece of 'lounge music' written by Chris Franke for the brothel scenes.

Dialogue to Rewind For: The Soul Hunters' creed: 'No heaven. Nothing beyond. Only the dark, impenetrable wall of death.'

Ships That Pass in the Night: The ship that attacks Bryson's team in the pre-title sequence is attracted by the warning emitted by the violated Whispering Gallery. It's almost certainly a Soul Hunter vessel, although not of a type we have seen before.

Other Worlds: The Soul Hunter suggests to the souls that his people will 'return' the Soul Sphere to the Soul Hunters' own world. This strongly indicates that the devastated world we see in the opening sequence is actually a Soul Hunter world.

We also get to see visions of Rauga – a world now depopulated by the Soul Hunters.

I've Seen That Face Before: Ian McShane (Dr Bryson) is a British actor best known at the moment for his recurring role as the antique-dealer detective Lovejoy. His film career is also reasonably impressive: look for him in particular in the film *Gangster* with Richard Burton.

Martin Sheen (the first Soul Hunter) has a film career ranging from the sublime (*Apocalypse Now*) to the ridiculous (*Spawn*).

Wayne Alexander, who appears as the first alien from the Soul Sphere to talk to Dr Bryson, previously played Jack the Ripper (episode 221 – 'Comes the Inquisitor'), a Narn (episode 320 – 'And the Rock Cried Out, No Hiding Place'), Lorien (the first six episodes of season 4), a Drazi (episode 418 – 'Intersections in Real Time') and a Drakh (episode 517 – 'Movements of Fire and Shadow') in the series.

Accidents Will Happen: Mr Garibaldi tells Dr Bryson that his work is being funded to the tune of around 2 million credits per year, but then goes on to talk about 'dollar amounts' in the ledgers.

'The amount of energy and equipment necessary to generate a three-dimensional image like that isn't portable,' Lochley tells Zack. So, how come Warren Keffler gets a three-dimensional-image letter from his girlfriend in episode 201 ('Points of Departure')?

This whole business of the souls taking over holograms makes no sense whatsoever. A hologram is a projection of light. If a Cary Grant movie had been playing in the Babylon 5 cinema, would the souls have taken over Cary Grant's image? If Zooty and Rebo's *New Sons of the Desert* had been playing on Babcom, would their images have been taken over too? How were the holograms supposed to touch, as they were seen doing? It's scientific nonsense, compounded by the fact that Captain Lochley's holographic image is clearly seen to have a shadow.

Questions Raised: Bryson tells Garibaldi that he has been looking for what he has found for twenty years. How did he know about it?

A Call To Arms

Transmission Number: Not Applicable
Production Number: TNTCF4

Written by: J Michael Straczynski
Directed by: Mike Vejar

Dureena Nafeel: Carrie Dobro
Galen: Peter Woodward
Samuel Drake: Tony Maggio
Captain Leonard Anderson: Tony Todd
Drazi: Ron Campbell

Plot: Almost flawless: a balls-to-the-wall SF adventure with no distractions, no subtleties and a crashing, ticking score that serves to distance the movie from its predecessors.

The 'A' Plot: It's the fifth anniversary of the Interstellar Alliance. President John Sheridan has put Michael Garibaldi in charge of a construction project: the reverse engineering of Vorlon and Minbari technology in order to construct a new fleet of ships. Together they set out to look over the first two ships at their secret construction yard, but their White Star is followed by a spy device reporting back to Galen, a Technomage hidden away with others of his kind. When they arrive the project co-ordinator – Samuel Drake – reports that there have been some problems with the development of the vehicles. While Garibaldi attempts to sort the problems out, a message arrives for Sheridan from Delenn, but when he attempts to view it all he sees is a flickering pattern of images.

Sheridan falls asleep, and dreams of a burning planet where he is confronted by Galen, the Technomage who had been tracking his White Star earlier on (and who, it turns out, sent the vision to Sheridan disguised as a message from Delenn). Galen alerts Sheridan to the fact that the burning planet is called Daltron 7, and that it has been destroyed as a test of some kind by unnamed aliens.

On Babylon 5, an alien woman named Dureena Nafeel arrives. She appears to be a thief, and attempts to make contact with the local Thieve's Guild. Knocked unconscious by a Guild member, she also has a vision of Daltron 7 and Galen.

At the secret construction yard the new ships (the *Excalibur* and the *Victory*) are being tested. While watching the firepower demonstration, Sheridan finds himself hallucinating that he is on the planet the Technomages are using as a refuge. There he watches Galen argue with his colleagues. Galen then tells Sheridan that the Drakh are preparing to move, and will start their war by attacking Earth. He ends by showing Sheridan the faces of three others who will join him in his quest to stop the Drakh – a human male, a Drazi male and a female alien of an unknown race. He also hints that Sheridan should start his quest on Babylon 5. When Sheridan awakes, he heads straight for the station in a White Star ship.

On Babylon 5, Sheridan gives Lochley sketches he has made of the three faces he saw in the vision. One of them – the alien female – is picked up by security pretty quickly. It is Dureena Nafeel, the thief who has been hallucinating Daltron 7, and she blames Sheridan for the destruction of her world by the Shadows during the Shadow War. Another – the human male – appears within a few hours. It is Captain Anderson, an Earthforce captain. The Drazi fails to appear.

The three of them head out to the secret construction yard where the new ships are being developed, and steal them. They then head for Daltron 7, where they find that the planet has been devastated by something disturbingly similar to the Shadow deathcloud used in the Shadow War. They pick up a distress call of Drazi origin and, heading down to the planet in a shuttle, discover a dead Drazi – the one who was meant to be part of their group. He has left behind a testament of sorts explaining how he arrived at Daltron 7 as it was being attacked by the deathcloud.

Sheridan and his ships encounter the deathcloud themselves, and are attacked by Drakh warships. They flee, and Sheridan alerts Captain Lochley to the fact that the deathcloud is headed towards Earth. He also tells Garibaldi, but Garibaldi has his own problems – Samuel Drake has turned out to be a Drakh agent.

The Drakh and their deathcloud arrive in Earth orbit and Sheridan and Anderson lead a fleet of Earthforce ships against them. The deathcloud appears invulnerable to their weapons, and so rams his ship into its controlling node, causing its destruction. The retreating Drakh poison Earth's atmosphere with a biogenetic plague, one that will take five years to accustom itself to humanity before wiping it out. Earth is completely quarantined, its only hope a search amongst left-over First One ruins for a cure. The Drakh also hit the secret construction dock for the new ships as they withdraw, wiping out any possibility that new ones can be built.

The Arc: This TV movie acts as a scene-setter for the spin-off series *Crusade*. Both Dureena Nafeel and Galen will be regular characters in that series. J Michael Straczynski has said that, had he attempted to show the seeding of Earth with the Shadow virus in an episode of *Babylon 5* then he wouldn't be able to do it properly, and so he made the decision to show these events in a TV movie.

The Shadow deathcloud was last seen in episode 406 ('Into the Fire'). The Drakh were last seen in episode 518 ('The Fall of Centauri Prime').

The 'telepath crisis' has only recently finished, with great loss of life. There are hints towards the end of season five that such a crisis is brewing, and we can probably assume that it coincides with Lyta Alexander's return to the solar system to find out how well Garibaldi has been supporting the telepath resistance (as set up in episode 519 – 'The Wheel of Fire').

The Technomages were previously seen in episode 203 ('The Geometry of Shadows') where they left known space so that their knowledge would not fall into the wrong hands during the Shadow War. They use superior technology to give the impression of magic.

Observations: The jumpgate CGI effect has been redone to make it more dramatic. This presumably indicates that jumpgate technology has altered in the handful of years since episode 521 ('Objects at Rest'). Odd, then, that Sheridan's White Star in episode 522 ('Sleeping in Light') used the old effect.

We're told that leftover Shadow technology has been used a few times since the Shadows went 'beyond the Rim'.

Dialogue to Rewind For: Sheridan's answer-screen message: 'Hello, this is the President. I'm busy with affairs of state and can't come to the link right now. At the chime leave a message and I'll get back to you at the earliest opportunity.'

Captain Anderson on the Drakh fighters: 'They're either Drakh or the weirdest looking pizza delivery trucks I've ever seen.'

Dureena Nafeel: 'There's no sense belonging to a secret group if you tell everybody about it.'

Ships That Pass In The Night: The new Interstellar Alliance ships (the *Victory* and the *Excalibur*) are based on a reverse engineering of Vorlon and Minbari technology. They possess a gravitetic propulsion system (whatever that is) and a skin that can repel 80 per cent of incident energy. Their primary weapon system is so powerful that it renders the ship immobile and powerless for at least a minute after firing.

The Earth Alliance destroyers *Charon* and *Hermes* both make an appearance. The Drakh motherships and fighters also reappear, and they appear to have some previously unseen ships with them.

Other Worlds: Zander Prime was destroyed by the Shadows during the Shadow War – it was Dureena Nafeel's home planet. Daltron 7 is devastated by the Drakh. Trepani VII also gets a mention.

Culture Shock: Drazi have a pouch under the left arm that's a part of their reproductive organs. Drazi smugglers hide things there if they don't want them found.

I've Seen That Face Before: Peter Woodward, who plays Galen, is the son of well known British actor Edward Woodward (who is himself best known for the film *The Wicker Man*, the British TV series *Callan* and the American TV series *The Equalizer*).

Tony Todd, who plays Captain Anderson, will perhaps be recognised for his work in *Star Trek: Deep Space 9* as a future

Jake Sisko, in *Star Trek: Voyager* as a Hirogen, in *Hercules: The Legendary Journeys* as a gladiator and as the eponymous hero of the film *Candyman* and its sequel.

I don't need to tell you who Wayne Alexander is. He plays the various Drakh seen during the course of the episode.

Questions Raised: Drake/Drakh, Drakh/Drake. Was anybody really surprised by Drake turning out to be a traitor?

THE BOOKS

Jeanne Cavelos, writer of the seventh *Babylon 5* novel, *The Shadow Within*, was the person responsible for getting the books off the ground in the first place. 'I was immediately drawn to the series when it came on the air,' she says. 'I loved the idea of a five-year storyline. That seemed an incredible idea to me. When the pilot came on I was still working at Dell Publishing as a senior editor. I went to the editor-in-chief and told her we should do a series of *B5* novels. She agreed, and we started the series. When I left Dell, they asked me to continue editing the manuscripts as a freelancer.' She adds, 'I think the books are growing as the series grows. We're all finding the tone of the series and learning some of the major themes that we should be exploring. In the beginning, the authors had very little to go on. The authors of the books only have the episodes to go by. They do not have inside informa-tion. I think a few of them had a couple of questions answered by JMS by e-mail. The authors also had a bible to consult, but it was written at the time of the pilot and had limited, dated information. All of the books have been written in about three to eight weeks, and have been edited by me in three days. Any changes done in the editing phase have to be done quickly, usually over the phone. That's why you may catch errors or inconsistencies. A lot of editing, as with many media tie-ins, I think, involves filling in descriptions, trying to make the dialogue and actions consistent with the charac-ters, trying to eliminate the dreaded nits, and then some more standard editing issues: making the plot as suspenseful and exciting as possible, and making the writing strong and vivid. JMS has become more involved in choosing the authors for the books and in the book series in general. I think this is helping to improve the books and make them more of a reflection of what is important and distinctive about *B5*.'

Following the publication of the ninth book, Kathryn M Drennen's *To Dream in the City of Sorrows*, the books were put on hiatus for a while. It was obvious that, with perhaps three exceptions, the books were written too quickly and with no real feel for the strengths of the series and the voices of the characters. The licence to publish *Babylon 5* books had been issued on a three-book-by-three-book basis, and for book numbers 10 to 12 J Michael Straczynski passed the licence to Del Rey.

Statements from J Michael Straczynski indicate that, following the first three Del Rey novels (a Psi Corps trilogy written by John Gregory Keyes) he was planning a Centauri Prime trilogy. He also hinted that he might want one day to tell the story of Kosh in the novels.

The Shadow Within

Published by: Dell
Book Number: 7

Written by: Jeanne Cavelos

Date: The book is set between November and January 2256, placing it before the series proper actually starts.

Plot: A book that's a *real* book, rather than just a TV tie-in knock-off. Jeanne Cavelos has put her experience to good use and has produced an absorbing and affecting science-fiction novel. If it had the zeal and depth of Jim Mortimore's *Clark's Law* then it would be brilliant; as it is, it's just excellent.

The 'A' Plot: Anna Sheridan, an archaeologist, is investigating a strange artefact found during an excavation on an alien planet – an artefact that appears to be half biological and half mechanical – when it explodes, driving every telepath rated P5 or less within a three-mile radius into a catatonic state. An expedition is mounted to the planet believed to be the source of these artefacts and, on the eve of her wedding anniversary, Anna is recruited to join it by her boss, Dr Chang. She soon realises that the expedition is not under Chang's control: a Psi Corps operative named Donne is present on the ship, as is an Earthforce archaeolinguist named Morden. They arrive at the planet – designated Alpha Omega 3 – and start investigating the alien ruins they find. Things begin to go wrong straightaway: their equipment is sabotaged, artefacts go missing and, eventually, so do most of the expedition. Anna Sheridan discovers that the expedition has another, more sinister reason for its existence: an alien ship of advanced design was discovered on Mars three years before during an archaeological dig, and was rescued by another ship of the same type. A beacon planted on the first ship led Earthforce to Alpha Omega 3, and they encouraged Interplanetary Expeditions to mount the exploration in an attempt to discover what was going on. Anna and Morden find out that the majority of the expedition members have been captured by the recently reawoken inhabitants of the planet, and are being turned into biological components for their alien technology. Anna attempts to activate one of the telepathic bombs in order to kill herself and Morden, thus saving them from the clutches of the aliens, but Morden succumbs to their blandishments and stops her.

The 'B' Plot: John Sheridan takes command of the Earthforce vessel *Agamemnon* and discovers it to be run by a shoddy and dispirited crew. Sheridan schedules as many drills and inspections as possible, and does his best to instil some kind of team spirit, but he finds resistance at every turn. Earthforce instruct him to use the *Agamemnon* to monitor a rendezvous between a Narn transport ship and a Homeguard vessel, during which a consignment of explosives is to be transferred to the Homeguard ship. Earthforce believe that the explosives will be used to destroy the Babylon 5 space station during its commissioning ceremony, and Sheridan is ordered to stop the Homeguard ship from getting to Babylon 5. Despite inefficiency and sabotage, he pulls his crew together, unmasks the saboteur and destroys the Homeguard ship with only moments to spare.

The 'C' Plot: Commander Jeffrey Sinclair is preparing for the commissioning of his new command – the Babylon 5 space station – when the Minbari Ambassador Delenn contacts him. She tells him that an Earth ship is approaching an uninhabited planet on the rim of the galaxy, and asks Sinclair to have it recalled. He tries, but Earthforce refuse.

The Arc: The book explains the background to the events we already know from episodes 308 ('Messages From Earth') and 322 ('Z'ha'dum') – the Shadow ship on Mars, the waking of the Shadows and the involvement of the crew of the *Icarus*

– without adding any more important information. What it does instead is to deepen our understanding: what before was a series of facts now has an emotional resonance for us, as we have come to know the people involved.

The Shadows appear to have weapons that can be used against telepaths – bombs that can drive them into catatonic states when activated by mental effort.

The Shadows have 'servants' on Z'ha'dum – humanoid aliens who may be the same as the aliens who appear in issues 5 to 8 of the *Babylon 5* comic ('Shadows, Past and Present').

The Homeguard previously appeared in episodes 107 ('The War Prayer') and 111 ('Survivors').

Observations: The *Icarus* is said to have had a crew of 130 and a scientific team numbering ten. This accords with the number given in episode 217 ('In the Shadow of Z'ha'dum').

Dr Morden is an archaeolinguist. His wife and daughter died when terrorists blew up the jumpgate at Io, destroying the spaceship they were travelling in.

The Shadow ship on Mars was discovered some three years before, putting it around 2253. This agrees with episode 308 ('Messages From Earth'), which is set in early to mid-2260 and states that the Shadow ship was discovered on Mars seven years before.

'I love the show,' Jeanne Cavelos, the novel's author, says, 'and I thought I could contribute something to it. Also, as the freelance editor of the *B5* series of novels, I felt that we should do books that could not be episodes of the series, that would do things episodes could not do. JMS felt similarly, and he wrote an open letter to be given to potential *B5* book authors. In it, he suggested possible backstories that could be made into novels. He mentioned many possibilities, one of which was Anna Sheridan's story on the *Icarus*. That intrigued me, and I started to think about what might have happened.

'I had eight weeks to write this,' she continues. 'I believe I'm the first author who had the opportunity to talk to JMS in the early stages of writing the manuscript. I felt this was necessary, since I was writing about a time period not covered by the series, and JMS was willing. I asked him questions for about a half hour, mainly things like, "Is it OK if I do this?" (for example, Is it OK if I put someone from Psi Corps aboard the *Icarus*?). And he told me whether it was or not. JMS also helped in getting me an early copy of the script of "*Z'ha'dum*", which I didn't even know about when I wrote the proposal for my novel. I wrote the proposal I think near the end of 1995, then was asked in August 1996 to write the book. Only when I started contacting my *B5* trivia experts did I learn of the upcoming episode regarding Anna Sheridan, which was not scheduled to air in the United States until after my manuscript was due. I was in quite a panic for a while, until JMS circumvented red tape and sent me the script. I also had a friend send me a copy of the episode taped off British TV about a month later, as soon as it aired there.

'I'm proud to say, as JMS has noted on the Internet, that he made not one single note on my manuscript – no corrections, no changes.'

Koshisms: After arriving at Z'ha'dum and watching as the humans wake the Shadows: 'The avalanche begins.'

Ships That Pass in the Night: The *Galatea* was John Sheridan's first command as captain. The *Athena* is an Earthforce ship that took part in the Earth–Minbari War. The *De Soto* is an explorer vessel, and the *Curie* gets a mention as well.

'One point of interest,' says Jeanne Cavelos, 'is that I gave almost every new ship mentioned in the book a female name, since I thought ships with female names were under-represented on the show.'

Other Worlds: Theta Omega 2, Anfras, Alpha Omega 3 (better known as Z'ha'dum).

Culture Shock: An extinct alien race known as the J/Lai are an offshoot of the Brakiri, while little is known about another extinct alien race known as the Krich. The Kandarian language gets a name check. The Anfran come from the planet Anfras, while Piridian sculpture and Gigmosian ceremonies are both mentioned. 'The Gigmosians are based in part on characteristics of my iguana, Igmoe,' Jeanne Cavelos admits.

Literary, Mythological and Historical References: The book is prefaced with a quotation from TS Eliot's poem 'Burnt Norton' from his *Four Quartets* collection (but see **Accidents Will Happen** below). Thomas Mann is also quoted at the beginning of another section.

There is a brief reference to a poem entitled 'High Flight', by John Gillespie Magee Jnr. In the book, a character thinks of a spacecraft slipping the surly bonds of gravity. The poem talks about an aircraft slipping 'the surly bonds of Earth'.

The Kandarian language is a reference to Sam Raimi's film *The Evil Dead*.

I've Seen That Face Before: Morden takes a major role in the book (his first name appears to be 'Doctor'). 'I asked JMS if Morden already had a first name,' Jeanne Cavelos recalls, 'since I needed one for him. When JMS said no, I asked if I could give him one. JMS said he always thought of Morden as Morden, without any first name. He didn't really want Morden to have one. This posed a problem, since I wanted to portray the growing friendship and closeness between Anna and Morden. So I invented the whole idea of the archaeologists going by their last names to get around this.'

Accidents Will Happen: The opening quotation from TS Eliot is incorrect. The quotation (from the poem 'Burnt Norton') as printed in the book is, 'The present and the past are perhaps both present in the future and the future is contained in the past.' The correct version is, 'Time present and time past are both perhaps present in time future / And time future contained in time past.'

Questions Raised: If the Shadows have weapons that can drive telepaths into catatonic states, why do they never use them in the Shadow War?

Who actually woke the Shadows? The IPC expedition or someone beforehand?

Personal Agendas

Published by: Dell
Book Number: 8

Written by: Al Sarrantonio

Date: The book is set before episode 404 ('Falling Toward Apotheosis') but after episode 403 ('The Summoning'), indicating that it occurs around February 2261.

Plot: This book is an embarrassment. It lacks everything – style, wit, characterisation, plot, enjoyability … It has 67 chapters in 207 pages, meaning that each chapter lasts around three pages – and feels shorter. The best thing about it is the cover, and that's not saying very much.

The 'A' Plot: Five Narn are smuggled to Centauri Prime in an attempt to rescue G'Kar from captivity. G'Kar discovers this, and knows that they cannot be allowed to succeed if he is to fulfil his side of the bargain and kill Emperor Cartagia in exchange for the freeing of the Narn Homeworld. He tells Londo of their presence, and forces Londo to promise that they will be stopped but not killed. The Narn fail in their first attempt to free G'Kar, and so kidnap Londo and attempt to make an exchange. Vir manages to save Londo by persuading the Narn that G'Kar should be kept in captivity for the greater good of the Narn Homeworld.

The 'B' Plot: Vir is invited to a party to be held by the parents of his bride-to-be – Lyndisty. He is scared to go, because he knows that their marriage date will be announced at the party and he doesn't want to go through with it. All his ploys to get out of going fail, but he manages to avoid the party by tracking down G'Kar's supposed rescuers and persuading them to free Londo.

The 'C' Plot: Garibaldi, Ivanova and Franklin travel to Centauri Prime, disguised as Centauri, in an attempt to free G'Kar. They succeed, but G'Kar persuades them to return him to his cell. Reluctantly they comply, and are then captured by the crack Narn team who are trying to rescue G'Kar themselves. They are freed along with Londo when Vir persuades the Narn that their purpose would be better served by leaving G'Kar where he is.

The 'D' Plot: Sheridan is bored, and so he and Delenn try to track down some toy smugglers (smugglers of toys, rather than very small smugglers). In order to spice things up, they dress up as spies in trench coats and hats – Sheridan having been reading some James Bond books. The toy smugglers turn out to be smuggling weapons in their toys, and Sheridan and Delenn are kidnapped by them. They escape by using the dismantled toys to build a bomb, and take the smugglers prisoner.

Observations: We're told that Babylon 5 is 75 human light years from Centauri Prime, and 12.2 human light years from the Narn Homeworld. This fits in with episodes 107 ('The War Prayer') and 112 ('By Any Means Necessary'), thus proving that, whatever else Al Sarrantonio might be, at least he does his research.

Culture Shock: The Trivorians get a name check. They were previously mentioned in Neil Barrett Jnr's book, *The Touch of Your Shadow, the Whisper of Your Name*.

Literary, Mythological and Historical References: There're a lot of references to Ian Fleming's masterspy James Bond in the book, particularly in the Sheridan/Delenn subplot, but they barely go beyond a simple name check. It's pretty obvious that Sarrantonio has never read a James Bond book in his life – just seen the films.

I've Seen That Face Before: We get guest appearances from Emperor Cartagia and Vir's wife-to-be, Lyndisty.

Al Sarrantonio, the writer of the book, has previously written some 25 novels and has been nominated for several prestigious awards. How?

Accidents Will Happen: It's tempting to list the entire book as an unfortunate accident. Perhaps the author had only twelve hours to write it or something.

Ivanova fails to recognise the term SMERSH (the secret organisation that James Bond fought against) even though it is a contraction of a Russian term ('*Smiert Spionam*' – 'Death to Spies').

To Dream in the City of Sorrows

Published by: Dell
Book Number: 9

Written by: Kathryn M Drennan

Date: The main bulk of the book occurs from January 2259 to late in the same year, although it has a wraparound prologue and epilogue that take place some time between August and December 2260.

Plot: There's a series of events that occur one after the other, but nothing as ambitious as a coherent plot.

The 'A' Plot: Jeffrey Sinclair has been reassigned from Babylon 5 to Minbar as the new Ambassador, but pretty soon he realises that the people who sent him and the people who received him both have their own agendas. President Clark and his people just wanted Sinclair out of the way so he wouldn't make trouble about the assassination of President Santiago, while the Minbari leader Jenimer believes Sinclair to be the prophesied 'Minbari not born of Minbar' who will lead the Anla'shok – the organisation set up a thousand years ago by the semimythical Minbari leader Valen to fight against the Shadows. Against the wishes of the Warrior caste, and much to his own surprise, Sinclair accepts the position, and immediately throws open the doors of the Anla'shok not only to the Worker caste but also to humans. He is briefed on the Shadows and their return, and is shocked at how much he had not been told. Sheridan sets up rigorous training courses for the Anla'shok, and is proud when the new students pass their training and begin to operate out in the galaxy at large. Increasingly unhappy at the way he is becoming desk-bound and restricted, he goes against the wishes of the Minbari and the Vorlons by leading a mission to repair a time rift that the Shadows wish to use to go back in time and destroy all opposition to their plans. The mission is successful, but Sinclair's girlfriend, Catherine Sakai, is lost in time.

The 'B' Plot: Marcus Cole, head of a mining colony on Arisia, is upset when he discovers that his brother William has travelled to Minbar. When Marcus is visited at the mining colony by William he finds that his brother has joined a semimystical Minbari organisation known as the Anla'shok. An attack on the colony by mysterious and powerful aliens known as the Shadows leads to William Cole's death. Marcus travels to Minbar to join the Anla'shok and takes part in a mission to heal a rift in time that the Shadows wish to use for their own purposes.

The 'C' Plot: Catherine Sakai, fiancée of Jeffrey Sinclair, is on a lone planetary expedition when she discovers that the surface of the planet Ymir has been destroyed. Later she travels to Minbar to be with Sinclair, but finds him in charge of a semimystical Minbari organisation known as the Anla'shok. She joins too, in order to give herself something to do, and, during a mission to heal a rift in time that the Shadows are attempting to use, her ship is caught in the time rift and lost in the past.

The Arc: It's basically the story of Sinclair after he left Babylon 5 and before he becomes Valen, so in a sense the entire book is arc-related material. That said, we discover little that we did not already know from the series.

Observations: References are made to the first four issues ('In Darkness Find Me') and the second four issues ('Shadows Past and Present') of the *Babylon 5* comic, as well as episodes 106 ('Mind War'), 108 ('And the Sky Full of Stars'), 117 ('Legacies'), 120 ('Babylon Squared'), 122 ('Chrysalis'), 211 ('All Alone in the Night') and 316 and 317 ('War Without End' Parts One and Two).

Marcus's first visit to B5 took place during episode 211 ('All Alone in the Night') at the height of the Streib crisis.

We discover here that the Vorlon ambassador to Minbar (as seen in episodes 316 and 317 ('War Without End' Parts One and Two) is named Ulkesh Naranek (as opposed to Kosh Naranek, of course).

The Minbari word for Rangers is *Anla'shok*. Ranger One is *Anla'shok na*.

Ranger One and *Entil'zha* are not synonymous terms. Ranger One is the title of the leader of the Rangers, while *Entil'zha* is an honorific term reserved for Valen's successor.

Many jumpgates were built 7,000 years before by a nameless alien race who have since vanished (possibly one of the First Ones, although nobody ever mentions this in the series).

Diridium gas is a valuable natural commodity.

The title of the book is taken from a line of dialogue said by Jenimer, the Minbari leader: 'It is said that to dream in the City of Sorrows is to dream of a better future.'

Sinclair's brother's name is Malcolm. Marcus Cole's brother's name is William.

The events of this book are a late add-on to the arc, rather than an always-planned part of it. Shortly after the first showing of episodes 316 and 317 ('War Without End' Parts One and Two), which follows on chronologically from the events shown in this book, J Michael Straczynski said that Catherine Sakai and Jeffrey Sinclair split up when he went to Minbar. 'Sakai certainly wouldn't have wanted to get tied down to life on Minbar,' he said, 'and Sinclair knew that his life would be difficult now with the Rangers, so they parted ways.' This statement contradicts what occurs in this book.

Koshisms: 'It is important to remember: every door has two sides.'

'It is wise for the arrow to remember it does not choose the target.'

To Sinclair: 'You are what we say.'

To Sinclair: 'You must forget what is personal. Concentrate on the cause.'

'It is important to select information; too much information can be harmful.'

Other Worlds: Arisia III (see **Literary, Mythological and Historical References** below). Planet UTC43-02C, otherwise known as Fensalir. Planet UTC45-03A, otherwise known as Ymir. Planet UTC5-03B, otherwise known as Glasir. Planet

UTC67-02C, otherwise known as Mjollnir. Planet UTC59-02B, otherwise known as Skirnir.

Literary, Mythological and Historical References: Sinclair has a copy of *The Meditations of Marcus Aurelius* with him on Minbar. Marcus Aurelius (Marcus Aurelius Antoninus, formerly known as Marcus Annius Verus) was born in AD 121 and became one of the most respected of Roman emperors. His *Meditations* is a collection of his thoughts, philosophy and beliefs, and is one of the great works of mankind.

The planet Arisia III is probably a reference to the books of EE 'Doc' Smith, in which the planet Arisia is home to the Arisians (prototypes of the Vorlons in many ways).

Sinclair quotes the Austro-German poet Rilke at one stage, and both he and Catherine Sakai seem to quote Alfred, Lord Tennyson, at every opportunity.

I've Seen That Face Before: The book contains guest appearances by Rathenn (the Minbari who first appeared in issue 1 of the *Babylon 5* comic ('In Darkness Find Me') and later in episodes 316 ('War Without End' Part One) and 319 ('Grey 17 is Missing')), Catherine Sakai, Shai Alyt Neroon (the Minbari leader who appeared in issue 4 of the *Babylon 5* comic and has now been named as Jenimer) and Ulkesh Naranek. The Minbari Turval and Durhan appear: they also turn up in episode 505 ('Learning Curve'). Durhan is also mentioned in episode 319 ('Grey 17 is Missing').

William Cole (brother of Marcus) also appears. He has been mentioned before, but not seen.

The writer, Kathryn Drennan, is married to J Michael Straczynski.

Dark Genesis

Published by: Del Rey
Book Number: Officially 10, but it's a new publisher and the design has changed to reflect a fresh start

Written by: J Gregory Keyes

Date: The book starts in 2115 and ends around 2189

Plot: Given that this novel is the first in a trilogy that purports to tell the true history of Psi Corps, from its inception until 'now', the plot of the first book is, of necessity, a little disconnected. It takes place over some eighty years or so, starting with the detection of the first few telepaths and ending with the birth of Alfred Bester, but large chunks of the book are spent telling the stories of a handful of people.

The 'A' Plot: The book's primary focus is Kevin Vacit, who begins working for Senator Lee Crawford, head of the Earth Alliance's Metasensory Regulation Authority (MRA), in the year 2132. The MRA has been set up to monitor and control the increasing number of telepaths that are being discovered on Earth, and, given humanity's distrust of this new, strange breed, the head of the MRA has to be a normal, rather than a telepath. The MRA takes its responsibilities so seriously that it is opposed by the Resistance, a movement made up of telepaths who attempt to disrupt its operations: helping telepaths who do not want to be controlled by the MRA to escape and bombing MRA facilities. Vacit takes over the MRA around 2156, just as it is in the process of becoming Psi Corps, but unknown to almost everyone Vacit is himself a telepath and is actively supporting the Resistance. He is aware, from alien devices discovered some years before on Mars by Interplanetary Expeditions and from telepathic evidence picked up at an alien landing site in the Antarctic, that telepaths will one day be a weapon in a great war, and he is hoping that the conflict between Psi Corps and the Resistance will lead to stronger telepaths in the future. In 2189, Vacit becomes aware that more alien artefacts may exist on Venus, and so mounts a mission to the planet. While there he is intercepted by, and taken on board, a Vorlon spacecraft. As a result of his encounter with the Vorlons Vacit decides to pull all the telepaths on Earth into Psi Corps, for only an organisation of them can stand against the war he knows will come – a war that will encompass the galaxy. He decides to destroy the Resistance that he helped keep going, but first he ensures that his grandson, whom he had placed in the protection of a friend in the Resistance, is safe. Unfortunately he can do this only at the expense of the life of his daughter.

The 'B' Plot: A group of teenage telepaths – Blood, Monkey, Mercy, Teal and Smoke – have been using their telepathic powers to set up a fake religion in the wilderness of Alaska and use it for the gratification of their desires, but the increasing pressure on telepaths to conform forces them to abandon their temple and move deeper and deeper under-cover. When they can run no more they make an offer to Senator Lee Crawford, that they will come out of the shadows if he will give them positions of power. Monkey disagrees, and withdraws from the group, taking with him a small child they had adopted after his mother died. Blood sacrifices her life to save that of Lee Crawford, and Monkey – whose real name is Jack O'Hannlon – goes on to head up the Telepath Resistance. The small child grows up into Kevin Vacit, first head of Psi Corps, and he asks Monkey to bring up his daughter Fiona. Monkey is eventually killed by Psi Corps and the leadership of the Resistance passes to Fiona and her partner Matthew Dexter. They are also eventually killed by Psi Corps, but their son – named Alfred Bester by his grandfather – lives on.

The 'C' Plot: Mysterious aliens named Vorlons have been fighting a war with an evil enemy for millennia. Telepaths are an important weapon in this war, and so two Vorlons came to Earth between 2059 and 2062 in order to alter the genetic make-up of certain humans so as to produce telepaths. The telepaths were created; one of the Vorlons died, in Antarctica, but the other remained on Venus, waiting to be found. When finally discovered by humanity, it carried out its last duty, placing a hidden compulsion inside one particular human, and left.

The Arc: As we already knew, the Vorlons created telepaths on many worlds in order to act as weapons in the war against the Shadows. The telepaths on Earth were created around 2060 by genetic manipulation carried out by two Vorlons. One of them died on Earth; the other travelled to Venus where it waited to be discovered. When the trail of clues was followed, and its hiding place located, it placed further instructions into the mind of one of its discoverers – Lyta

Alexander's grandmother. When the Shadows finally revealed themselves again, those instructions would cause the carrier to seek out the Vorlons for further work to be done. This explains the strange compulsion Lyta Alexander felt which dragged her to the Vorlon homeworld, and sets up the further alterations they made in her as shown in episode 507 ('Secrets of the Soul').

In passing, this book introduces us to the ancestors of some of the characters who later turn up in the series itself. Blood, the rebel who becomes a loyal MRA member, is actually Desa Alexander. Her daughter is Brenna Alexander, her granddaughter is Michelle Alexander, her great-granddaughter is Natasha Alexander. An Ironheart appears as a background character, and Alfred Bester turns up, newly born, at the very end.

Observations: The book is subtitled 'The Birth of the Psi Corps'.

There's a small cross-reference between the events of this book and those shown in issue 11 of the *Babylon 5* comic, 'Psi Corps and You'. Earth Alliance President Elizabeth Robinson appears in both, and she makes reference in the book to her life having been saved by a man named William Karges – events shown in the comic.

Koshisms: 'I am here. I have always been here.'

'The mirror never sees itself. The reflection never is itself.'

'Evolution crawls to imperfection. It ends in extinction.'

To Natasha Alexander: 'It will be you, if the Darkness comes soon, or one in your line, if the Darkness comes later. You, or the echo of you, will hear the call, and you will come to us, and we will finish the work we began in you.'

Literary, Mythological and Historical References: Kevin Vacit is familiar with the SF books of Alfred Bester, and names his grandson Alfred Bester in acknowledgement of this.

THE COMICS

In October 1995, after the last 'regular' issue of the DC *Babylon 5* comic was issued but before the 1997–8 four-issue comic 'In Valen's Name', J Michael Straczynski promised more *B5* comics as one-shots and miniseries. Tim DeHaas was to do one set during the Earth–Minbari War and there was to be a four-issue mini tentatively entitled 'The Book of the War', featuring the new Ranger character.

Based on what Straczynski has said, the assumption has to be that the planned Earth–Minbari-war comic transmutated (at least as a project) into the TV movie *In the Beginning* while the material introducing the new Ranger character (i.e. Marcus Cole) later turned up in the novel *To Dream in the City of Sorrows*.

'In Valen's Name'

Written by: J Michael Straczynski (Parts One and Two)
Peter David (based on a premise by J Michael Straczynski)
(Parts Three to Six)

Drawn by: Michael Collins (penciller)
David Roach (inker)

Plot: Interesting, but filled with unanswered questions and missed opportunities. The reappearance of Babylon 4 should have been the key to something much bigger than actually occurs. The main plot seems to be a thin excuse to allow flashbacks of Valen.

The 'A' Plot: At some time following the end of the Shadow War but before the War to Retake Earth starts up in earnest, Babylon 5 intercepts a signal from the vanished Babylon 4 station. It appears to have reappeared in 2260, having previously been sent back a thousand years into the past to become a base for the fight against the Shadows. Sheridan, Delenn, Ivanova and Garibaldi take a White Star ship to find out why it has returned. Managing to enter the massive hulk, they discover that ancient Minbari edifices have been built along the inside. The party are attacked by energy weapons fired by spacesuited figures, but manage to escape to Babylon 4's Command and Control section. There they discover two things: the station will fall into the atmosphere of the nearest planet within 72 hours and one of the aliens has just blown up their White Star. Mr Garibaldi discovers an ancient Minbari vessel in the bowels of the station and manages to get it working again just as a fleet of alien ships arrives. Sheridan attempts to hold off the fleet by using the ancient Minbari fighter, but ends up firing on them instead. The aliens attack the station, and are about to kill everyone when they recognise the name 'Delenn' (after Sheridan shouts it). The aliens – named the Tak'cha – venerate Valen as a prophet and great leader, and their records tell of a 'Delenn' whom he talked about. They too had been attracted to Babylon 4 when its distress call was received, as their holy books tell of its existence. Hostilities over, the Tak'cha agree to return the four adventurers to Babylon 5 as Babylon 4 burns up in the atmosphere of the unknown planet.

The 'B' Plot: While on Babylon 4, Delenn manages to access a record of the last War Against the Shadows left by Nukenn of the Religious caste and Rashok of the Warrior caste. Delenn discovers that the creatures who are attacking the station are the Tak'cha, a race who joined with Valen and the Minbari during the last War Against the Shadows but who were rejected by Valen when he could not tame their aggressive natures.

The 'C' Plot: A thousand years ago, during the War Against the Shadows, Valen attempted to prevent the war between the Minbari and humanity that was to come by leaving a message for Delenn. The Vorlons, however, warned him not to.

The Arc: Following the end of the last Shadow War, Babylon 4 was moved to a secret location to become a monument to what had occurred. 'In Valen's Name' gives us some indication of Jeffrey Sinclair's actions after he became Valen, of how he gave hope to the almost defeated Minbari and of how he pulled together an alliance of other races, but it hints at more than it tells.

As with Kathryn Drennan's *To Dream in the City of Sorrows,* there is an indication that Catherine Sakai also travelled back in time and was reunited with Jeffrey Sinclair.

Observations: This comic strip was first published in Titan's *The Official Babylon 5 Magazine* issues 3 to 8 (November 1997 to May 1998). DC Comics republished it in three parts, dated March, April and May 1998.

Ivanova's Life Lessons: 'Ivanova's Rule #34: Always make sure that whatever looks dead, stays dead, and will not have any ideas about not being dead at any time in the foreseeable future.'

Culture Shock: A race known as the Pakkel get a mention, and a race known as the Tak'cha take a starring role. They had joined in the original War Against the Shadows, but were thrown out by Valen when he discovered their warlike nature. The Yolu are also seen briefly – a Yolu representative appeared in episode 114 ('TKO').

Literary, Mythological and Historical References: In Part One, Ivanova quotes JBS Haldane's 'The universe is not only stranger than we imagine, it is stranger than we *can* imagine.'

I've Seen That Face Before: Nice to get a glimpse of one of the Zathras brothers, acting as Valen's most trusted friend.

Accidents Will Happen: Referring to Babylon 4, Garibaldi states, 'Twice before we almost didn't make it out.' Fair enough, but he went inside only once. He was left behind the second time.

The Yolu seen in this comic strip bears little resemblance to the one seen in episode 114 ('TKO').

In the fourth from last panel, Jeffrey Sinclair (as Valen) sends a message to the future. 'Delenn, Catherine, Susan, Michael . . .' he says, 'if any of you see this somehow . . . don't cry for me . . .' He then goes on to add, '. . . I've found her at long last . . . I've found her.' The only person he could have found, as far as we know, is Catherine Sakai, but he appears to be talking to her as well. In fact, the mention of her name four panels from the end is an oversight on the part of the writer and of J Michael Straczynski.

THE GAMES

'The Babylon Project'

Written by: Joseph Cochran (with additional material by Ronald Jarrell, Charles Ryan and Zeke Sparkes).

Date: The suggested events of the role-playing game are set between 2250 and 2259, placing it before the Shadow War gets started.

Plot: Well, that's up to you, isn't it?

The Arc: The example scenario included in *The Babylon Project* is tied into the Homeguard's attempts to destroy the Babylon stations. The Homeguard previously appeared in episodes 107 ('The War Prayer') and 111 ('Survivors'), while their destructive interest in the Babylon stations was referred to in the seventh *Babylon 5* novel, *The Shadow Within*.

Observations: Some dates of interest: the Centauri arrived in Earth's solar system in April 2155, and provided Earth with its own jumpgate technology in 2161. By 2220, Earth was involved in border skirmishes with both the Centauri and the Narn. The war with the Dilgar started in 2231.

The role-playing-game source book contains minor references to Jha'Dur (episode 109 – 'Deathwalker') and G'Sten (episode 220 – 'The Long, Twilight Struggle').

EarthGov has diplomatic ties with some sixty races and knows of around forty others.

Senator Calvin Natawe was the founder of the Babylon stations.

Babylon 1 was destroyed thanks to substandard building materials. Babylon 2 blew up, either by accident or thanks to a bomb. Babylon 3 was definitely destroyed by bombs.

The first name of Major Krantz (episodes 120 – 'Babylon Squared' – and 317 – 'War Without End' Part Two) is Gerald.

Earth in 2250-ish has sixteen colonies and eight military outposts.

Ships That Pass in the Night: Earth Alliance Starship *Eisenhower*, Earthforce Cruiser *Asia* (destroyed in 2169),

Earthforce Carrier *Avenger* (operational in 2170, so probably destroyed or decommissioned by the time the series commences), Narn transport *Ta'mazad*, Civilian Transport *No Strings Attached*.

Other Worlds: Proxima III, Tau Ceti IV, 61 Cygnus A II (otherwise known as the Signet outpost), Ross 128 IV and Orion VII are all Earth colonies. Sh'lek'k'tha is a Minbari world; Tr'es's'na another. Immolan V is a Centauri colony.

Culture Shock: A race known as the Koulani attacked the Earth colony at 61 Cygnus A II in 2169. Similarly, a race known as the Ch'lonas attacked the Earth colony at Ross 128 IV in 2170. Both of these attacks were just border skirmishes and did not lead to any major conflict.

The Drazi ceremonial conflict highlighted in episode 203 ('The Geometry of Shadows) is known as the *Dro'hannan*.

Minbari are given childhood names but choose new names when they reach the age of majority.

All Minbari telepaths are members of the Religious caste.

The Minbari Federation covers twenty worlds in eighteen systems.

The Minbari caste structure cuts across a number of clans. The most important clans are the Wind Swords (generally militant), the Star Riders (who usually become starship personnel), the Night Walkers (who act as the custodians of the Minbari homeworld), the Fire Wings (generally explorers and inventors) and the Moon Shields (the guardians and healers). See the entry on episode 109 ('Deathwalker') for further details. The Narn capital city is G'Kmazas.

The Centauri Republic's first contact with alien races was when an alien ship crashed on Centauri Prime.

Accidents Will Happen: The Narn oath of vengeance – the *shon'kar* – is referred to consistently as the *Chon'kar*.

ESSAYS

Cast ... in a Bad Light

How Changes in the Cast of *Babylon 5* Affected the Arc

'To lose one parent . . .' Oscar Wilde wrote, 'may be regarded as a misfortune; to lose both looks like carelessness.' The same principle applies to television series and their actors. Most shows would find it hard to recover if their leading man left. For one to lose a leading man *and* twelve other primary members of the cast and yet still survive – not only survive, but prosper – it must be a very good show. Or, of course, very lucky.

Losing cast members is considerably worse for *Babylon 5* than for almost any other TV show. Most series plan only a few episodes ahead: characters can be dropped and replaced with reasonable ease (and the hope that the audience will either not notice or not care). The recent major alterations in the casts of *Star Trek: Voyager*, *Star Trek: Deep Space Nine* and *Millennium* are cases in point. With *Babylon 5*, however, an overarching plot exists in which the major characters all have their part to play. That's not to say that nobody is indispensable, of course – events have proved that only too well – but it's unarguable that the loss of a regular actor or actress will affect the arc that has been so painstakingly constructed. Despite claims by the show's creator and co-Executive Producer J Michael Straczynski that there are built-in trapdoors through which he can get rid of all the main characters if necessary, the *Babylon 5* we ended up with at the end of season 5 was not the one we were meant to be getting when episode 101 ('Midnight on the Firing Line') started filming.

The first four casualties were inflicted between the transmission of the pilot episode ('The Gathering') and episode 101 ('Midnight on the Firing Line'). Changing and refining the cast in the period between pilot episode and series is nothing unusual in American television: at the time

Straczynski said simply that he wanted to raise the 'energy level' of the ensemble cast (a phrase that probably meant more to him than it does to us). One of the four actors with the wrong 'energy level' was Johnny Sekka, who had played the head of medlab – Dr Benjamin Kyle. His role was originally intended to continue into the series proper, during which he would have developed into a father figure for Commander Sinclair. Elements of Dr Kyle's character, such as his time spent hitchhiking around the galaxy on alien spacecraft exchanging his medical services for food and lodging, were transferred to his replacement, Dr Stephen Franklin (as played by Richard Biggs), and the character has occasionally been mentioned during the series. Indeed, during season 5 Stephen Franklin is asked to take over from Benjamin Kyle as Head of Xenobiology back at EarthDome on the occasion of Kyle's retirement.

Tamlyn Tomita – the actress who played *Babylon 5*'s second in command Laurel Takashima (originally referred to as the Vice-Commander) – also failed to reappear when the series was commissioned. The majority of her role was bequeathed to the incoming Claudia Christian (playing Susan Ivanova), including her secret coffee plant in the hydroponics section. Some of her more hidden aspects were, however, shared among the other characters. Had she not left the series, it would have been revealed by the end of season 1 that she was part of the assassination attempt on Ambassador Kosh (a fact given away in the pilot episode – 'The Gathering' – when the assassin uses her security code to gain access to areas of the station), and she would then have betrayed Garibaldi in episode 122 ('Chrysalis') either by giving him over to those involved with the assassination of President Santiago or by shooting him herself, a task that fell to Garibaldi's new and satanic-looking aide Jack. Early descriptions of her character by Straczynski also indicate that she would become involved in drug abuse – a vice picked up by Stephen Franklin.

Commander Sinclair's girlfriend, Carolyn Sykes (Blair Brown), also failed to reappear in the series. Although a reasonably minor character, she did play a part in scenes that were cut from the transmitted version of the pilot episode.

During one such scene she confronted Ambassador Delenn and demanded to know why she had been lying to Sinclair. Delenn explained that she didn't know what was going on herself. This cut scene indicates a connection between Delenn and Sykes that Sinclair was unaware of – everyone around him appears to be keeping something from him. Blair Brown was replaced by Julia Nickson playing the very similar part of Catherine Sakai, although both her link to Delenn and the plot strand that would have involved her getting into trouble with one of the big Earth corporations were quietly dropped.

The fourth character to vanish between pilot episode and series, and perhaps the most interesting one of all, was the station's resident telepath, Lyta Alexander (played by Patricia Tallman). Straczynski has said that he wrote the part specifically for the actress and that it was her choice, not his, that she left. Patricia Tallman has, however, indicated that she was manoeuvred off the series behind Straczynski's back, and that she would have loved to continue. She was replaced by another resident telepath – Talia Winters, played by Andrea Thompson – but the character never got much to do in the series. It surprised nobody when Patricia Tallman returned as Lyta Alexander for a few guest-starring roles in season 2 and then as a full member of the regular cast in season 3. Her absence actually helped the show, providing her character with an opportunity to have visited the Vorlon homeworld – a plot element that would be referred to all the way to the end of season 5.

Although none of the four cast changes had major effects on the arc plot, the loss of the only two people in the pilot episode to have seen what a Vorlon looks like inside its encounter suit also gave Straczynski an opportunity to play up the paranoia level in the series. A reference was made to Dr Kyle and Lyta Alexander having been recalled by Earthforce and, following her return, Lyta Alexander tells Sheridan that she was questioned on everything she knew about the Vorlons and had to escape to Mars to avoid further interrogation. That actually helped, in that it raised the general level of concern about the state of things on Earth.

Once the series itself had been commissioned and started

filming, Straczynski probably thought his cast problems were over. He, like Londo Mollari, hadn't banked on the Narn.

The opening credits of episode 103 ('Born to the Purple') lists the character of Ko'Dath as being played by Mary Woronov. Woronov is listed not as a guest star but as a regular member of the cast. Ko'Dath was meant to be the continuing head of G'Kar's diplomatic staff, but the actress had a major problem with the make-up and had to back out of her five-year option in a hurry. Ko'Dath was killed off in an off-screen airlock accident, and another actress – Susan Kellerman (sister of the film *M*A*S*H*'s Sally Kellerman) – was given the newly created role of Na'Toth. There must have been something pretty bizarre about that make-up, because, as Billy (Lennier) Mumy recalled, she too left in a hurry. 'On my first day there was an actress who was playing a Narn,' he has said. 'Actually, she was one of the actresses cast to play Na'Toth. Unfortunately this one never got on camera because as they were making her up she was freaking out and having an anxiety attack, calling her agent and running out of the studio. This was the first thing I saw – this woman with latex going, "I can't do it, I can't do it, I can't do it!"'

Desperate for an actress who would be willing to play the part of an alien under heavy make-up, *Babylon 5*'s casting director called in a favour from the actress Julie Caitlin Brown. She played her first episode as Na'Toth wearing a variation on the Ko'Dath mask because there hadn't been time to make up a mask of her own face. After five episodes in the make-up, she found that not only was it causing her skin problems, but that she was also having to turn down leading parts in big-budget films so she could appear in an unrecognisable part in a television series. After much soul-searching and discussion with J Michael Straczynski, she left the series at the end of the first season. By that point in the ongoing plot arc, however, Na'Toth was the only person who knew that G'Kar had gone in search of the Shadows and with whom he could talk on his return, and so for arc-related reasons she had to somehow be maintained. Julie Caitlin Brown's replacement was Mary Kay Adams – an actress who had experience of acting under heavy make-up when she played a Klingon female in the *Star Trek: Deep Space Nine* episode 'The House of Quark'. It was soon obvious to Straczynski that a mistake had been made, however: Adams was not playing the part in the way he had intended, and she was asked to leave the series after appearing in only two episodes. Fortunately, the character had, by then, done everything that had been required for the arc plot, and so, rather than recast it again, Straczynski took the opportunity to readjust the characters he was writing for. Julie Caitlin Brown later reappeared as Na'Toth in episode 510 ('A Tragedy of Telepaths'), but that appearance was not pivotal to the series' arc and, had the episode in which it occurred never been made, then the series would not have changed.

Julie Caitlin Brown wasn't the only performer to leave at the end of the first season, and (despite the necessity of recasting her part) her leaving didn't cause anywhere near as many problems as the loss of the series' leading man. It's tempting to look for hidden motives and dark conspiracies when any leading actor leaves a major series unexpectedly, and it's also tempting to look for one single reason when the explanation might consist of half a dozen. Unfortunately for conspiracy theorists, the bottom line seems to be that the decision to change the station's commander was an amicable one – suggested initially by Straczynski and happily agreed to by the actor Michael O'Hare.

Straczynski has said that Sinclair's connection to the Minbari soul arc *and* to the Shadow War would have strained credibility too much, and so he took the decision to split the arc between two different characters – Jeffrey Sinclair and John Sheridan – but this one simple act had major repercussions on the arc as originally envisioned. The events of episodes 316 and 317 ('War Without End' Parts One and Two), in which Sinclair is transformed into a full-blown Minbari, were always meant to occur, but they were certainly not meant to occur in season 3. 'You talk like a Minbari, Commander,' Alyt Neroon tells Sinclair in episode 117 ('Legacies'), foreshadowing the later revelation that Sinclair has a Minbari soul, and more subtle references occur later on.

'There's a scene in "Confessions and Lamentations"

[episode 218],' Straczynski points out, 'when Delenn says she was in the temple as a child and someone appeared to her and said, "I will not allow harm to come to my little ones, here in my great house," which is, of course, Valen. If you recall, in "Soul Hunter" [episode 102], when Delenn is down on the deck, she says [to Sinclair], "I knew you would come." Certain elements of that were always being hinted at throughout the whole first season – that was definitely the direction I was planning to go in.'

It may have been the direction Straczynski intended to go, but the timing was way off. The original arc of the series, as formulated before the pilot movie was even written, had Jeffrey Sinclair as the hero. Had Sinclair been transformed into a Minbari halfway through the series and travelled back in time, who then would have won the Shadow War and retaken Earth? It is possible that one of the other main characters would have taken over the lead slot, but the way American television is made means it is unlikely that Warner Brothers would have risked losing some of their audience by actually agreeing to changing the lead actor. No, the most likely explanation is that Sinclair's transformation was originally intended not to occur in 'War Without End' but at the end of season 5. Practically and dramatically, that's the optimal solution. Watching 'War Without End' carefully, you see that there's a certain amount of fudging goes on to keep Sinclair on Babylon 4, travelling into the past.

The whole business with the premature ageing, and the presumption that if he travels back with Sheridan and Delenn, he will age to death, feels forced. It's far more likely that the grey hair and lined face make-up applied to Michael O'Hare for episode 120 ('Babylon Squared') was intended to make him look as he would at the end of season 5 – supposedly set twenty years in the future. Remember, similar make-up was applied to Bruce Boxleitner for episode 522 ('Sleeping in Light'). When it became necessary to rewrite the plot such that Sinclair became Valen far earlier than intended, a new reason had to be introduced to explain why Sinclair looked so old in 'Babylon Squared' – and so much of 'War Without End' was born.

So – the original arc had a naturally aged Sinclair travelling back in time to become Valen at the end of season; whereas the revised arc had a prematurely aged Sinclair travelling back in time to become Valen in the middle of season 3 and a naturally aged Sheridan going 'beyond the rim' at the end of season 5. The pieces were shuffled around, but the eventual result was the same.

Almost unnoticed in the kerfuffle over Michael O'Hare's leaving, Julia Nickson, who played Sinclair's girlfriend Catherine Sakai, quietly slid from the series at the same time. In his absence, there was no reason for her to appear any more. The *Babylon 5* novel *To Dream in the City of Sorrows* tells us that the character travelled to Minbar after Jeffrey Sinclair and was lost in the past before he was, although (unconvincingly) they found each other again in the past.

Bruce Boxleitner was, of course, brought in as the new commander – Captain John Sheridan – in episode 201 ('Points of Departure') but the same episode also introduced Lieutenant Warren Keffer, a Starfury pilot whose sole plot function seemed to be to give us an idea how it felt to be in at the sharp end of the series, having to implement command decisions without actually knowing how they were made. Keffer appeared in six episodes of the series, and died in the last episode of season 2, killed by the Shadows. He was always disposable, and his loss changed the series not one jot.

At the end of season 3, the actor Jason Carter was distressed when he was told by Bill Mumy (Lennier) that his character – Marcus Cole – was going to be killed off. Rushing into J Michael Straczynski's office to find out whether it was true or not, he found Straczynski writing the scene in 'Grey 17 is Missing' where Marcus and Neroon are fighting. 'Marcus steels himself for the death blow,' read the line that Straczynski was typing. When Carter protested, Straczynski realised what Bill Mumy had done and played along, telling Carter that he would not be returning. It was a joke, of course, but it turned out to be a foreshadowing of things to come – something that happens a lot in this series. The character of Marcus Cole was actually killed off at the end of season 4, although the fact that alternate scenes were filmed in which he lived suggests that the decision was never hard and fast. Marcus Cole's usefulness was essentially linked to the character of Susan Ivanova: when Claudia Christian left, there was nothing else for him to do.

And why did Claudia Christian leave? That really *is* another story . . .

There's Always a 'Boom' Tomorrow

Ivanova's Departure: A Tale of Misunderstandings

The biggest drama to have hit *Babylon 5* during its five-year tenure on our screens, and the one to have left the bitterest taste in the mouths of the fans, was the departure of Claudia Christian between seasons 4 and 5. Members of the cast had departed before – voluntarily or involuntarily – and they would do so again, but this parting of the ways was played out largely in public, in part at a convention and later on the Internet. Bitter words have been spoken, statements have been issued that contradict each other, and two people who once appeared to be good friends have been badly hurt. So incensed were some of the fans (and one has to assume, if only for one's peace of mind, that they are the extreme lunatic fringe) that death threats were made against J Michael Straczynski, provoking him to examine whether or not he should employ a private security firm. It would be the understatement of the decade to say that the situation was unfortunate.

As with any situation fleetingly observed from afar, it would be misleading to make any definitive statements. It's not even clear that the two prime movers in the situation fully understand the facts themselves, given that they each appear to believe (or, at least, publicly state) incompatible points of view. It would be tempting to assume that one or even both are deliberately misrepresenting the facts. Tempting, but wrong. As the Vorlons have said, 'Understanding is a three-edged sword.' It is much more likely that misunderstandings have arisen and, with time, these misunderstandings have forced a divergence of what is believed. Everything we say, everything we do, is based on assumptions. If even one of those assumptions is wrong then what we say will be skewed, and we may not even realise.

For the sake of clarity, I should make it clear that

the quotations below are taken from statements made by J Michael Straczynski and by Claudia Christian that have been posted on the Internet (a notorious source of rumours, wild surmises and impersonations). These statements were distributed widely at the time, and neither of the supposed authors has denied that they made them, either then or since. It can only be assumed, therefore, that these are their own words. Any interpolations within square brackets are my own comments, intended to clarify some of the statements with regard primarily to people or to dates. According to convention, ellipses (. . .) have been used to mark points at which I have removed material irrelevant to the argument.

It had been increasingly clear for some time, based on her comments at conventions, that Claudia Christian was not happy about the scale of her role in *Babylon 5*. 'During season 4,' she pointed out after leaving the series, 'I mostly read off of a teleprompter for "The Voice of The Resistance" or said "Aye Captain" into my link. I was creatively frustrated but continued to float along thinking I would get my chance to stretch my acting muscles. It wasn't until episode 421 that Joe [Straczynski]wrote a scene for Richard Biggs and I that I am very proud of and was thrilled to be able to do.' An ironic statement, considering the line that J Michael Straczynski wrote for her character in the first-season episode 'Believers': 'I think I'll just walk to and fro for a while, maybe over to my console. After that, maybe I'll try pacing fro and to, you know, just for the kick of it.'

By the end of filming on season 4, however, Christian had filmed the scene in which Ivanova is given command of *Babylon 5*, Sheridan having been promoted to become President of the Interstellar Alliance. This, and conversations she is known to have had with Straczynski in which he told her about the Byron subplot she was to have in season 5, should have convinced her that the role of Ivanova would have been expanded.

Towards the end of filming on season 4 (the summer of 1997), and before any firm word had been reached on the fate of season 5, Christian began to audition for other roles, in case *Babylon 5* was over for good. 'I auditioned for the Borg on Voyager during season 4, when we were told that it did not look good for season 5 . . .' she said later. 'All of the actors were auditioning for lots of things since we thought the series was over.'

Christian's frustrations came to a head in mid-1997, following the expiry of the contract options that tied the many actors on the series to a possible season 5 and during the discussions that were to lead to the transfer of *Babylon 5* from the defunct PTEN network to the TNT cable company. Straczynski explained it thus: 'In early June, WB [Warner Brothers] asked for, and received, one-month extensions on their contract options from all cast members except Claudia, for the purposes of allowing WB time to work out the co-financing deal with TNT for year 5 of B5. There was a great deal of red tape left over from the PTEN deal to finish unravelling, and other business aspects, to work out in going from syndication to cable, and it was taking longer than expected.'

Claudia Christian's comments agree with this version of events. She has said, 'On June 20th [following the expiry of her contract], I was called into the B5 office to find out the fate of the 5th season. With three other cast members present we were told that we could make the fifth season . . . We were then asked to give up the residuals for that season . . . Well, nonetheless I said OK – I even volunteered to talk the rest of the cast into it.'

Straczynski continued, 'Claudia said, repeatedly, that she was on board for the fifth season, but that she didn't want to give the extension for business reasons of her own. We took her at her word and allowed her to not give the extension. Assurances were made to us, and to her fellow cast members.'

Christian confirmed that she, unlike the rest of the cast, did not sign up to an extension of her contract. 'I had expressed my hesitation in extending my contract renewal,' she said, 'because I wanted to get their assurance that in the 5th season I could get at least 4 episodes off to do a film. That was the only thing I was asking for. No raise – accepting a pay cut – simply less episodes, period.'

People close to Claudia Christian have since suggested that her actions were dictated by additional considerations: the fact that she was attempting to change agents. Had Christian extended her original contract and then signed a new contract for season 5, her old agent would have still received a percentage of her season 5 earnings, as the contract would have been based on the one he originally negotiated. By forcing a gap between contracts and then allowing a new agent to negotiate a fresh deal for which he, not the old agent, would have received a commission, they claim that she was creating an added incentive for him to take her on.

Whatever her reasons for not signing, Christian's comments about accepting a pay cut struck an obvious nerve with Straczynski, who said afterwards, 'Nobody was asked to, or accepted, a cutback in salary. Every cast member got their salary bumps this year.' The truth, however, lay somewhere between the rumour and the denial. The actors were receiving money from two different directions – their salary for being in the show and their 'residuals', which are fees paid for every showing on television of an episode they are in. In moving from PTEN to TNT, *Babylon 5* had crossed the line from network to cable, and the residuals for syndication are less than for network showings. While the actors' salaries may have increased, their residuals had dropped. Straczynski, to be fair, acknowledged this, admitting, 'There are different formulas for residuals in network, syndication, and cable. The network formula is the largest fee per rerun, followed by syndication and then cable.' As Claudia Christian pointed out about residuals, however, '. . . those are the things that pay the rent, since syndication isn't exactly lucrative.'

Accepting that the actors would be making money less quickly (which may or may not have added up to less money in total), and ignoring the argument over whether this constitutes a pay cut or not, it is clear that both Straczynski and Christian agree that, although she had given oral assurances that she would appear in season 5, she did not sign the extension on her contract. She did, however, agree to appear at the Wolf 359 *Babylon 5* convention in the UK (11–14 July 1997) with Straczynski and some of the other actors.

Although Christian was committed to the series, other developments in her life meant that she needed other work – especially if the new *Babylon 5* deal meant reduced residuals. 'I had a car accident that ended up costing me my savings account . . .' she explains. 'Along comes a producer who wants me to star in a film that will help get me on my feet again . . . barely . . . and satisfy my acting needs in a challenging role. I really wanted to do it. I asked [J Michael Straczynski] for the time off and I was told I would get it. I explained I needed it in writing . . . There was no way they would hire me without this permission note . . .'

'While we were all together (cast, some crew, and I) in Blackpool for Wolf 359,' Straczynski has said, 'word reached us of . . . articles in Variety and Reuters reporting that Claudia would not be returning to B5, and was looking for other work. This was the very first indication we had that she would not be in season 5. TNT was upset by this, WB was upset by this, and we were called on the carpet asking why we had trusted her about the fifth year.'

Christian denies that she instigated these press reports. 'While I was in Europe,' she reports, '. . . I heard about the gossip column in Variety. It is a gossip column, nothing more. I have no idea who planted the gossip and frankly, I didn't think much of it since Hollywood is based on gossip. Because the producers and Joe were in Europe, I assumed negotiations for the 5th season would continue when we all returned. I was told quite curtly that my request for time off had been denied and that Ken Parks from Warner Bros. had told my agent to tell me to "Find another job, we'll replace her". At that point, I was in shock but I still went to Blackpool thinking that they would come around and give me the time I needed off. I knew Ivanova was in the first episodes. I figured we could sit down with my agent and come to a deal.'

Christian continues, 'In Blackpool I was told by JMS that he would give me the episodes off but I could not get anything in writing. I trust him; however, I know that he was not writing all of the episodes for the fifth season so I really felt that I had to have something in writing.'

'When spoken to in Blackpool,' Straczynski continues,

255

'she was still, at that point, saying that she was going to be in season 5 . . . but did nothing to address the situation with WB. She was told that WB had to know, for sure, if she was in or out by last Friday [11 July]. All she had to do to be in season 5 was to pick up the phone, or have her agent do so, and call WB and say, "I'm in."'

Although Straczynski and Christian agree on the facts up to their joint appearance at Blackpool for the Wolf 359 convention, it is from this point that each of them begins to emphasise a different aspect. To Straczynski, the important point was that Christian sign an extension of her contract covering her potential appearance in all 22 episodes of the new season in order to allow Warner Brothers and TNT to conduct their detailed negotiations over the future of the series. As far as Straczynski was concerned, he was happy to arrange at a later date for Christian to drop out of four or five episodes in order for her to appear in a film. Such an arrangement had been made during season 4 for Stephen Furst. 'Yes, she's right,' he says, 'in that the contract could not be changed so that she could go out and do movies at a moment's notice. By contract, we must have first call on an actor's services. That is a requirement of *any* contract with an actor who is a series regular. That cannot be changed for *any* actor, *any*where. That said . . . I already *told* Claudia that, even though we couldn't put it in the contract, I would be happy to work with her *informally* on this, and that if she said she needed to be gone from X-date to Y-date, I would write her out of those episodes so that she could do the movies . . . I've already done similar things for her and other cast members on the show, which is how many of them have appeared in other projects.'

According to Christian, however, this time she couldn't get the film project without having an agreement *in writing* that she could take that time off from the series. There was no point in her signing a contract committing her to 22 episodes if there was no equivalent statement explicitly excusing her from some of them. Stalemate.

This is where the first of the major discrepancies appears between what Straczynski has said and what Christian has said. Straczynski indicates that a contract could have been written to cover Christian's wishes, and claims that Christian '. . . was told that if she wanted to be *paid* for 22 episodes, then the contract would have to stipulate that she was hired for 22 episodes. The problem was that she wanted to have the contract read that she was being paid for 22 episodes, but appearing in 18, which constitutes a per-episode pay increase, which would invalidate our contracts with all the other cast members, who are on a favoured-nation basis. Had her people said, "Just pay us for 18 episodes and we'll just do 18 episodes," there would never have been a problem.'

Christian's recollection is different. 'I was never offered 18 episodes at a different price,' she says. 'I was told "If TNT wants you for all 22 – you have to do all 22" period.' Expanding upon this statement, she has said, 'It turns out my fears were justified, because when my agent spoke to John Copeland [the series Producer] and mentioned Joe's offer to write me out of a few episodes, Mr Copeland responded by saying "That's not possible. If TNT wants her in every episode then she has to do all 22. That's the deal, take it or leave it." '

The second major discrepancy now occurs: and, rather than concerning what was or wasn't on offer, it concerns when that offer was to expire. 'As of June 15th,' Straczynski states, 'when Claudia did not give the extension, her contract expired and she no longer worked for B5, or WB; neither had any call or hold on her. What had to happen then was for WB to put an offer on the table for her services. This was done. A deadline was finally put on for a Friday [11 July], because of the pressures of production. She did not accept the offer, and by that Friday, the offer was withdrawn.'

Christian disagrees. 'At this point,' she says, 'I was told that I had until Monday [14 July] to call Warner Bros. to tell them I was on board. Well . . . an actor does not call a studio. Our union has rules. The producers of B5 never called my manager or agent to tell them of this deadline. Instead, I was told by Jeff Conaway. I called my agent and left word. We missed each other. On Monday, I found out that on the previous Friday my agent had received a fax stating that the offer for me to be in B5 was withdrawn.'

Straczynski continues the story: 'Friday came, and went. It was clear that she had no intention of being in season 5, and wanted instead to pursue movies . . . Cast members prevailed upon her to change her mind over the weekend. Bruce, Jeff Conaway, others took it upon themselves to try and talk her back on to the show, tried to get her to call on Monday in case she might be able to repair the bridges burnt the prior week. On Monday, she left the convention early, and never called WB, never called Doug [Netter], never called anyone.'

'In essence, I was fired,' Christian claims. 'This fax was received on Friday, so what kind of game was being played by giving me false hopes throughout the weekend in England?'

Straczynski disagrees. 'You cannot fire someone who does not work for you. That is the one part of this conversation everybody keeps forgetting.'

From this point, the stories converge again. Claudia Christian did not return to the series, a voice-over was altered slightly in the last but one episode of season 4 to explain the sudden disappearance of her character and a new part was created to fill the dramatic space thus vacated. A mark of the lingering bitterness felt by J Michael Straczynski can be seen in the fourth episode of season 5 ('The View From the Gallery'), where one of the characters says that he has heard a rumour that Ivanova 'quit because she wasn't getting paid enough money'. Straczynski has gone on record since as saying that this was a dig at the fans and the magazine article writers who were making this claim, but it could be equally applicable to his perception of Claudia Christian's actions.

It's hard not to see this whole situation as a tragic misunderstanding blown up out of all proportion. Straczynski certainly feels hurt on a personal level by what has happened, and the same feeling comes through in what Christian is saying. She will reappear in the series – her parts in the TV movie *Thirdspace* and in the final episode of the series, 'Sleeping in Light', had already been recorded when the disagreements happened – but Ivanova's contribution to the arc has effectively been curtailed. In response to questions on the Internet over whether he could reintroduce Ivanova into the later season five episodes of *Babylon 5*, Straczynski has said that, as it was Christian who walked away from the series, there is nothing he can do to get her back. He carefully ignores the possibility that, if a sufficiently good deal were on the table, she might walk back of her own accord, and that in itself is telling. Too much is remembered to be forgotten.

Babylon 5 survived the loss of its leading man early on, and it survived the loss of one of its leading women late on, but both events have tainted the series, dragging it away from the five-year arc that was envisioned before the first ray of light hit the first frame of film. Is it better for the changes? Perhaps we should leave the last word to Susan Ivanova herself: 'Does the phrase, "No way in hell", ring a bell?'

Beyond the Rim to the Sea

Death in *Babylon 5*

Over the course of five years, *Babylon 5* has shown us a panoply of alien races, each with their own particular religious beliefs. Unlike, for instance, *Star Trek*'s various incarnations, where religious faith is almost invariably shown as being due to the actions, conscious or unconscious, of aliens with superior powers, *Babylon 5* has gone out of its way to indicate that each religion may have an insight into something that the others perhaps don't. No one religion has the answer, it says, but each is in its own way striving towards that answer, and should be praised for that rather than criticised.

What *Babylon 5* has also done that no other SF series has managed is to show us that there *is* something beyond death which cannot be explained. There is a generally accepted truth that something survives after death – but precisely what is open to question and interpretation.

Some of the characters in *Babylon 5* – and presumably some of the races as well, have no belief in any sort of afterlife. 'I never believed in anything beyond death,' Mr Garibaldi said in episode 508 ('Day of the Dead'); although he was 'brought up a good Catholic boy' he has since divested himself of his unquestioning acceptance of the resurrection of the body and the life everlasting. Zack Allen, on the other hand, makes it clear in the TV movie *The River of Souls* that he implicitly believes in Heaven and Hell.

By contrast, the Minbari, the race about which we know the most, believe that living creatures are the universe's way of finding out about itself. Whatever it is about the universe that is conscious is, they avow, split into an uncountable number of fragments, fragments that we call souls. Each living creature contains a small piece of the universe, and when we die these fragments coalesce again, bringing back what they have learned. 'They will join with the souls of all our people,'

Delenn explains in episode 102 ('Soul Hunter'), 'melt one into another until they are born into the next generation of Minbari.' The souls cycle round, moving from body to body, a process interrupted periodically by the minor inconvenience of death. There's a certain amount of evidence for this belief: the Minbari were able to determine, for instance, that the soul of their mythical hero Valen had been reborn not into a Minbari body but into that of a human. They were wrong in detail – in fact, Jeffrey Sinclair later travelled back in time to become Valen – but right in the generalities; Sinclair and Valen did in fact share the same soul.

The *Shag'Toth*, known colloquially as the Soul Hunters, also believe in souls, but they do not accept that they are eternal and eternally reborn into other bodies. 'A quaint lie,' a Soul Hunter retorted when Delenn attempted to explain Minbari theology to him in episode 102 ('Soul Hunter'): 'the soul ends with death.' It is the creed of the Soul Hunters that the soul – 'the long exhalation of the spirit' as they have called it, can be collected, bottled so as to sustain the essence of a creature even after the dissolution of the body. 'We are not thieves,' they explain when accused of taking a soul without permission, 'we are preservers. We are drawn to the moment . . . the moment of surrender.' The Soul Hunters firmly believe that, were they not allowed to collect the soul as it leaves the body then it would be lost forever. 'No heaven,' they state in the TV movie *The River of Souls*. 'Nothing beyond. Only the dark, impenetrable wall of death.'

There is a certain amount to be said for the Soul Hunters' point of view. Whatever it is that they collect, it would appear to be the essence of a being. It can be communicated with, and it can dispense wisdom. What happens to these souls when released from the Soul Hunters' clutches is, however, a moot point. It could be that they will simply cease to exist, as the Soul Hunters themselves believe, or perhaps will coalesce into some amorphous mass of souls and then be reborn, as the Minbari believe. All we know is that most of the souls who have been given a choice have opted to be released rather than kept in a collection and revered.

The Brakiri have another attitude entirely. They firmly

believe that, every one hundred and eighty years, they are permitted to talk to the dead. While this could be considered a quaint custom, there is evidence that they could be correct. In episode 508 ('Day of the Dead') a number of non-Brakiri saw 'ghosts' from their own past, and communed with them for several hours. An illusion, perhaps, created from memories and wishes by disturbed minds? Perhaps, but during the episode one of the ghosts accurately predicted the future for the person he was visiting. Another passed a message from a ghost that had not returned to someone else on the station. The message didn't make sense at the time, but later came to have a certain amount of significance.

The Brakiri belief in raising ghosts (if only for a few hours every couple of centuries), backed up by the evidence seen by at least some of the inhabitants of Babylon 5, leads to three important conclusions. Firstly it presupposes that those who have died retain some form of integrated personality, rather than either fading away or being reborn into another body. This more or less destroys the beliefs of both the Soul Hunters and the Minbari. Secondly it indicates that the dead reside together: all races co-located in one place. Otherwise how else could a Vorlon ghost ask a human ghost to pass a message back to the land of the living during a Brakiri ceremony? Thirdly, it implies that there are certain rules and regulations that even the dead must obey. '. . . When this night is done, so am I,' the ghost of Adira tells the living Londo Mollari, and the ghosts of Morden and 'Dodger' Derman both know how long they are allowed to visit for.

Perhaps this mysterious land in which the dead live is located somewhere out in space, beyond the rim of our galaxy. Certainly there would appear to be some other realm, distinct from the normal laws of time and space, that lies beyond what is known. 'There are beings in the universe much older than either of our races . . .' Delenn tells Sheridan in episode 217 ('In the Shadow of Z'ha'dum'). 'Once, long ago, they walked among the stars like giants – vast and timeless – taught the younger races, explored beyond the Rim, created great empires. But to all things there is an end. Slowly, over a million years, the First Ones went away. Some passed beyond the stars, never to return. Some simply disappeared . . .' Here Delenn appears to indicate that the Rim (presumably the rim of our galaxy) is more or less an arbitrary boundary: the First Ones explored beyond it and, presumably, resumed before passing 'beyond the stars' again. Later, in episode 406 ('Into the Fire') the Rim is more of a barrier than a boundary: there is a strong implication that once the First Ones pass beyond the Rim they can never return – something similar to death, although perhaps not quite the same. Later a dying Sheridan meets again with Lorien, First of the First Ones. Lorien has resumed from the Rim to collect Sheridan. Sheridan cannot live where he is any more, his time is ended, but if he goes with Lorien then more time will be made available to him. 'We have been waiting for you,' Lorien says. 'Beyond the Rim,' Sheridan realises, and then asks, 'can I come back?' 'No,' Lorien replies, 'this journey is ended. Another begins. Time to rest now.'

Lorien's words are those one uses to someone who is dying, as we know Sheridan is. Granted access to a realm of existence from which he can never return, he leaves us in a state of some confusion. Lorien came back, so why can't Sheridan? Is it because he hasn't got the powers of the First Ones? Perhaps so, but Adira, Zoe, 'Dodger' and Morden came back, albeit briefly, and they aren't First Ones. Are they in the Afterlife too? It would seem so, because Kosh's ghost got a message to Sheridan telling him in roundabout terms how to get to the Afterlife beyond the Rim, but what was the point? Kosh and Adira apparently got to the Afterlife from Babylon 5 with no help from anyone else. 'Dodger' got there from Akdor; Morden from Centauri Prime. Why does Sheridan need to be at a certain place at a certain time, and why does he need help?

At best, all we can say is that the mystery of death remains exactly that, and that no one race has all the pieces of the jigsaw. At worst, we have to conclude that the treatment of death and what happens afterwards within *Babylon 5* is inconsistent.

Of course, we still don't know what the Drazi make of death. Or the Gaim. Or the Vree. Their beliefs might be significantly different to those of the Minbari, the Brakiri and the *Shag'Toth*. And, if we looked closely enough, there might be evidence suggesting that there was at least a grain of truth in their beliefs.

Perhaps it's best not even to think about it, and to assume that death is indeed the end.

More Questions Than Answers

Plot Elements That Were Set Up But Never Fully Explained

Life isn't as neat as fiction: not all loose ends get tied up. In that respect, *Babylon 5* is more like life than fiction. Although J Michael Straczynski assured us that 'By the time the series has run its five-year course (Neilsen willing), there will only be one unanswered question left: "now what?" ', the truth is that there are more loose threads hanging off the end of the last episode than from a cheap Hong Kong suit.

Some of the plot elements that haven't been resolved are unimportant: things that the fans considered a potential part of the arc but which were little more than background colour, extraneous detail that made the series that little bit more convincing. Others were important to begin with, but that importance was lost as other elements were reshuffled or as rewrites and replotting occurred. A third set comprises those plot elements that were always an integral part of the arc but which, either because he ran out of time or because he wanted to hold their resolution over to *Crusade* or the spin-off novels, J Michael Straczynski never actually closed off in *Babylon 5* itself. A fourth set is those questions which appear not to have been answered, but in fact were (if not terribly clearly).

And so, as this is the last volume of *The Babylon File*, it seemed only right and proper that we list those questions which we would have liked to know the answer to, or to which we had expected different answers, in rough order of increasing importance.

Why was San Diego blown up? We know from the start of season one (episode 101 – 'Midnight on the Firing Line') that terrorists exploded a nuclear device in San Diego at some stage in the past, rendering it uninhabitable. We saw the blasted ruins in episode 206

('Spider in the Web'). In episode 518 ('The Fall of Centauri Prime') Stephen Franklin makes reference to the device having been left over from the fall of the Soviet Union in the late 20th Century. So, we know what happened and how it happened; what we don't know is why. Early in the course of the series there was an automatic assumption that anything referred to but left unexplained had to be a part of the overall plot arc. In the case of San Diego we were wrong: it's just a part of Earth's history that has little relevance to what is happening 'now'.

Who blew up Babylons 1, 2, and 3? As with the bombing of San Diego, one has to assume that the loss of Babylons 1, 2 and 3 was unrelated to the overall plot of the series. According to *The Babylon Project* – the *Babylon 5* role-playing game – Babylon 1 was destroyed by accident during construction when substandard building materials failed in the harsh conditions of space. Some of Babylon 1 was salvaged and rescued in the construction of Babylon 2, but that station exploded just as the fusion reactors were brought online. The official reports referred to the explosion as an accident, but there were rumours of sabotage. Babylon 3 was definitely destroyed by terrorist bombs shortly after the station's superstructure was complete. Babylon 4, of course, vanished backwards in time in order to form a base for the War Against the Shadows, and Babylon 5 hung around for some twenty three years before being deliberately destroyed on the orders of EarthGov to prevent it being a danger to shipping.

What does 'Naranek' mean in 'Kosh Naranek'? This is reasonably trivial, but still exercised the brains of many fans (well, me) throughout the first three seasons. Initial series documentation specifically referred to the Vorlon Ambassador to Babylon 5 as Kosh Naranek. The novel *To Dream in the City of Sorrows* specifically refers to the Vorlon representative on the Minbari Homeworld as

Ulkesh Naranek. So what does 'Naranek' mean? It may just be a family name, but there were suspicions that it referred to something deeper: another example of too much being read into the series.

What were the four plans President Clark set in motion against Babylon 5? In episode 407 ('Epiphanies') President Clark sets in motion a four-pronged attack against Sheridan and Babylon 5. Psi Corps, Earthforce, Nightwatch and the Ministry of Peace are each given one 'prong', and none of them know what the others are doing. Psi Corps' plan is to use their Black Omega starfuries to make it look as if Sheridan has carried out atrocities against Earthforce ships (episode 407 – 'Epiphanies'). ISN (presumably at the instigation of Nightwatch, as Nightwatch seem to be running the propaganda battle) use falsification and distortion of the truth to attempt to turn public opinion against the rebellion (episodes 407 – 'Epiphanies' and 408 – 'The Illusion of Truth'). What were Earthforce and the Ministry of Peace up to? The truth is that we will never know. The plots were probably started up, but never became obvious before President Clark's suicide and the fall of his regime. More prosaically, J Michael Straczynski may have intended that the plots would have come to fruition towards the end of season four, but abandoned those episodes when he had to finish off the War to Retake Earth in season four rather than letting it slide into season five as originally planned.

Who are Bureau 13? Who is their agent on the station? In episode 206 ('Spider in the Web') a hidden organisation known as Bureau 13 uses a cybernetic agent to sabotage negotiations between a prominent businessman and a member of the provisional Martian Government: negotiations that might lead to an increased recognition of an independent Mars. Bureau 13 have a base in the ruins of San Diego, and appear to be linked to EarthGov (if only because their cybernetic agent is the result of old

Earthforce experiments). We never see Bureau 13 again, and are presumably meant to assume that they either conduct the rest of their operations in secrecy or become absorbed into some other aspect of President Clark's operations. The cybernetic agent was created using telepathic conditioning, so there's a good argument that Bureau 13 is a part of Psi Corps (especially since one of their operatives used to be in Psi Corps before being listed as dead).

The real reason why Bureau 13 never reappeared is that J Michael Straczynski had inadvertently given the organisation the same name as an organisation in an existing computer game. 'We hadn't heard of the Bureau 13 game when we did the episode,' Straczynski has said, 'it was just something we came up with 'cause it sounded neat. Later, we found out there was a game by that name. At which point I decided that it wouldn't be appropriate to use that name again, and had a good conversation with some folks at the game company about it. There was no problem, I just didn't want to walk on their turf intentionally or otherwise. Logically, any secret group is going to change its name from time to time *anyway* (it's not like they're in the yellow pages or anything), so the organisation would remain under varying names.'

The really interesting thing is that Bureau 13 have an agent on Babylon 5. During a conversation between a Bureau 13 member and their unseen 'Control', that agent is referred to as male, which rules out Talia Winters (who, you will recall, is a Psi Corps agent with a secondary personality). Who is it? We will never know.

Why do the Vorlons need encounter suits with such high shoulders if their wings are just an illusion they create in the minds of those beings who see them out of their encounter suits? This question illustrates something that appears not to have been thought through properly in the show. The Vorlons appear to most races within encounter suits that (a) stop them from being recognised

('By whom?' Sheridan asks in episode 217 – 'In The Shadow of Z'ha'dum' – and Kosh replies, 'By everyone,') and (b) allows them to breathe their own atmosphere (methane, carbon dioxide and some form of sulphur compound, according to the pilot TV movie *The Gathering*). The encounter suits have high shoulders (indeed, this was one of the few specifications from J Michael Straczynski to the original designer), and when we finally see Kosh outside his encounter suit in episode 222 ('The Fall of Night') his form is indeed winged. The twin Vorlons we see out of their encounter suits in episode 317 ('War Without End' Part Two) also have wings. All the races who see Kosh's true form assume him to be a supernatural entity, for they all have legends of winged beings (angels and so on). However, when we *really* get to see the true form of Kosh (episode 404 – 'Falling Toward Apotheosis') he is a large, translucent jellyfish-like being, as is his colleague, Ulkesh. Three as-yet-unanswered questions raise their ugly heads. Firstly, why do Kosh and Ulkesh choose to go round in encounters suit that have large shoulders to hide their wings if they haven't got any wings (especially if the last thing they want is for people to think they *have* got wings)? Secondly, if Kosh can control how people see him, why does he claim that he doesn't want to be recognised and then deliberately choose to be seen in an angelic form that he knows will be instantly identified? Thirdly, why is Kosh's encounter suit filled with methane, carbon dioxide and a sulphur compound when he (and later Ulkesh) seem quite happy breathing the station's own atmosphere?

Who built the Great Machine on Epsilon 3? What is it for? The Great Machine on Epsilon 3 doesn't appear to have taken part in the last War Against the Shadows. Although it has records of that time, there has been no indication that it took an active or decisive role, which, given its sheer power, one might have expected. The assumption on the part of the viewers during the first few seasons of the show was that it was to be a decisive influence on the War that was to come. 'Do not let them take the Machine,' Varn, the Keeper of the Machine, implores Sinclair when aliens attempt to wrest control of it. 'It's not for them. It's not for this time.' Draal, the new Keeper, later tells Sinclair, 'When the time is right we will be here, waiting for you.'

It's legitimate to ask what the Great Machine was actually for, as Sheridan managed to decisively finish the Shadow threat for good without its help, and all it did during the War to Retake Earth was to amplify the Voice of the Resistance's signals – a tactic which may or may not have done Sheridan's forces any good. The answer actually lies in the past: the sole function of the Great Machine was to send Babylon 4 backwards in time to become a base for the last War Against the Shadows (and incidentally to take Sinclair back as well). 'It's not for this time', Varn said. He's right, it's for a thousand years ago.

It's a fair bet that, in J Michael Straczynski's original formulation, the moving of Babylon 4 and the transformation of Sinclair into Valen was intended to take place at the end of season 5 rather than mid-way through season 3. Thus in the original formulation the rationale for the Great Machine's existence would have tantalised us for five whole seasons, rather than being revealed half way through the show's run, leaving it hanging around as something of an embarrassment for some fifty-odd episodes.

What we still don't know, of course, is who built the Great Machine and what relationship Zathras's race have with it. And, of course, was the location of Babylon 5's construction accidental (of all the planets in all the galaxies we could be built in orbit around, why did it have to be this one?) or did the Minbari influence the location?

Who actually woke the Shadows up? Who was piloting their ships in 'War Without End' Parts One and

Two? In episode 217 ('In The Shadow of Z'ha'dum') Delenn tells Sheridan that the crew of the Icarus awoke the Shadows when they landed on Z'ha'dum. This is reiterated in the *Babylon 5* novel *The Shadow Within*, which dates this awakening to early 2257. However, episode 120 ('Babylon Squared') reveals that Babylon 4 vanished four years before the events of that episode, i.e. some time in late 2254. In episodes 316 and 317 ('War Without End' Parts One and Two) we see that Babylon 4 vanished shortly after being attacked by Shadow fighters whose pilots were attempting to attach a fusion bomb to it. The question is: if the Shadows were not woken until 2257 then who was piloting their ships in 2254? Although this was a bit of a poser in season 3, it's more explicable by the time we get to season 5. We've now seen the Shadows' allies – the Drakh and others – and so we can quite believe that the Shadow fighters were under the control not of the Shadows but of the Drakh, ensuring that any threats to their sleeping masters were eradicated. In fact, the Drakh may actually be in *The Shadow Within* – on page 236 we are introduced to a group of aliens aiding in the awakening of the Shadows whose skin is blue and whose heads are large and ungainly: an almost perfect description of the Drakh as seen in episode 518 ('The Fall of Centauri Prime').

There are other, more recent, questions which have as yet only incomplete answers. What plans do the Drakh have for the unborn David Sheridan? What events lead up to the captivity of Sheridan and Delenn by Emperor Mollari as seen in episode 317 ('War Without End' Part Two), and what will be the aftermath? Will Lyta Alexander's plot to take her revenge against Psi Corps work as she hopes? J Michael Straczynski has said that these questions will be addressed in future incarnations of *Babylon 5* – the follow-on series *Crusade* and the spin-off books being published by Del Rey. We can only hope that some of the questions listed above are addressed as well.

WHAT WAS, AND WHAT WILL BE . . .

Crusade

During April 1999 an official announcement was made that a spin-off series from *Babylon 5* would go into production. Entitled *Crusade* (originally *The Babylon Project: Crusade*), the series began filming on August 3, 1998 for a proposed transmission date in January 1999 following the transmission of the cross-over TV movie *A Call to Arms*.

Set between the years 2267 and 2272, the series deals with the exploits of an experimental Interstellar Alliance ship, the *Excalibur,* and the efforts of its crew to search for the cure to a plague based on Shadow technology that threatens humanity. Their search takes them to various First One cities and unexplored planets, where they discover all kinds of dangerous and wondrous things.

Initial reports gave the main cast as follows:

> Gary Cole as (Captain) Matthew Gideon
> Peter Woodward as Galen
> Marjean Holden as Dr Susan Chambers
> Daniel Dae Kim as Lt Matheson
> David Allen Brooks as Max Eilerson
> Carrie Dobro as Dureena Nafeel

Gary Cole's face is familiar from his roles as a late night radio show host in *Midnight Caller* and as the evil Sheriff in *American Gothic*. Peter Woodward is one of actor Edward Woodward's sons.

Regular guest appearances were originally going to be made by a number of regular Babylon 5 cast members, including Jeff Conaway (Zack Allan), Richard Biggs (Stephen Franklin) and Tracy Scoggins (Elizabeth Lochley). Although the last two have already taken part – with Scoggins expected to appear in 13 episodes of the first season – Jeff Conaway was not invited aboard *Crusade*. Pat Tallman declined to return as Lyta Alexander for a flashback sequence, and plans for other cast members to appear have also fallen through.

Problems arose during production when TNT asked for a number of changes to be made, including the incorporation of a number of 'introductory' episodes before the planned first episode. J Michael Straczynski says of TNT's requests: 'One of the issues brought up by TNT had to do with a decision we all made early on that the first episode up, "Racing the Night", would just jump right into the story, without doing the usual pilot-episode thing of showing the team coming together, which was our other option. On reflection, TNT figured that the best thing might be to do that "coming together" episode after all, to set the stage for all that follows. It's a lateral change, really, you could have it or not, either way, it's dealer's choice. But if we're going to do that, we may as well get the sets and other stuff ready to go for that first episode and the ones that will immediately follow. We're also making some adjustments to the wardrobe (and I've come up with a pretty funny way to make the transition in the story). All of the prior produced episodes are still in, and still going to be broadcast, nothing's changed that as far as I know. Anyway, things continue to progress, the script for the alternate first ep is in, and all should be cool from this point on. Which is not to say there haven't been some knife-fights ... but we seem to have reached some understandings ... '

Although transmission was originally set to commence in January 1999, the imposition of TNT's demands has led to a delay. The series is currently scheduled for June 1999 (although persistent rumours suggest that it may be moved up to March or April).

The current list of episodes is as follows, with the expected transmission and production numbers illustrating where the disjunction has occurred.

Title	Expected Transmission Number	Production Number
War Zone	101	108
The Long Road	102	107
The Well of Forever	103	106

We can only wait and see what *Crusade* is like: TNT's sudden change of mind after production had started does not bode well, but initial (unbiased) reports are encouraging and *A Call to Arms* sets up the background and some of the characters excellently. During January 1999 TNT announced that they would not be continuing with *Crusade*, and J Michael Straczynski was suddenly faced with the prospect of finding a replacement backer. But as Susan Ivanova says at the end of episode 522 ('Sleeping in Light'): '. . .there can always be new beginnings.'

Afterword

by Pat Tallman

In looking back a few months to the filming of the last episodes of *Babylon 5*, I realise how much my perspective has already changed. My temper has cooled, and love entered my life in the wondrous form of Jeffrey Willerth. In a few years this perspective shift will be dramatic. Time will mellow me and give me a graceful view of a famous television show known for its mysteries and its eccentric creator. At this moment, however, there are some basic truths from my view that I don't think will ever change.

Babylon 5 was a powerful time in my life. As my character struggled, and grew and changed, so did I. We did the pilot as a fresh new team of professionals with a varied degree of experience but a common motivation: to produce the best science fiction television pilot ever made. We knew the script was dark, different and really special. The cast was unusual, with stage actors instead of known TV personalities. We worked our butts off and were proud of what we were doing. I was thrilled to be doing advance PR with JMS at conventions. I was incredibly excited when Joe called to say the series was a go. The devastation I went through when my deal went south for the series is beyond my power of words to describe. It was a typical Hollywood manoeuvre, just business to them. Just business.

I came back to the show in its second season a new mom. My son was 5 months old. I had gone back to my roots in the theatre, joined a class headed by Charles Nelson Reilly who I believe saved my career by salvaging my self-esteem. He made me work, and I remembered how it feels to be an actor.

The cast was mostly new with few familiar faces. But they were champs, who made my first day back fun, and friendships were formed then that I believe will always be there. Our Director of Photography, John Flinn, was still there. His presence on the set really creates a tone I have come to depend on. Yes, we had what you may have heard was a family feeling to our production. A warm and wonderful family feel that became increasingly dysfunctional as we headed into the fifth season. I'll get back to that.

I had a lot of fun in the fourth season. Finally a regular, great storylines, great friends. I was working on *Deep Space Nine* one day when one of their castmembers asked me: 'I hear you can just walk into your producers' office and talk to them. Is that true?'

Absolutely! And I have their home phone numbers. Just don't call Joe before noon. (He writes until 4am!)

Our producers' offices were in the same building as the sound stages. Unless there was a meeting or casting or rewriting going on, you could just walk in to talk with Joe or John whenever you needed to. Jeffrey Willerth was always around if you had a question you didn't want to go to them for. Extraordinary.

I felt very protective of Joe, towards the end of that season. I think we all did. He was writing every episode, doing cons, talking to everyone about a fifth season and writing two *B5* movies. The man was a walking timebomb. I gave him some vitamins one day. He jokingly accused me of trying to poison him! He used that in a scene between Robin Atkin Downes and me.

Everyone took the news of moving to TNT as a very positive thing. We'd at least get to tell the rest of the story, although moving on without Claudia was very bittersweet for me. I have heard that I benefited with a better storyline because she left. But I missed her terribly, and I think the fans did too.

What immediately impressed me while shooting *Thirdspace* was how enthusiastic TNT was. We finally felt valued. That helped morale considerably.

Lyta had some major changes coming up in the fifth season. This is where my character benefited from Claudia's departure, I think. Robin's character, Byron, was introduced. Byron and Lyta began a long storyline that occupied much of the first half of the season. That love affair would have been between Byron and Ivanova. What Lyta would have been doing I don't know.

Not much, I imagine. I found things in scripts I needed more explanation on, so I sought out Joe more than ever. His has always been a policy of keeping plots very close to the vest. The actors were on a need to know basis for the most part. I can totally understand the wisdom of this, but it made making acting choices very difficult at times. Lyta makes choices concerning the telepaths that I found implausible. Joe would do his best to help me to see why this was necessary; I give him a lot of credit for his patience. He even did add a bit to one script when during our talks he realised something more was needed to make the transition more believable. He made sure to tell me he did it because it made the script better, not because I thought it was important. When season 5 began to air, I received very mixed reviews on the show as a whole. Viewers had come to expect the grander, more important storylines, and the new season seemed disjointed. I heard stronger opinions from the UK fans, who were really into Lyta, but where was this going? I told them to hold on and wait, things would become clearer. Luckily, the fifth season had so much going on, they couldn't help but want to see the outcome.

The season ended, and so did our show. The analysis continues and will go on for some time I imagine. At this point I can't help but feel a sixth season was needed to tie things up from the fifth! Maybe there will be more *Babylon 5* cable movies to finish up storylines and start new ones, but that is a risky place to put one's hopes. Why didn't Joe let us continue one more year? Everyone else seemed to want to.

I don't know for sure why there was no sixth season. I do know how things were handled when it came to the cast during those last weeks. We didn't know if we had a sixth season, what the movies were about, who was in them, if *Crusade* was a go, and who was in that! The scripts for the movies came out but we didn't see them. No one's agent was called. It was an awful, depressing time. None of the cast or crew understood why we were being treated like this. Meanwhile we continued to shoot our last episodes while rumours flew through the stages.

While I was in Colorado Springs with Robin for a convention, Joe, John and Doug had the official meeting. I called a castmate for the scoop only to find there really wasn't one. No news other than what we had already surmised.

I was one of the first of the regular cast to leave. My last day on the set was quiet. John Flinn, always the gentleman, had everyone give me a cheer, his trade mark. I didn't see any of the producers. As I walked out of the stage for the last time, I turned to look down the hall. At the back of the stage was a figure, I couldn't tell who it was, one of the grips I think, and he waved. I waved back. That was it.

Heading back to my trailer, I saw my door was open. Jeffrey Willerth, longtime friend and castmate was sitting there with a bottle of champagne. We toasted the show and had a good laugh. Then I got in my car to pick up my son.

I hadn't spoken to Joe or John when I got a call to do an episode of *Crusade*. A flashback storyline was all I was told. I couldn't shoot it, I was to be out of town at that time, which I told them. Joe did call me then to ask why I wasn't available, to say it was a good couple of scenes for Lyta, and it set up the movie. Joe said he'd send a script. He never did. Weeks went by, the TNT shutdown had happened, so no word from the *B5* office. I left town to do the movie *Chill Factor*. While away, I talked to a friend who was in a meeting with Joe. When Joe heard I was out of town, he said, Fine; we'll recast her. Okay.

Home once again, I got a call from casting. Would I be available such and such a date? Then the money. I dreaded hearing the offer. I knew it would be tight but I was so shocked I laughed. It was one-sixth what I had been paid on *B5*, and I wasn't paid much! I had flashbacks to the contract negotiations of five years ago. My self respect just wouldn't let me do it. The final offer was one half what I had been paid. I turned it down. Hey, it's just business to me. Just business.

The impression here could be that we all have sour grapes concerning the show, which is not accurate at all. The longer we are away from *B5*, the fonder our tones as we talk about it. Just don't bring up contract negotiations or the end of the show. I love the wonderful cast and crew I had the honour of working with. Joe Straczynski was totally unique. I'd never seen a producer/creator with such a loyalty among the whole team. He cared for us and we for him.

We did have fun, which we'll tell you over and over again when we meet at conventions. We made a great show. I'm sorry that there is any negative comments at all to make about the whole experience. But what family doesn't have its problems? The producers would have the cast feel that we were disposable and replaceable, that we had nothing to do with the success of the series. But we all know that isn't true. It's just business to us. Just business.

Bibliography (Volumes 1 & 2)

Cinemania 92 CD-ROM, Microsoft

Foundation, Number 64, Summer 1995

The Hutchinson Encyclopedia, 9th edition, Hutchinson

The Official Guide to J Michael Straczynski's Babylon 5 CD-ROM, Sierra

The Oxford Dictionary of Quotations, 3rd edition, Oxford University Press

The World Almanac 1996, World Almanac Books

The Official Babylon 5 Magazine, Vol. 1 Issues 1 to 9, Vol. 2 Issues 1 to 3

Bassom, David, *The A to Z of* Babylon 5, Creating *Babylon 5*, Boxtree

Bischof, Ledford J, *Interpreting Personality Theories*, Harper & Row

Bottéro, Jean *et al* (eds), *The Near East: The Early Civilizations*, Weidenfeld and Nicolson

Campbell, Joseph, *The Hero With a Thousand Faces*, Fontana Press

Clute, John and Nicholls, Peter, *The Encyclopedia of Science Fiction*, Orbit

Drury, Neville, *Dictionary of Mysticism*, Prism Unity

Gardner, Helen (ed), *The New Oxford Book of English Verse*, Oxford University Press

Hinsley, FH, *British Intelligence in the Second World War*, HMSO

Hyde, Maggie and McGuinness, Michael, *Jung For Beginners*, Icon Books

Killick, Jane, Babylon 5 *Season by Season: Signs and Portents*, Boxtree
　　Babylon 5 *Season by Season: The Coming of Shadows*, Boxtree
　　Babylon 5 *Season by Season: Point of No Return*, Boxtree
　　Babylon 5 *Season by Season: No Surrender, No Retreat*, Boxtree
　　Babylon 5 *Season by Season: The Wheel of Fire*, Boxtree

Leeming, David Adams and Leeming, Margaret Adams, *Encyclopedia of Creation Myths*, ABC-CLIO

Oates, Joan, *Babylon*, Thames and Hudson

Rees, Nigel (ed), *Brewer's Quotations*, Cassell

Rolleston, TW, *Celtic Myths and Legends*, Senate

Storr, Anthony, *Jung*, Fontana Press

Straczynski, J Michael, *The Complete Book of Scriptwriting*, Writers Digest Books

Suetonius, *The Twelve Caesars*, Penguin